THE ACTS OF THE APOSTLES

Latin Reader

The
ACTS OF THE APOSTLES
Latin Reader

By Dale A. Grote, PhD

Foreword by Wes Callihan

CiRCE
Concord, NC

Published in the USA by the CiRCE Institute
© 2020 by Dale A. Grote, PhD

ISBN: 978-1-7347853-0-2

All rights reserved. This publication may not be reproduced, stored in a retrieval system, or transmitted, in any form, or by any means, without the prior written consent of the CiRCE Institute.

For information:
CiRCE Institute
81 McCachern Blvd.
Concord, NC 28025
info@circeinstitute.com
www.circeinstitute.com

Cover design by Graeme Pitman.

Printed in the United States of America.

The CiRCE Institute is a non-profit 501(c)3 organization that exists to promote and support classical education in the school and in the home. We seek to identify the ancient principles of learning, to communicate them enthusiastically, and to apply them vigorously in today's learning settings through curriculum development, teacher training, leadership development events, online training, and a content-laden website.

To learn more please visit circeinstitute.org.

CONTENTS

Foreword ix
Introduction xi
Acts Chapter 1 1
Acts Chapter 2 11
Acts Chapter 3 19
Acts Chapter 4 25
Acts Chapter 5 33
Acts Chapter 6 41
Acts Chapter 7 45
Acts Chapter 8 57
Acts Chapter 9 67
Acts Chapter 10 77
Acts Chapter 11 85
Acts Chapter 12 91
Acts Chapter 13 99
Acts Chapter 14 111
Acts Chapter 15 117
Acts Chapter 16 125
Acts Chapter 17 133
Acts Chapter 18 141
Acts Chapter 19 147
Acts Chapter 20 155
Acts Chapter 21 161
Acts Chapter 22 169
Acts Chapter 23 177
Acts Chapter 24 185
Acts Chapter 25 191
Acts Chapter 26 197
Acts Chapter 27 207
Acts Chapter 28 219
Glossary 225
Appendix A: Three Accounts of Paul's Conversion 253
Appendix B: Sources for Paul's Death 257
Appendix C: Suggestions for Further Reading 261

FOREWORD
by Wes Callihan

Dale Grote has given the world yet another outstanding resource for teaching students of Latin. His first was the immensely valuable *Comprehensive Guide to Wheelock's Latin*, which made my own Latin teaching career, and my students' Latin studies, immeasurably easier and more pleasant, as it did for countless other teachers and students.

As a result of using his *Comprehensive Guide*, I became personally acquainted with Dale and eventually, he and I teamed up to lead close to a dozen student tours of Greece, and I got to know him as a friend and even a mentor (though he doesn't know that last part). His perspective on education, the classics, and life, in general, has been as big an influence on me as anyone's aside from my father's. I know more now about the chaos of the Byzantine world, eccentric modern classicists (and why I want to be one), and the joys of small engine repair—or at least how to think more interestingly about those topics—because of late evening conversations with Dale over dinner in Greek cafes. I would like to think that I've been improved by his down-to-earth attitude to life and learning.

So when his *The Vulgate of Mark* came out, I knew it would be good, and it was. It gave Latin teachers a tool for teaching that would generate more interest than Cato or Cicero, or at least provoke more reactions, as he points out in the introduction to that book ("I chose provocation over boredom") because working through a Gospel would give students a sense of accomplishment in an area they are more likely to really care about. Now he has given us, in *The Acts of the Apostles: Latin Reader*, another rich book with which to interest, stimulate, and provoke Latin students of all ages with a fresh look at the Latin text of Luke's second history.

The text has a quick, accessible, and intriguing summary account of the Acts, then a very brief account of the layout of the book, and then it launches straight into it. The book is straightforward and well-planned: a brief section of Latin text is accompanied by a short vocabulary list (the full glossary is in the back of the book) and some notes and essential commentary on the words and sometimes the background where necessary. There are some

helpful maps and pictures, but otherwise, it is geared toward moving the student rapidly through the Latin text of Acts and could easily be used as a complete standalone text for a Latin course. This is the kind of book I would have expected from Dale. He doesn't mess around but gives people just what they need, with clarity, brevity, and grace.

INTRODUCTION

The Acts of the Apostles probably isn't the first book of the New Testament one might pick up to read. It sits in the shadow of the four Gospel accounts of Matthew, Mark, Luke, and John, the theologically rich letters of Paul and others, and the mysterious cataclysmic ending of the New Testament in Revelation. Furthermore, the story it tells is, by now, old news.

At the beginning of Acts, we see a small handful of disciples huddled together with the resurrected Jesus. After his assumption into heaven, they await the imminent outpouring of the power of the Holy Spirit, and the installation of the promised Kingdom of Heaven. The Holy Spirit does come, like a mighty wind, and the disciples speak in foreign languages they never knew before. But the end of time doesn't come. Gradually, Jesus' followers face the difficult challenge of reconciling their faith that the Kingdom of Heaven is imminent with the need to get on in this world.

Far from being swept up by a unanimous consensus about what was to be done, the disciples quarreled with one another, often with an acrimony that distresses modern Christians. The romantic notion that the disciples marched out of Jerusalem after the Pentecost united in their aspiration to convert the world to Christianity doesn't hold up to any five contiguous pages of Acts. Most of Jesus' original disciples apparently threw their hands up and walked away, never to be heard of again in the canonical Scriptures. What information we get comes from later accounts that the first Christians didn't include in their most sacred texts. Only the two sons of Zebedee, James and John, and Peter do anything in Acts. The other eight—nine if you include Judas' replacement—are mentioned only once during a head count.

The first internal fractures appear early. After Jesus is taken up before their eyes, the disciples organize themselves into a kind of love communalism and pool their possessions for the good of the whole. Soon, however,

some Greek speaking Christ believers[1] complain that they weren't receiving their fair share of the funds they needed for their dependents. In response, the disciples appointed a board of seven Greek-speaking deacons to oversee the matter.

Another problem appears when these early believers are persecuted by the Jewish authorities. Some of the disciples are driven out of Jerusalem, but others curiously are allowed to remain. Why would that be, unless there had developed at least two distinct sets of believers within the Jesus movement, one that was tolerated by the Jewish authorities and one that wasn't?

Because of this persecution, not in spite of it, the Gospel of Jesus is carried outside of Jerusalem and its immediate environs by these Greek-speaking Christ believers and into the lands of half-Jews (Samaria) and even of pagans (first in Caesarea, about seventy miles from Jerusalem). Thereupon a serious rupture breaks out over the question of non-Jewish converts.

Peter and John are sent by the brethren in Jerusalem to Samaria to inspect these "half-Jews" who are being converted by the exiled Philip (one of the seven Greek-speaking deacons). Clearly, the disciples back in Jerusalem were concerned about what was becoming of their movement, as part of it, which had been driven out of Jerusalem, was continuing to act and acting with increasing autonomy.

It's at this point that Paul, who'd been appointed by the Jewish authorities to root out this new Jesus faction, appears in Jerusalem, professing to be one of the believers. He's granted temporary status among them because of the intercession of the trustworthy believer Barnabas, but soon Paul runs afoul of them by preaching enthusiastically among Greek speakers in Jerusalem. They send him out of the city and back to his hometown in Tarsus. For a time, there's a truce between them and the Jewish authorities in Jerusalem.

---

[1] This is the expression I use in the book in place of "Christian," which connotes a fully developed body of beliefs and liturgical practices that are only nascent at the time of Acts. For the same reason, I avoid the term "church" for a local body of Christ believers. "Church" suggests at the very least a building. The first Christ believers met in private houses and had yet to imagine the specialized architecture needed for their worship gatherings.

INTRODUCTION

Soon the matter of pagan converts comes up again. This time God sends Peter a vision, which he interprets to mean that it was acceptable for Gentiles (i.e., non-Jews) and Jews to eat together. He then assists in the conversion of a non-Jewish pagan, Cornelius, in Caesarea. Peter returns to Jerusalem and defends the notion that Gentiles can become Christ believers. The floodgates had been opened, but many questions remain unanswered.

Next there are large numbers of Gentile converts in Antioch who need instruction and guidance. The disciples in Jerusalem send out Barnabas to Antioch to instruct them. He summons Paul from Tarsus to help. It's at this point that the disciples and their converts are first given the name "Christians," which was almost certainly meant as a slur. Whatever its intention, it makes it clear that they are increasingly seen as a distinct sect within Judaism. The growth of Christ believers in Antioch was followed by even more Gentile converts even farther away from the traditional Jewish homelands.

Following another persecution of the Christ believers in Jerusalem, Paul sets off on his first missionary journey. Jews in the cities outside of Jerusalem are alarmed at the large numbers of Gentile converts he's winning over, and they run him off. In Lystra he is actually stoned by the Jews and left for dead. Their complaints about what Paul is saying filter back to the Jerusalem brethren.

Paul is summoned back to Jerusalem to explain what he has been telling these new converts. A compromise is worked out: the non-Jewish converts would not need to be circumcised, but they would be expected to observe a small handful of laws. Apparently not trusting Paul to represent the decision accurately, they provide him a letter and send him out on his second missionary journey.

At the beginning of his mission, a permanent rift opens up between Paul and his friend Barnabas over a young man named John Mark. Barnabas wants him to accompany them on their journey, and Paul is opposed to it. In the end, they can't resolve their disagreement, and they go their separate ways.

On this, his second missionary journey, Paul is beaten and imprisoned in Philippi, driven from Thessaloniki at the instigation of local Jews and laughed out of Athens by pagan philosophers. Despite spending a year and half in Corinth, his followers soon broke into factions after his departure, requiring at least one follow up visit that we know of. His experience in Ephesus is even worse.

Though Acts tries to convey a more positive impression, Paul's work there can only be called a qualified disaster. He inspired a riot in the city, and he stayed away, even when other Christ believers were being threatened. He stops preaching openly and instead opens up a kind of school, where he teaches the Gospel for nearly two years. Later, on his way back to Jerusalem after his third missionary journey, he pointedly avoids Ephesus and addresses only some representatives from Ephesus whom he'd summoned to a nearby city. The speech he gives them is essentially an *apologia pro vita sua*, in which he defends himself against what appears to be a series of specific charges that had been leveled against him, including, it seems, stealing other people's clothing. He warns them against perverters of his message, who were presumably flourishing in Ephesus and elsewhere.

In Jerusalem, he is again cross-examined by the Christ believers for his teaching about the Law. He's instructed to submit to a purification ritual as a public act of penance. While he was thus engaged, a new and more serious accusation is leveled against him: that he allowed a Gentile to accompany him into an area of the Temple that was restricted to Jews—a charge, incidentally, leveled by men from Ephesus. It's this charge that set into motion the course of events that would bring him into Roman custody and ultimately to Rome itself.

Though the author of Acts tries his best to paper over these divisions, it's not hard to see how Jesus' original followers were deeply divided about Paul and about the future of their movement. Even if the Holy Spirit is ultimately the engine behind it all, there are times when its will is hard for them to discern. As such, Acts is a compelling chronicle of human weakness and uncertainty mixed with courage and devotion in the light of the extraordinary events of Jesus' life and crucifixion.

So much for the human and divine drama of Acts. What is Acts as a text?

INTRODUCTION

What Is Acts?

It has rightly been said that Acts is the center of a scholarly storm, where even the most basic facts are disputed: Who wrote Acts, when, where, and why? What is Acts? Is it an effort, though incomplete, to report historical fact accurately, or just another type of fiction, like a novel, written in the second century BC for the entertainment of Christians.

The author of Acts tells us at the beginning that his work is a continuation of the third Gospel. Both texts were written to one man in particular, someone named Theophilus. We don't know anything about Theophilus, and in a sense it doesn't matter. We can deduce from the third Gospel and Acts that Theophilus asked two questions: what is this Christianity, and how did it get to Rome? The first question is answered in the Gospel account. The second was answered in Acts.

The first Christians, so far as we can tell, were nearly unanimous that the author of both was Paul's companion Luke. This is been largely endorsed by contemporary scholarship. For this reason, both works can be put together under the title "Luke-Acts."

The Chronology of Acts

The story of Acts is set in the first three decades of the Christian movement. It begins forty days after Jesus' crucifixion in the early 30s, and ends with Paul waiting in Rome for his appeal to be heard by the emperor in the mid to late 60s.

Judged as an historical narrative, Acts falls well short by modern standards. There's no explicit chronology, for example, to set the dates in the context of the wider world. In the first several chapters, years go by that are covered by little more than a speech or two. By contrast, in the later chapters, events are recorded in detail, even down to the time of day, the names of ships, precise sailing routes, and the exact number of passengers and crew on the ship taking Paul to Rome: 276.

Getting a fix on the absolute chronology of the narrative involves cross-referencing it with events that are otherwise datable from other sources. For example, in chapter 12 we're told that the Romans' puppet king, Herod Agrippa I, begins a crackdown on the Jesus believers in Jerusalem. Shortly thereafter he dies in Caesarea. We know from other sources that Agrippa ruled from 41-44, so this establishes both a *terminus post* and a *terminus ante quem* for chapter 12. By combining materials such as this where available, and relying on conjecture when they're not, modern scholarship can piece together a consensus chronology.

Acts and the Letters of Paul

Perhaps one of the most surprising things about Acts is the complete silence about Paul's career as a letter writer. There are many possible explanations for this omission and all have been proffered in one form or another. At one end of the spectrum, Luke knew about Paul's letter writing but didn't think it served his larger purpose in Acts to mention it. At the other end, the author of Acts, whoever he was, made up Acts as a work of fiction, and Paul qua letter writer didn't make for an exciting hero.

Like all other subjects related to Acts, the scholarship on how to fit Paul's letters into the chronology of Acts is as massive as it is fascinating. For the beginner, however, Acts enlivens Paul's letters by giving them a living context, and even demystifying their titles. Something happened in Galatia in Acts. Paul spent two years in Ephesus and ran into trouble there. There's Philippi where Paul made his first European convert, a woman named Lydia. The Thessalonians lived in Thessaloniki, a city Paul was driven out of by angry Jews. Acts also populates his letters with real people. We read in Acts when, where, and how Timothy joined his second missionary trip. In chapter 18 of Acts, Paul completes the baptism of Apollos, a follower of John the Baptist, and later sends him to help shore up the brethren in Corinth. Then we read in 1 Corinthians that Apollos became the leader of one of the factions that had developed among the believers in the city. Recognizing Apollos and knowing his story gives depth and color to this aspect of Paul's letters to the Corinthians.

All this notwithstanding, my notes will make scant mention of Paul's letters, for no other reason than to keep the nose of the camel where it should be for a book like this—outside the tent with the rest of its body.

INTRODUCTION

Parts of This Book

After this introduction, the book lays out the text of Acts, divided into chapters and smaller subsections. Each subsection has a very brief running vocabulary to help with words with no obvious English derivatives or which can't be considered to be part of an introductory curriculum.

The text is accompanied by notes and commentary, the purpose of which is neither pastoral nor interpretive. Their main objective is to help with occasional grammatical/syntactical peculiarities and to throw some light on what the words meant to Christians in Luke's original audience. That necessarily involves some comments on wider issues, but I've tried to keep them at the bare minimum required just to keep the flow of text going.

After the text and commentary comes the complete glossary for this text of Acts. The entries provide only translations that are useful for the context in which the words appear.

Following the glossary are three appendices: A) a side-by-side comparison of the three different accounts of Paul's conversion for easy reference, B) a compendium of later accounts of Paul's ultimate fate after he is delivered to Rome, C) a short annotated bibliography for further reading.

Artwork has been added to give you an idea of how artists have portrayed Paul throughout history. If you'd like to learn more about the pieces included, they can be found on the website of The Metropolitan Museum of Art (www.metmuseum.org).

I hope you profit as much from using this book as I did from writing it.

Dale A. Grote
Charlotte, NC

Pro Tanto Beneficio
My sincere thanks to members of my church's Seekers Class (Adult Sunday School), who read through the entirety of Acts with me in the 2018-2019 year. My notes benefited immensely from their numerous insights and comments. Their support and encouragement also helped me persevere to the conclusion of such a large undertaking.

ACTS

AD 30/33

Luke announces the theme of his work: the story of the followers of Jesus after the resurrection. While he is with them, Jesus promises his disciples the power of the Holy Spirit and says they will bear witness throughout the world. He is taken up into heaven after forty days. Peter tells the apostles they need a replacement for Judas. Matthias is chosen by lot.

1–2: Luke refers to his earlier work about what Jesus taught and did.

sermo, sermon • **facio**, to make • **omnis**, all, each • **coepi**, to begin • **doceo**, to teach • **elego**, to select • **usque in**, up until • **praecipio**, to instruct • **elego**, to select • **adsumo**, to take up

Primum quidem sermonem feci de omnibus, O Theophile, quae coepit Iesus facere et docere, ²usque in diem quā, praecipiens Apostolis per Spiritum Sanctum quos elegit, adsumptus est.

Primum sermonem: This is widely accepted to be the Gospel of Luke. For this reason the two texts are often referred to collectively as "Luke-Acts." **Theophile**: There is nothing known about Theophilus. It's not even certain that he was a real person. His name means "God-Lover," so he might be nothing more than a personification of the entire body of Christ believers. Assuming that there was a Theophilus, based on what we have in Luke-Acts, we can infer that he asked Luke two questions, "(1) What is Christianity, and (2) how did it spread throughout the empire, eventually arriving in Rome itself?" In response to the first, Luke wrote his Gospel; in response to the second, he wrote Acts. **Quae**: accusative neuter plural; its antecedent is *quibus*: "about all the things which." **Coepit...facere et docere**: The first followers of Jesus were surely discouraged that their Messiah had been executed in the most disgraceful manner possible. Crucifixion was more than a gruesome method of execution; it was meant to humiliate its victim. The Romans used it only for slaves and rebels. **Per Spritum Sanctum**: Despite how familiar the "Holy Spirit" is now in Christian liturgy and theology, its origins are not easy to trace. In Acts, it resembles a kind of energy, which gives its recipients enhanced powers and even tells them where to go and what to do. Under its influence and direction they can perform miraculous cures (even raise the dead) and speak with authority and confidence when challenged. What's not knowable is whether the Holy Spirit was thought of at this point as a divine being in its own right or simply the power that God sends out. However it is to be understood, this Holy Spirit is the *éminence grise* of Acts, so much so that Acts has been called the *Book of the Holy Spirit* or the *Acts of the Holy Spirit*.

3–5: Jesus stays with his followers for forty days and tells them to await the "promise of the Father" in Jerusalem.

praebeo, to show • **ipse**, the very one • **vivus**, alive • **argumentum**, discussion • **dies**, day • **quadraginta**, forty • **appareo**, to appear • **loquor**, to speak • **convescor**, to eat • **discedo**, to leave • **expecto**, to wait for • **promissio**, promise • **audio**, to hear • **os**, mouth • **dico**, to say • **quia**, that • **aqua**, water • **hic**, this

³Quibus et praebuit se ipsum vivum post passionem suam in multis argumentis per dies quadraginta apparens eis et loquens de regno Dei. ⁴Et convescens praecepit eis ab Hierosolymis ne discederent sed expectarent promissionem Patris, "quam audistis per os meum" [dicens], ⁵quia "Iohannes quidem baptizavit aquā; vos autem baptizabimini Spiritu Sancto non post multos hos dies."

Quibus: "those to whom he showed himself," i.e., the eleven remaining apostles. *Per dies quadraginta*: There is no specific significance to the number of days Jesus is with the disciples before his ascension. Generally speaking the number "forty" is used for a standard amount of time for a sacred event: Jesus was tempted in the desert for forty days, for example; the Hebrews were forced to wander in the wilderness for forty years before being allowed into Canaan; etc. *Convescens*: This is a present active participle from the deponent verb *vescor*, one of only two active forms a deponent verb will have. Taking food is further proof that Jesus has been resurrected bodily. Thus Luke makes it clear that the disciples are not conversing with a ghost. *Praecepit eis ab Hierosolymis ne discederent*: Move *ab Hierosolymis* after *discederent* in the indirect command for more natural English word order: "He gave instructions to them that they not depart from Jerusalem." After Jesus' crucifixion, it would have been understandable if the disciples and others had wanted to return to Galilee, where Jesus' ministry began.

CHAPTER 1

6–8: Jesus tells them that they are not to know when the kingdom is to arrive. They are to wait to receive the power of the Holy Spirit, and then to bear witness about him to the entire world.

---

convenio, to gather • **interrogo**, to ask • **tempus**, time • **regnum**, kingdom • **restituo**, to restore • **vester**, yours • **nosse** < **nosco**, to know • **vel**, or • **pono**, to put • **potestas**, power • **virtus**, miracle • **supervenio**, to come on • **testis**, a witness • **ultimus**, farthest

---

⁶Igitur qui convenerant, interrogabant eum, dicentes, "Domine, si in tempore hōc restitues regnum Israhel? ⁷Dixit autem eis, "Non est vestrum nosse tempora vel momenta quae Pater posuit in suā potestate, ⁸sed accipietis virtutem supervenientis Spiritūs Sancti in vos, et eritis mihi testes in Hierusalem et in omni Iudaeā et Samariā et usque ad ultimum terrae."

Qui: "those who." ***Si in tempore hōc restitues***: The disciples assume the arrival of the Holy Spirit will be contemporaneous with the establishment of the Kingdom of God, which they still expect will be a political, earthly kingdom. ***Restitues***: "re-establish" because the Kingdom of God was understood to be in part a resurrection of the old Davidic kingdom. ***Vestrum***: neuter nominative singular of the adjective *vester*: "It is not yours . . . ," which we can translate as "It is not for you . . ." ***Nosse***: This is a syncopated perfect active infinitive (*novisse*) from the verb *nosco*. Even though the form is perfect, it's translated as if it were a present: "to know," not "to have known." Verbs that have the *-sc-* ingressive infix have their perfect tenses shifted forward: the perfect = our present; the pluperfect = our perfect; the future perfect = our future. ***In suā potestate***: The word *potestas* (*exousia* in the Greek) can mean "rule," which fits the context here perfectly. ***Supervenientis***: *super-venientis* because the Holy Spirit will arrive from on high. ***Et eritis mihi testes***: This is an effective summary of the geographic vectors of Acts. The evangelizing of Jesus' disciples begins in Jerusalem, expanding outward through Judea — the area directly around Jerusalem — finally to encompass the entire world. ***Et Samariā***: The Jews of Judea considered the entire area of Samaria to be polluted by fallen half-Jews, observing heretical ritual practices mixed with paganism. It was virtually a Gentile, non-Jewish region, and off-limits. In John 8:48, some Jews disparage Jesus' followers as mere Samaritans, probably possessed by demons, and in Matthew 10:5-6, Jesus himself tells his apostles to avoid the towns of Samaria on their evangelizing mission. Our expression "good Samaritan," which is can be used of someone who is ignorant but means well, retains some of the original contemptuous feel of the word. By specifying Samaria as the next area for expansion, Jesus opens the message of salvation even to the most marginal of Jews. It's also accurate. The first converts outside of the district of Jerusalem after Jesus' resurrection are Samaritans (Chapter 8).

9–11: Jesus is taken up into the heavens before their eyes. Two angels appear and tell them that he will return just as he was taken.

elevo, to raise up • **oculus**, eye • **nubes**, cloud • **intuor**, to look upon carefully • **eo**, to go • **ecce**, behold • **duo**, two • **vir**, man • **adsto**, to stand near • **iuxta**, close to • **vestis**, clothing • **albus**, white • **sto**, to stand • **aspicio**, to look upon • **caelum**, sky • **quemadmodum**, just as • **eunte** < **eo**

⁹Et cum haec dixisset videntibus illis, elevatus est, et nubes suscepit eum ab oculis eorum. ¹⁰Cumque intuerentur in caelum, eunte illo, ecce: duo viri adstiterunt iuxta illos in vestibus albis. ¹¹Qui et dixerunt, "Viri Galilaei, quid statis, aspicientes in caelum? Hǐc Iesus, qui adsumptus est a vobis in caelum, sic veniet quemadmodum vidistis eum euntem in caelum."

Videntibus: "as they were looking on." This emphasizes the fact that the event was witnessed and not simply hearsay. ***Eunte illo***: ablative absolute, "while he was going." ***Duo viri***: There are also two "men in white" at Jesus' tomb in Luke and John. There's no reason to suppose Luke means these very men, and no reason to assume he doesn't. ***Quemadmodum vidistis***: It's very likely that many were claiming to have seen him in the years after his resurrection. This clause makes it clear that there will be nothing ambiguous or hidden about his return.

12–14: Those present at Jesus' ascension return to Jerusalem and reunite with the other disciples.

reverto, to return • **mons**, mountain • **voco**, to call • **Oliveti**, Mount Olive • **iter**, journey • **introissent** < **intro + eo** • **cenaculum**, dining hall • **ascendo**, to go up • **maneo** to stay • **persevero**, to persevere • **unianimiter**, in one mind • **oratio**, prayer • **mulier**, woman • **mater**, mother • **frater**, brother

---

¹²Tunc reversi sunt Hierosolymam a monte qui vocatur Oliveti, qui est iuxta Hierusalem, Sabbati habens iter. ¹³Et cum introissent in cenaculum, ascenderunt ubi manebant—Petrus et Iohannes, Iacobus et Andreas, Philippus et Thomas, Bartholomeus et Mattheus, Iacobus Alphei et Simon Zelotes et Iudas Iacobi. ¹⁴Hi omnes erant perseverantes unianimiter in oratione, cum mulieribus et Mariā, matre Iesu, et fratribus eius.

Oliveti: Strictly speaking, this is inconsistent with Luke's Gospel, which places Jesus' ascension at Bethany, a village approximately a mile to the east of Mt. Olive. It's possible, however, that Luke thought of Bethany as a part of the hill where Mt. Olive is situated. *Sabbati habens iter*: *habens* agrees with *Oliveti*, which is nominative, and takes the neuter noun *iter* as its object: "having a Sabbath journey" or better "being one Sabbath day's journey away." A Sabbath day's journey is how far one was allowed to walk on the Sabbath: about one half mile. This is simply a way of measuring distance. The ascension did not occur on the Sabbath. *Ubi manebant . . .*: This is the canonical twelve apostles, less Judas. *Petrus*: Peter, meaning "rock" in Greek, is the nickname Jesus gave Simon or Simeon (Matthew 16:18). *Iacobus*: By tradition and convention, *Iacobus* is translated into English as "James." *Cum mulieribus*: Who were these women? Were they the wives of the disciples, or perhaps disciples themselves? Luke refers to women being among the throng of people following Jesus during his missions and even supporting him and his followers financially (1:1-8). *Et fratribus eius*: Did Jesus have brothers, or does *fratibus* in this context mean his cousins or perhaps half-brothers from his "step-father" Joseph? The question has spawned intense debate since the second century.

ACTS OF THE APOSTLES

15–22: Peter tells the other apostles they must find a replacement for Judas.

exsurgo, to arise • **medius**, the middle • **turba**, crowd • **fere**, almost • **nomen**, name • **centum**, one hundred • **viginti**, twenty • **oportet**, it is necessary • **impleo**, to fill up • **praedico**, to predict • **sortior**, to obtain by lot • **sors**, lot • **ministerium**, service • **possedeo**, to own • **merces**, price • **iniquitas**, crime • **crepo**, to explode • **defundo**, to spill out • **viscera**, guts • **sanguis**, blood • **notus**, well-known • **habito**, to live in • **appello**, to name • **ager**, field • **lingua**, language • **commoratio**, a dwelling place • **episcopatum**, role • **accipio**, to take • **alius**, another • **congrego**, to gather • **intro**, to come among • **exeo**, to depart

---

¹⁵Et in diebus illis exsurgens Petrus in medio fratrum, dixit (erat autem turba nominum simul fere centum viginti), ¹⁶"Viri, fratres, oportet impleri Scripturam quam praedixit Spiritus Sanctus per os David de Iudā, qui fuit dux eorum qui conprehenderunt Iesum, ¹⁷quia connumeratus erat in nobis et sortitus est sortem ministerii huius." ¹⁸(Et hĭc quidem possedit agrum de mercede iniquitatis, et suspensus crepuit medius et diffusa sunt omnia viscera eius. ¹⁹Et notum factum est omnibus habitantibus Hierusalem ita ut appellaretur ager ille linguā eorum, Acheldemach. Hoc est, Ager Sanguinis.) ²⁰"Scriptum est enim in libro Psalmorum, 'Fiat commoratio eius deserta, et non sit qui inhabitet in eā,' et 'Episcopatum

In diebus illis: sometime within the ten days after the ascension and the arrival of the Holy Spirit. ***Petrus***: The history of the Christian Church as an institution begins at this moment. Until this speech, none of the disciples anywhere in the New Testament had spoken at length or made a decision. The disciples are now on their own. ***Fere centum viginti***: There is no significance to the number. Luke admits that it's only approximate. ***Quam praedixit Spiritus Sanctus per os David***: The reference is probably to Psalm 40:10. ***Et sortitus est sortem ministerii huius***: *Sortem* is the direct object of *sortitus est*: "he won a share of this ministry by lot." We can't take this to mean it was sheer luck that Judas was chosen. A general notion in antiquity is that of casting lots. It meant giving the deity the right to decide by directing the outcome. ***Et hĭc quidem . . .***: This is almost certainly an editorial remark made by Luke and not a part of Mark's original speech to the apostles. Ancient texts had no punctuation marks, so modern editors have to make decisions about how to apply these modern conventions. Sometimes it's clear, and other times it involves some difficult questions and requires judgment calls. ***Pronus factus***: Some late manuscripts and editions have *suspensus* instead of *pronus factus*. This is probably an effort to harmonize Luke's account of Judas' death with that related in Matthew, where he hangs himself. The Greek original is *prēnēs*, "headlong," best translated as *pronus factus*. ***Acheldemach***: The origin of the name of the field is also inconsistent with Matthew's account. In Matthew the priests of the Temple bought the land with the bribe money Judas returned to them. That's why it's called the "field of blood"—because it was bought with Jesus' blood. ***Scriptum est***: Peter splices together

eius accipiat alius.' ²¹Oportet ergo ex his viris qui nobiscum congregati sunt in omni tempore quo intravit et exivit inter nos Dominus Iesus, ²²incipiens a baptismate Iohannis usque in diem quā adsumptus est a nobis, testem resurrectionis eius nobiscum fieri unum ex istis."

two different passages: Psalms 69:25 and 109:8. That Peter should have been able to cite these relatively obscure verses and see the meaning they had for the present situation would seem to prove the working of the Holy Spirit. Peter was a fisherman by profession, and almost certainly illiterate. **Episcopatum**: "area of responsibility," where Judas was the "overseer." In John 12:6—and in none of the other Gospels—Judas served as the accountant: "He said this [that the expensive perfume Mary had poured on Jesus' head could have benefited the poor], not because he cared about the poor, but because he was a thief, and having charge of the moneybag he used to help himself to what was put into it." Eventually this Greek term will take on the specialized use in church governance we recognize in words like "episcopal," "episcopate," and even "bishop," which is derived from it. **Oportet**: The accusative infinitive expression that completes the verb comes only at the end of the sentence: *Oportet fieri unum ex istis—ex his viris qui* . . . Jesus' baptism was witnessed by many people, and surely would have generated some interest in him (Luke 4:21-23). Even though he didn't officially call the twelve disciples to follow him until later, Jesus would still have had a following "beginning from the baptism," from whom the candidates for Judas' replacement could have been chosen.

ACTS OF THE APOSTLES

23-25: Matthias is chosen by lot to replace Judas.

cognomino, to nickname • **nosti** < **nosco**, to know • **cor**, heart • **praevaricor**, to deceive • **abeo**, to go away • **locus**, place • **do**, to give • **cecidit** < **cado**, to fall • **adnumero**, to count among

---

²³Et statuerunt duos, Ioseph qui vocabatur Barsabban, qui cognominatus est Iustus, et Matthiam. ²⁴Et orantes dixerunt, "Tu, Domine, qui corda nosti omnium, ostende quem elegeris ex his duobus unum ²⁵accipere locum ministerii huius et Apostolatūs, de quo praevaricatus est Iudas, ut abiret in locum suum." ²⁶Et dederunt sortes eis, et cecĭdit sors super Matthiam. Et adnumeratus est cum undecim Apostolis.

Ioseph . . . Barsabban: Neither of these two appeared in any of the four Gospel accounts and we hear nothing more about either of them in Acts. ***Nosti***: This bizarre looking form is a syncopation of *no[vi]sti*. Remember that the perfect subjunctive regularly drops the -vi- infix. Hence *laudasset* instead of *laudavisset*, and so on. See the note at 1: 6-8 for the translation. ***Quem . . . unum***: "which one." ***Elegeris***: This is best understood as a perfect subjunctive in an indirect question, from the original direct question, "Which one did you pick?" Again the casting of lots was thought to be leaving the choice to God, not to chance. ***Accipere***: An infinitive showing purpose is common in Vulgate Latin. Classical Latin might have written, *qui accipiat*. ***Apostalatūs***: "apostleship." Judas wasn't just another disciple; he was one of the twelve central apostles, and in Peter's mind it's critical that twelfth position be occupied. ***Ut abiret in locum suum***: Judas proved false with regard to his apostleship with the result that "he went to his own place," not to the place assigned to him by God.

The Eastern Mediterranean World in Paul's Time

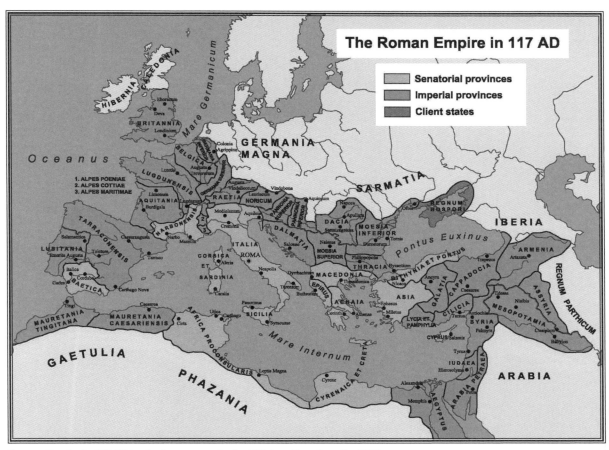

Roman Empire in 117 CE by Andrew nacu, *Ancient History Encyclopedia*. 2012. .

ACTS 2

AD 30/33

Fifty days after the resurrection, the Holy Spirit gives the disciples the power of speaking in different languages. Visitors to Jerusalem are astonished to hear their native languages being spoken fluently. Some think the disciples are drunk. Peter replies that they are not drunk but filled with the Holy Spirit, as Joel had predicted. He continues that Jesus is the fulfillment of the prophecies in David's psalms. The people are ashamed that they participated in Jesus' execution and want to know what they can do to atone. Peter tells them they should repent and be baptized. Three thousand convert. This new community pools its worldly possessions for common use.

1–4: The Holy Spirit gives the disciples the ability to speak in tongues.

conpleo, to fulfill • **pentecostes**, fifty • **pariter**, equally • **idem**, the same • **repente** suddenly • **tamquam**, like • **sonus**, sound • **vehemens**, powerful • **repleo**, to fill up • **totus**, all • **sedeo**, to sit • **disperitus**, differing • **ignis**, flame • **prout**, in so far as • **eloquor**, to speak

¹Et cum conplerentur dies pentecostes, erant omnes pariter in eodem loco. ²Et factus est repente de caelo sonus tamquam advenientis spiritūs vehementis, et replevit totam domum ubi erant sedentes. ³Et apparuerunt illis dispertitae linguae tamquam ignis seditque supra singulos eorum. ⁴Et repleti sunt omnes Spiritu Sancto, et coeperunt loqui aliis linguis prout Spiritus Sanctus dabat eloqui illis.

Pentecostes: This is simply the Greek word for the number fifty. It served as the name of the great harvest feast that occurred fifty days after an event during the Passover week. The details of its celebration need not delay us here (for which see Exodus 23:14-19, Leviticus 23: 9-21 and Deuteronomy 16:9). Suffice it to say that Jerusalem would have been filled with Jewish visitors of different nationalities on the day the disciples received the Holy Spirit. *Pariter*: An adverb < *par, paris*, "equally," or "of one accord." *Advenientis spiritūs vehementis*: genitives, "like [the sound] of an approaching powerful wind." *Sedit*: The number of the verb emphasizes how the individual tongues (*dispertitae linguae*) came to land on each of the disciples individually. *Aliis linguis*: This is the first time speaking in tongues, or glossolalia, as it is called by modern scholars, is mentioned anywhere in the Bible. We would wish for more details from Luke. What is clear, however, is the first gift of the Holy Spirit is the power to speak a human language, one that was previously unknown to speaker, not some incomprehensible utterance requiring further interpretation.

ACTS OF THE APOSTLES

5–13: The people in Jerusalem are astonished to hear them speaking foreign languages.

autem, moreover • **religiosus**, religious • **natio**, nation • **vox**, voice • **mens**, mind • **confusus**, confused • **quoniam**, since • **unusquisque**, each one • **stupeo**, to be astonished • **miror**, to marvel • **nonne**, is it not that • **nascor**, to be born • **pars**, region • **advena**, visitor • **proselytus**, foreigner • **magnalia**, mighty works • **ad invicem**, to one another • **quidnam**, whatsoever • **vult > volo**, to want • **inrideo**, to laugh • **quia**, that • **mustum**, new wine • **plenus**, filled with

⁵Erant autem in Hierusalem habitantes Iudaei viri religiosi ex omni natione, quae sub caelo sunt. ⁶Factā autem hāc voce, convēnit multitudo et mente confusa est, quoniam audiebat unusquisque linguā suā illos loquentes. ⁷Stupebant autem omnes et mirabantur, dicentes, "Nonne omnes ecce: isti qui loquuntur Galilaei sunt, ⁸et quomodo nos audivimus unusquisque linguā nostrā in quā nati sumus?"—⁹Parthi et Medi et Elamitae, et qui habitant Mesopotamiam et Iudaeam et Cappadociam, Pontum et Asiam, ¹⁰Frygiam et Pamphiliam, Aegyptum et partes Lybiae, quae est circa Cyrenen et advenae Romani ¹¹Iudaei quoque et proselyti Cretes et Arabes—audivimus loquentes eos nostris linguis magnalia Dei. ¹²Stupebant autem omnes et mirabantur ad invicem, dicentes "Quidnam hŏc vult esse?" ¹³Alii autem inridentes dicebant quia "Musto pleni sunt isti."

Galilaei sunt: The passersby wouldn't have known they were from Galilee by their accent, since presumably the gift of the Holy Spirit made them perfectly fluent in the new tongues. Perhaps they wore distinctive clothing or were known to people in the district. **Parthi et Medi . . .** : Efforts to detect any linguistic or geographical structure to this list of nations and peoples have not proven successful. At best it can be said that Luke accurately portrays the commotion of the typical street scene in Jerusalem at the time of this festival: a swirling mass of people speaking different dialects and different languages. **Quidnam hŏc vult esse**: "What does this mean?" **Alii**: The accusation that the disciples were intoxicated could not have been made by those hearing their own languages spoken perfectly. Excessive drinking doesn't suddenly make one fluent in a foreign language. There must have been others who were attracted by the commotion. Not being close enough to hear anything distinctly, they might have dismissed the scene as another example of drunkenness at the festival.

CHAPTER 2

14–21: Peter begins a three-part speech in which he first tells the most orthodox Jews in the crowd that the prophet Joel's predictions of the end of times have been realized.

undecim, eleven • **universus**, each/all • **auris**, ear • **percipio**, to receive • **sicut**, just as • **aestimo**, to suppose • **ebrius**, drunk • **hora**, hour • **tertius**, third • **novus**, late • **caro**, flesh • **propheto**, to speak out courageously • **filius**, son • **filia**, daughter • **iuvenis**, young person • **senior**, elder • **somnium**, a dream • **somno**, to dream • **servus**, servant • **ancilla**, female servant • **prodigium**, wonderous sign • **sursum**, upward • **deorsum**, downward • **vapor**, vapor • **fumus**, smoke • **sol**, the sun • **converto**, to turn • **tenebra**, gloom • **luna**, moon • **antequam**, before • **quicumque**, whosoever • **invoco**, to call upon • **salvus**, saved

¹⁴Stans autem Petrus cum undecim levavit vocem suam et locutus est eis, "Viri Iudaei et qui habitatis Hierusalem universi, hoc vobis notum sit et auribus percipite verba mea. ¹⁵Non enim sicut vos aestimatis hi ebrii sunt, cum sit hora diei tertia, ¹⁶sed hoc est quod dictum est per prophetam Iohel: ¹⁷"Et erit in novissimis diebus,' dicit Dominus, 'effundam de spiritu meo super omnem carnem, et prophetabunt filii vestri et filiae vestrae, et iuvenes vestri visiones videbunt, et seniores vestri somnia somniabunt. ¹⁸Et quidem super servos meos et super ancillas meas in diebus illis effundam de spiritu meo, et prophetabunt. ¹⁹Et dabo prodigia in caelo sursum et signa in terrā deorsum, sanguinem et ignem et vaporem fumi. ²⁰Sol convertetur in tenebras, et luna in sanguinem, antequam veniat dies Domini magnus et manifestus. ²¹Et erit omnis quicumque invocaverit nomen Domini salvus erit."

Viri Iudaei et qui habitatis Hierusalem universi: Peter's speech is a carefully engineered argument, with three themes each addressed to a widening section of the crowd. The first (verses 14-21) is addressed to *Viri Iudaei*. Here Peter tells them how the event the just witnessed is more evidence that the Old Testament prophecies about the end of times (Joel 2: 28-32) have been fulfilled. ***Horā diei tertiā***: that is, about 9 AM. ***Novissimis diebus***: The adjective *novus, -a, -um* means "new" or "of late/recent." ***Effundam***: It's not that an inspiring *spiritus* hasn't been around before. David is often said to have been inspired by the spirit. The difference is that in the end of time the spirit will be poured out in abundance on all *carnem*. Even ordinary Jews, not just prophets and priests, will be inspired. ***De spiritu meo***: The preposition *de* suggests that the *spiritus* was originally not a distinct being but a manifestation of the power of God. The conception of the Trinity, of which the Holy Spirit was an equal part, wasn't finally adopted as undisputed Christian dogma until the fourth century AD.

22–28: Peter now addresses the wider Jewish population.

adprobo, to approve • **sicut**, just as • **definitus**, fixed • **consilium**, plan • **praescientia**, foreknowledge • **trado**, to hand down • **iniquus**, unjust • **adfigo**, to brand • **interemo**, to kill • **solvo**, to break up • **infernus**, underworld • **teneo**, to hold • **coram** + *ablative*, in front of • **dexter**, right hand • **propter**, on account of • **laetor**, to be glad • **exulto**, to be joyous • **requiesco**, to rest • **spes**, hope • **derelinquo**, to abandon • **iucunditas**, joy • **facies**, face

²²"Viri Israhelitae, audite verba haec. Iesum Nazarenum—virum adprobatum a Deo in vobis virtutibus et prodigiis et signis quae fecit per illum Deus in medio vestri, sicut vos scitis— ²³hunc, definito consilio et praescientiā Dei, traditum per manūs iniquorum adfigentes interemistis— ²⁴quem Deus suscitavit, solutis doloribus inferni, iuxta quod inpossibile erat teneri illum ab eo. ²⁵David enim dicit in eum, 'Providebam Dominum coram me semper, quoniam a dextris meis est ne commovear. ²⁶Propter hoc, laetatum est cor meum, et exultavit lingua mea insuper, et caro mea requiescet in spe. ²⁷Quoniam non derelinques animam meam in inferno neque dabis sanctum tuum videre corruptionem. ²⁸Notas fecisti mihi vias vitae. Replebis me iucunditate cum facie tuā."

Viri Israhelitae: The second section of Peter's speech (verses 22-28) is addressed to a broader Jewish constituency that he invokes as *viri Israhelitae*, a body larger than the *viri Judaei* he addressed in the first section. To these he recalls how Jesus' recent crucifixion and resurrection was predicted by David in the Psalms. ***In medio vestri, sicut vos scitis***: According to the synoptic Gospels (Mark, Matthew, and Luke) Jesus performed only one public miracle during his time at Jerusalem during the Passover week. He blasted a fig tree outside of the city because it hadn't produced fruit yet (Matthew 21:18-22; Mark 11:12-14). It's fitting therefore that Peter directs this part of his address to Jews outside of Judea and Jerusalem, for only they witnessed Jesus' miracles. ***Adfigentes***: possibly a reference to the sign attached to Jesus' cross. As recorded later in John 19:19, it was written in Hebrew (i.e., Aramaic), Greek, and Latin: "Jesus, the Man from Nazareth, King of the Jews." John continues that the chief priest objected and wanted it changed to "He said, 'I'm the King of the Jews.'" Pilate replied, as translated into Latin, *"Quod scripsi, scripsi."* ***David enim dicit***: (Psalm 16 [15]: 8-11) Peter sets out the proof text that lays the foundation for a complex argument to come: 1) since David was a prophet, he cannot make a mistake about the future; 2) he says in the psalm that God will not let "his" body see corruption after his death; 3) but David's body was buried and saw corruption; 4) therefore David must not have been referring to his own body, but to the body of one of his descendants; 5) it must be that David was predicting Jesus' resurrection, not his own.

29–36: Finally Peter addresses the new and emerging community of Christ believers.

licet, it is permitted • **audenter**, boldly • **defungor**, to die • **sepelio**, to bury • **hodiernus**, present • **iureiurandum**, an oath • **fructus**, fruit • **lumbus**, loin • **sedes**, seat • **accipio**, to receive • **effundo**, to pour out • **donec**, until • **pono**, to place • **inimicus**, an enemy • **pes**, foot • **scabillum**, footstool • **ergo**, therefore • **domus**, home

---

²⁹"Viri, fratres, liceat audenter dicere ad vos de patriarchā David, quoniam et defunctus est et sepultus est, et sepulchrum eius est apud nos usque in hodiernum diem. ³⁰Propheta igitur cum esset et sciret quia 'iureiurando iurasset illi' Deus 'de fructu lumbi eius sedere super sedem eius,' ³¹providens locutus est de resurrectione Christi, quia 'neque derelictus est in inferno, neque' caro eius 'vidit corruptionem.' ³²Hunc Iesum resuscitavit Deus, cui omnes nos testes sumus. ³³Dexterā igitur Dei exaltatus et promissione Spiritūs Sancti acceptā a Patre, effudit hunc quem vos videtis et audistis. ³⁴Non enim David ascendit in caelos, dicit autem ipse, 'Dixit Dominus Domino meo, "Sede a dextris meis, ³⁵donec ponam inimicos tuos scabillum pedum tuorum."' ³⁶Certissime ergo sciat omnis domus Israhel quia et Dominum eum et Christum Deus fecit hunc Iesum, quem vos crucifixistis."

Viri, fratres: Finally the third section (verses 29–36) is addressed to the new and emerging community of Christ believers, the *viri, fratres*. To these he talks about the reality of the Kingdom of God and their own promised resurrection, as a signal that their salvation is both for the present and the future. So the outline of the speech is 1) the end of times is here, 2) we have all witnessed Jesus' crucifixion and resurrection, and 3) the promise of the Kingdom and life-everlasting has been fulfilled. **Audenter**: It would take some courage to suggest David's tomb refutes his earlier prediction. Peter asks for patience while he develops his argument that David's prediction was not mistaken, despite the evidence, and that he was actually referring to one of his descendants, and not to himself. **Iureiurando iurasset**: literally, "to have sworn by swearing an oath." *iurasset = iuravisset*. *Iureiurando* is a compound made up of *ius* and the gerundive *iurandum*. Hence both roots inflect: nominative, *iusiurandum*; genitive, *iurisiurandi*, etc. There follows a complex mélange of passages taken from Psalms: Psalm 132:11, *de fructu . . . sedem eius*; Psalm 16:10, *neque derelictus . . . corruptionem*; Psalm 110:1, *Dixit dominus . . . dextris meis*. **Certissime ergo sciat**: This completes the syllogism started at verse 14: The outpouring of the Holy Spirit evidenced by how the disciples were speaking in tongues is the sign that the entire nexus of prophecies about the end of times and the arrival of the Messiah is being tied together.

37–41: The people regret what they did to Jesus. Peter tells them they must repent of their sins in the name of Jesus Christ to be saved. Three thousand are baptized.

conpungo, to grieve • **reliquus**, the other • **paenitentia**, repentance • **ago**, to make • **remissio**, forgiveness • **peccatum**, a sin • **longe**, far off • **advoco**, to summon • **plures**, more • **exhortor**, to exhort • **salvo**, to save • **pravus**, depraved • **adpono**, to set next to • **anima**, soul/person • **tres**, three • **milia**, thousands

---

³⁷His auditis, conpuncti sunt corde, et dixerunt ad Petrum et ad reliquos Apostolos, "Quid faciemus, viri, fratres?" ³⁸Petrus vero ad illos, "Paenitentiam," inquit, "agite et baptizetur unusquisque vestrum in nomine Iesu Christi in remissionem peccatorum vestrorum, et accipietis donum Sancti Spiritūs. ³⁹Vobis enim est repromissio et filiis vestris et omnibus qui longe sunt, quoscumque advocaverit Dominus Deus noster." ⁴⁰Aliis etiam verbis pluribus testificatus est et exhortabatur eos, dicens, "Salvamini a generatione istā pravā." ⁴¹Qui ergo receperunt sermonem eius baptizati sunt, et adpositae sunt in illā die animae circiter tria milia.

Conpuncti sunt corde: Persuaded by the evidence and Peter's interpretation of these recent events in Jerusalem, the crowd asks how they may be forgiven. What follows is the first Christian baptism recorded. John the Baptist asked the converts to repent and be immersed in water. The new baptism adds the expression in *nomine Iesu Christi* and promises them the gift of the Holy Spirit, which is presumably the powers they've witnessed in the disciples. At Acts 19: 1-7, Paul *rebaptizes* twelve men in Ephesus who'd been previously baptized by John. They tell Paul they never even knew there was such a thing as a Holy Spirit. **Omnibus qui longe sunt**: We can't assume that this is yet meant to include Gentiles (non-Jews). There was a considerable diasporic Jewish world outside of Judea, and Peter may be referring only to them.

42–47: The body of believers sell their goods and share the proceeds.

fractio, a breaking • **panis**, bread • **timor**, honor • **metus**, fear • **credo**, to believe • **pariter**, equally • **communis**, in common • **substantia**, resources • **vendo**, to sell • **divido**, to divide • **prout**, such as • **cuique** < **quisque**, each one • **opus**, need • **cotidie**, daily • **quoque**, and also • **perduro**, to endure • **frango**, to break • **circa**, around • **sumo**, to take up • **cibum**, meal • **conlaudo**, to praise • **gratia**, favor • **plebs**, common people • **augeo**, to increase

⁴²Erant autem perseverantes in doctrinā Apostolorum et communicatione fractionis panis et orationibus. ⁴³Fiebat autem omni animae timor. Multa quoque prodigia et signa per Apostolos fiebant in Hierusalem, et metus erat magnus in universis. ⁴⁴Omnes etiam qui credebant erant pariter et habebant omnia communia. ⁴⁵Possessiones et substantias vendebant et dividebant illa omnibus, prout cuique opus erat. ⁴⁶Cotidie quoque perdurantes unianimiter in Templo et frangentes circa domos panem sumebant cibum cum exultatione et simplicitate cordis, ⁴⁷conlaudantes Deum et habentes gratiam ad omnem plebem. Dominus autem augebat qui salvi fierent cotidie in id ipsum.

Communicatione fractionis panis: This may not be the ritual of the Eucharist, but an expression of the fact that the community of Christ believers met to have a common meal, known as a "love feast," perhaps as a way of caring for the needy among them who might not have the resources to feed themselves. ***Timor***: In these contexts *timor* means the "reverence" or "awe" that one feels in the presence of a divine reality. Verse 43 has been suspected to be misplaced. Logically it would come before, not after, verse 42, as a way of summarizing the general feeling of people in Jerusalem in light of these events. Then Luke would turn to a discussion of how the first community of Christ believers were organizing their affairs. ***Possessiones et substantias vendebant***: It's clear that they didn't sell off all their possessions and turn the proceeds over to the apostles. People still had homes to go to where they would bake their bread (verse 46). As the number of Christ believers grew, the distribution of their common resources became more difficult. ***In id ipsum***: literally, "for this very thing." But what does that mean? The sense isn't transparent in Latin or Greek, where it's *epi to auto*, and there are several manuscript divergences as well. Some translations omit the expression altogether. It's best not to linger over this question as it doesn't substantially affect the narrative.

Province of Roman Judea

The Province of Roman Judea was established in AD 6. It is often referred to as "Roman Judea" to distinguish it from the region of Judea within it.

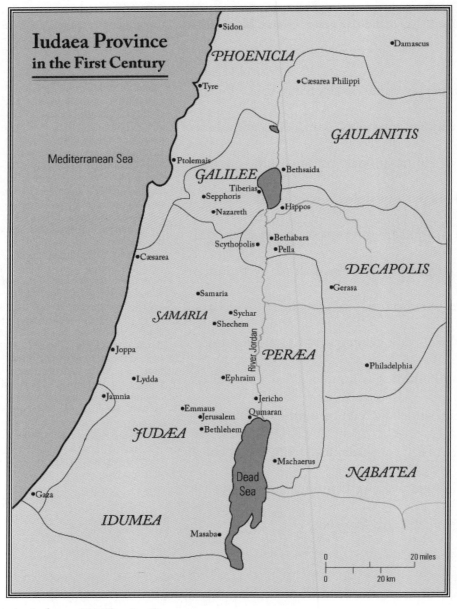

Iudaea Province by Andrew c, 2006 Creative Commons.

ACTS

3 AD 30/33-35

At the entrance of the temple, Peter heals a man paralyzed from birth. He explains to the people, who knew the man, that he drew from the power of Christ to effect the cure. Peter testifies that Jesus suffered to fulfill prophecies, and tells them they need to repent and be saved. If they do, they will become prophets of Jesus to the world.

1–8: Peter and John heal a man lame from birth.

---

nonus, ninth • **claudus**, lame • **uterus**, womb • **speciosus**, beautiful • **baiulo**, to carry • **peto**, to ask for • **elemosyna**, alms • **ambulo**, to walk • **protinus**, immediately • **consolido**, to become stonger • **basis**, foot • **planta**, sole of the foot • **intro**, to enter into • **exilio**, to jump up

---

Petrus autem et Iohannes ascendebant in Templum ad horam orationis nonam. ²Et quidam vir, qui erat claudus ex utero matris suae, baiulabatur quem ponebant cotidie ad portam Templi, quae dicitur Speciosa, ut peteret elemosynam ab introeuntibus in Templum. ³Is cum vidisset Petrum et Iohannem incipientes introire in Templum, rogabat ut elemosynam acciperet. ⁴Intuens autem in eum Petrus cum Iohanne dixit, "Respice in nos." ⁵At ille intendebat in eos, sperans se aliquid accepturum ab eis. ⁶Petrus autem dixit, "Argentum et aurum non est mihi. Quod autem habeo, hoc tibi do in nomine Iesu Christi

Ascendebant: Visitors could be said to be "going up" to the Temple because the complex was on a hill in Jerusalem, which itself is twenty-five hundred feet above sea level. ***Nonam***: i.e., 3 PM. There were two designated times of prayer each day, and in theory those who were near the Temple were to leave off from their business and pray in one of its *porticos*. **Quae dicitur Speciosa**: None of the entry gates to the Temple compound is known to have been called this. Presumably, it was one of the larger gates, where a beggar would hope for more alms because of the high traffic. ***Accepturum***: The future active infinitive regularly leaves out the complementary verb *esse*. ***Mihi***: dative of possession. Literally, "there is not to me gold or silver." ***Ei***: another dative of possession, "with his right hand having been taken." ***Protinus consolidatae sunt bases eius et plantae***: The tradition that Luke was a physician is strengthened by this anatomically precise description of the lame man's ailment and recovery.

Nazareni. Surge et ambula." ⁷Et adprehensā ei manū dexterā, adlevavit eum et protinus consolidatae sunt bases eius et plantae. ⁸Et exiliens stetit et ambulabat et intravit cum illis in Templum, ambulans et exiliens et laudans Dominum.

9–11: The people who knew the man are astonished and praise God.

cognosco, to recognize • **quoniam**, that • **stupor**, astonishment • **extasus**, stunned • **contingit**, happen to

⁹Et vidit omnis populus eum ambulantem et laudantem Deum. ¹⁰Cognoscebant autem illum, quoniam ipse erat qui ad elemosynam sedebat ad Speciosam Portam Templi. Et impleti sunt stupore et extasi in eo quod contigerat illi. ¹¹Cum teneret autem Petrum et Iohannem, concurrit omnis populus ad eos ad porticum, qui appellatur Salomonis, stupentes.

Ad elemosynam: *Ad* can indicate purpose: "for alms." *Cum teneret*: The subject is the man who'd been healed. This is how the crowd discovered the authors of the cure. *Qui appellatur Salomonis*: This portico ran along the eastern wall of the Temple and was frequently used as a place for public addresses.

12–18: Peter addresses them: "This was all done in the name of the man you crucified and who was risen by God from the dead."

miror, to mavel at • **quasi**, as if • **dimitto**, to forgive • **suscito**, to raise up • **interficio**, to kill • **integer**, pure

¹²Videns autem Petrus respondit ad populum, "Viri Israhelitae, quid miramini in hōc, aut nos quid intuemini, quasi nostrā virtute aut pietate fecerimus hunc ambulare? ¹³Deus Abraham et Deus Isaac et Deus Iacob Deus patrum nostrorum glorificavit filium suum, Iesum, quem vos quidem tradidistis et negastis ante faciem Pilati, iudicante illo, dimitti. ¹⁴Vos autem sanctum et iustum negastis, et petistis virum homicidam donari vobis. ¹⁵Auctorem vero vitae interfecistis, quem Deus suscitavit a mortuis, cuius nos testes sumus. ¹⁶Et in fide nominis eius, hunc quem videtis et nostis confirmavit nomen eius et fides, quae per eum est. Dedit integram sanitatem istam in conspectu omnium vestrum. ¹⁷Et nunc, fratres, scio quia per ignorantiam fecistis, sicut et principes vestri. ¹⁸Deus autem quae praenuntiavit per os omnium prophetarum—pati Christum suum—implevit sic."

Viri Israhelitae: Peter's second speech more or less reverses the thematic order of his first (2:14-36). In that speech he started with Old Testament prophecies, continued with the recent events of the crucifixion, and ended with the promise of Jesus' restorative power. In this speech, he begins with Jesus' power to heal, continues with the events of Jesus' death and crucifixion, and ends by citing Old Testament prophecies. *Virtute*: "power" not "virtue." *Hunc ambulare*: In Classical Latin this would be *ut hīc ambularet*. *Nostis*: a syncopated form of *novistis* < *nosco*, "you know." *Negastis . . . dimitti*: = *nega[vi]stis*: "whom you said not . . . to be released" = "whom you refused to have released." *Auctorem vero vitae*: This is a nice rhetorical play on *homicidem* just before: "you released a murderer but murdered the giver of life. *Confirmavit*: "healed; strengthened," not "confirmed." *Nomen et fides*: Peter must mean that his own faith granted him the gift of the Holy Spirit, and it's with this power that he can effect cures. It's the name of Jesus, actuated by this faith, that invokes the Holy Spirit and directs its healing power. In any case, the lame man is entirely passive in all this. His own faith, or lack thereof, has no bearing on the cure. *Omnium prophetarum*: This is hyperbole. Far from being found in all the prophets, there is not a single explicit prediction anywhere in the Old Testament that the Christ must suffer. (Isaiah 53 speaks of a suffering servant, but he is not identified with the Christ.) *Pati Christum*: This accusative-infinitive construction is what the prophets allegedly say: "that the Christ suffers." The present tense of the infinitive captures the gnomic force of the attribution, almost as if it were a proverb and not a temporal prediction: "the Christ suffers" and not "the Christ will suffer."

19–21: "You must repent to have your sins forgiven because the end of times that was predicted has arrived."

paeniteor, to repent • **deleo**, to erase • **refrigerium**, renewal • **saeculum**, generation

[19]"Paenitemini igitur et convertimini ut deleantur vestra peccata; [20]ut deleantur vestra peccata cum venerint tempora refrigerii a conspectu Domini et miserit eum qui praedicatus est vobis, Iesum Christum, [21]quem oportet caelum quidem suscipere usque in tempora restitutionis omnium, quae locutus est Deus per os sanctorum suorum a saeculo prophetarum."

Cum venerint tempora: They should want to have their sins blotted out both for the present age and for the time of restoration that will come when Jesus returns. *Refrigerii*: This seems to be an implicit agricultural metaphor. Just as the cool rains in the fall mark the time of the rebirth of the land, so the coming age will bring with it the promise of new life. *A saeculo prophetarum*: The last prophet in the canonical Old Testament is Malachi, who dates to the fifth century BC at the latest.

22–26: "This was prophesied in Scripture."

deinceps, one after another • **nequitia**, evildoing

²²"Moses quidem dixit quia 'Prophetam vobis suscitabit Dominus Deus vester de fratribus vestris, tamquam me ipsum. Audietis iuxta omnia quaecumque locutus fuerit vobis. ²³"Erit autem omnis anima, quae non audierit prophetam illum, exterminabitur de plebe.' ²⁴Et omnes prophetae a Samuhel et deinceps, qui locuti sunt, et adnuntiaverunt dies istos. ²⁵Vos estis filii prophetarum et testamenti, quod disposuit Deus ad patres vestros, dicens ad Abraham, 'Et in semine tuo benedicentur omnes familiae terrae.' ²⁶Vobis primum Deus, suscitans Filium suum, misit eum benedicentem vobis, ut convertat se unusquisque a nequitiā suā."

Moses: Peter continues his journey back into the deeper history of the Jewish people to Moses, the first of the prophets. The cutting-and-pasting of various Old Testament references that follows is difficult to navigate. Peter begins with a passage from Deuteronomy 18:15 where Moses says God will raise up a great prophet. Next he splices two different passages together, one from Deuteronomy 18:19 and another from part of Leviticus 23:29: *Prophetam de gente tuā et de fratribus tuis sicut me suscitabit tibi Dominus Deus tuus. Ipsum audies,* and *Omnis anima quae adflicta non fuerit die hoc peribit de populis suis.* Assuming that Luke is accurately reporting Peter's words, such a sophisticated use of Old Testament documents would have amazed the crowd. ***A Samuhel***: Strictly speaking Samuel was not a prophet, but there were prophets active during his reign. Think of this as "from the time of Samuel." ***Et in semine tuo***: Genesis 22:18. ***Vobis primum Deus***: The adverb *primum* anticipates the great debate that will dominate much of Acts over how and under what conditions non-Jews will enter into the covenant with the Jewish God.

The Temple of Jerusalem

Herod the Great's lavish rebuilding of the Temple stood less than one hundred years. It was destroyed by the Romans in AD 70 when they put down a wide-spread Jewish revolt against their rule. The Temple consisted of areas of increasing sanctity and restrictions. Beginning with the outer courtyards, where even pagans were allowed in, it ended with the Holy Place, which only the high priest could enter.

Holyland Model of Jerusalem by Berthold Werner, 2008. (Wikimedia Commons)

ACTS 4

AD 30/33-35

Peter and John are arrested for spreading the word of Jesus' resurrection. The two reject an order that they stop talking about Jesus, but they are released because the authorities fear the reaction of the crowd. Back with their friends, they all pray that God send them a sign of his protection. There immediately follows an earthquake and yet another outpouring of the Holy Spirit. The communal life of the Christ believers is described in more detail. One of them, named Joseph, sells his land and gives the money to the disciples for its distribution to the community.

1–4: The Jewish authorities have Peter and John arrested, but not before another five thousand are converted.

doleo, to feel pain • **inicio**, to lay upon • **crastinus**, the next day • **vespera**, evening

Loquentibus autem illis ad populum supervenerunt sacerdotes et magistratūs Templi et Sadducaei, ²dolentes quod docerent populum et adnuntiarent in Iesu resurrectionem ex mortuis. ³Et iniecerunt in eis manūs, et posuerunt eos in custodiam in crastinum, erat enim iam vespera. ⁴Multi autem eorum qui audierant verbum crediderunt, et factus est numerus virorum quinque milia.

Loquentibus autem illis: ablative absolute, "while they were talking." *Magistratus Templi et Sadducaei*: *Magistratus* is the Latin translation for the Greek *stratēgos*, which has a military connotation. He was, in effect, the supervisor of the priests in the performance of their duties. Our word "priest" signifies a mostly religious office, distinct from the lay members of a congregation. A priest in an ancient temple, by contrast, could be a security guard, tour guide, janitor, custodian, or a manager. The Sadducees are specified here because their sect was most firmly attached to the Temple and the traditional rituals mandated there. When the Temple was destroyed in AD 70 by the Romans, they all but disappeared from history. *In crastinum*: "until the next day." A session for a Sanhedrin court could be held only until the afternoon sacrifice at 3 PM. Hence even though Peter and John were arrested during the day, the court would not reconvene until the next morning.

ACTS OF THE APOSTLES

5–14: At the trial, the authorities are unnerved by Peter's eloquent defense and invocation of Jesus' power.

scriba, scribe • **hodie**, today • **diiudico**, to judge • **plebs**, people • **coram** + *ablative*, in front of • **lapis**, stone • **reprobo**, to reject • **aedifico**, to build • **angulus**, angle • **salus**, salvation • **conperto quod**, at the realization that • **idiota**, a common man

⁵Factum est autem in crastinum ut congregarentur principes eorum et seniores et scribae in Hierusalem. ⁶Et Annas, princeps sacerdotum, et Caiphas et Iohannes et Alexander et quotquot erant de genere sacerdotali, ⁷et statuentes eos in medio, interrogabant, "In quā virtute aut in quo nomine fecistis hoc vos?" ⁸Tunc Petrus, repletus Spiritu Sancto, dixit ad eos principes, "Populi et seniores, ⁹si nos hodie diiudicamur in benefacto hominis infirmi, in quo iste salvus factus est, ¹⁰notum sit omnibus vobis et omni plebi Israhel quia in nomine Iesu Christi Nazareni, quem vos crucifixistis, quem Deus suscitavit a mortuis. In hōc iste adstat coram vobis, sanus. ¹¹Hīc est lapis qui reprobatus est a vobis aedificantibus, qui factus est in caput anguli. ¹²Et non est in alio aliquo salus, nec enim nomen aliud est

Principes eorum: This is a hearing before the Sanhedrin, the administrative body for Jewish affairs, of which Luke identifies three parts: the leaders of the priests, the elders of the people, and the scribes, who were experts in the law. The present hearing may not have been before the entire Sanhedrin of seventy-one sitting as a court, but only part of it. The antecedent of *eorum* is the priests of verse 1. Not all the priests were called to serve on the court; only their leaders. *Et quotquot erant de genere sacerdotali*: The office of the High Priest was hereditary, being reserved for members of a certain clan, but behind the scenes the Romans were appointing and deposing them as fit their needs. Luke calls Annas the High Priest, but technically Caiaphas was the High Priest at the time. Annas was High Priest from AD 6-15, when he was deposed by the Romans and replaced with one of his sons, Eleazar, who ruled for one year from AD 16 to 17. He in turn was replaced by Annas' son-in-law Caiaphas, who ruled from 18 until his death in 36. (This, incidentally, gives us a firm *terminus ante quem* for this event.) Annas himself lived until somewhere around AD 40. Even though he was out of office, he continued to exercise great power over his successors. For this reason, he was called the High Priest in an informal recognition of who really was calling the shots. Nothing is known of John and Alexander, unless by "John," "Jonathan" is actually meant. Jonathan succeeded Caiaphas and ruled for a year from 37-38 CE. *In quā virtute*: They do not dispute the miracle, but demand to know where they received the power. The subtext appears to be that the miracle might have in someway profaned the Temple. If Peter and John invoked the power of a pagan god, for example, this would be a serious matter. *Hīc est lapis*: This is a rephrasing of Psalm 118:22, quoted also by Jesus himself (Mark 12:10). Probably what impressed the Sanhedrin the most

sub caelo datum hominibus, in quo oportet nos salvos fieri." ¹³Videntes autem Petri constantiam et Iohannis, conperto quod homines essent sine litteris et idiotae, admirabantur, et cognoscebant eos, quoniam cum Iesu fuerant. ¹⁴Hominem quoque videntes stantem cum eis qui curatus fuerat, nihil poterant contradicere.

is not that Peter knew the passage, but that he knew is so well he was able to recast it eloquently into his own address. This shows high rhetorical ability they didn't anticipate in someone not known to be an educated and skillful speaker. **Conperto quod**: *comperto* (< *comperio*) is an ablative of cause: "it being realized that," or "because of the realization that." **Nihil poterant contradicere**: The reality of the cure is undeniable, and since Peter and John claim it wasn't the work of a foreign, pagan God, but ultimately of the Jewish God, there is no case against them.

ACTS OF THE APOSTLES

15–22: They decide to release Peter and John, urging them not to talk anymore about Jesus.

foras extra, outside • **secedo**, to depart • **confero**, to confer • **divulgo**, to spread around • **comminor**, to threaten • **potius**, rather • **punio**, to punish

¹⁵Iusserunt autem eos foras extra concilium secedere, et conferebant ad invicem, ¹⁶dicentes, "Quid faciemus hominibus istis, quoniam quidem notum signum factum est per eos omnibus habitantibus in Hierusalem? Manifestum [est] et non possumus negare, ¹⁷sed ne amplius divulgetur in populum, comminemur eis, ne ultra loquantur in nomine hōc ulli hominum." ¹⁸Et vocantes eos denuntiaverunt ne omnino loquerentur neque docerent in nomine Iesu. ¹⁹Petrus vero et Iohannes respondentes dixerunt ad eos, "Si iustum est, in conspectu Dei, vos potius audire quam Deum iudicate. ²⁰Non enim possumus quae vidimus et audivimus non loqui." ²¹At illi comminantes dimiserunt eos, non invenientes quomodo punirent eos propter populum, quia omnes clarificabant Deum in eo quod acciderat. ²²Annorum enim erat amplius quadraginta homo, in quo factum erat signum istud sanitatis.

Conferebant ad invicem: Peter's defense has put the Sanhedrin in a bind. They can't deny that the man was healed, and pursuing the inquiry would give Peter and John a forum to evangelize the Gospel of Jesus. What had been a simple investigation into the possibility that the Temple had been profaned by the invocation of a pagan deity had the potential of becoming a full blown heresy within the Jewish religion itself. They decide (wisely, from a certain perspective) to cancel the proceeding and let them off with a warning. *Comminemur eis*: hortatory subjunctive, "Let's warn them," followed by the indirect command beginning with *ne*, "that they not . . . ," or "not to . . ." *ulli*, dative after *loquantur*, "to any one of men." *Si iustum est*: This is an indirect question, despite the indicative mood of the verb, after *iudicate*, "In the presence of God, you decide whether it is just to listen to you rather than to God." *Quae*: = *ea quae*, "that which" or "what." *Clarificabant*: "were glorifying." *In eo quod acciderat*: "in what had happened." *Annorum . . .* : A more natural word order in English would be: *homo enim, in quo factum erat signum istud sanitatis, erat amplius quadraginta annorum*. In other words, he wasn't a plant and this wasn't a scam. They'd known this crippled man for decades.

CHAPTER 4

23–31: Reunited with their friends, Peter and John pray that God will send a sign that he will be with them. The earth shakes and they are all filled again with the Holy Spirit.

quare, why • **fremo**, to growl • **meditor**, to think about • **ungo**, to annoint • **decerno**, to decide upon • **mina**, threat • **fiducia**, trustworthiness

---

²³Dimissi autem venerunt ad suos et adnuntiaverunt eis quanta ad eos principes sacerdotum et seniores dixissent. ²⁴Qui cum audissent, unianimiter levaverunt vocem ad Deum et dixerunt, "Domine, tu qui fecisti caelum et terram et mare et omnia quae in eis sunt, ²⁵qui Spiritu Sancto per os patris nostri David, pueri tui, dixisti, 'Quare fremuerunt Gentes et populi meditati sunt inania? ²⁶Adsiterunt reges terrae et principes convenerunt in unum adversus Dominum et adversus Christum eius?' ²⁷Convenerunt enim vere in civitate istā adversus sanctum puerum tuum, Iesum, quem unxisti, Herodes et Pontius Pilatus cum Gentibus et populis Israhel ²⁸facere quae manŭs tua et consilium decreverunt fieri. ²⁹Et nunc, Domine, respice in minas eorum, et da servis tuis cum omni

Quanta: is accusative neuter plural, object of *dixissent*: "as many things as," or "everything that." The verb is subjunctive of indirect question. ***Quare fremuerunt***: The reference is to Psalm 2:1-2. At the time, the Israelites were living in a kingdom, and the king was God's anointed one, the *Christos* in Greek. Thus opposing the *Christos* was to oppose God himself. Later, when the Davidic kingdom had been lost, the verses were thought to refer to a new, promised king and the restoration of the old Davidic kingdom. ***Gentes***: "the nations." This is the first time in Acts that this word is used for all non-Jews. It's the Latin equivalent of the Greek *ethnē*, which is itself a translation of the Hebrew *goy* (*goyim* in the plural). The adjective *Gentilis* derived from it is translated into English as "Gentile." ***Herodes***: This isn't Herod the Great, who ruled over the Jews for the Romans from 43-44 BC, but his son, Herod Antipas, who ruled over the region of Galilee from 4 BC to 39 CE. Only Luke (23: 6-12) has Herod Antipas play a role in Jesus' crucifixion, and then it's only a minor one. ***Quae***: It was of course God's plan that Jesus suffer and be crucified. This explains why the Gentiles and the opponents of the *Christos* rage in vain: they can do nothing but act as agents of God's will. ***Orassent***: ovavissent. ***Cum fiduciā***: This is not the same as speaking in foreign languages, as was reported when the Holy Spirit was first poured out on them. Now they are speaking out courageously, with conviction. Peter and John have just returned from being arrested—the first recorded persecution of the Christ believers—so it's natural that a certain amount of fear would be felt by the other disciples. They'd never personally been the object of the legal apparatus of the authorities before. Buoyed by the visible signs of miraculous healing and now the earthquake, their courage has been restored.

fiduciā loqui verbum tuum, ³⁰in eo cum manum tuam extendas sanitates et signa et prodigia fieri per nomen sancti Filii tui, Iesu." ³¹Et cum orassent, motus est locus in quo erant congregati, et repleti sunt omnes Spiritu Sancto, et loquebantur verbum Dei cum fiduciā.

32–37: The Christ believers form a communal society, in which all things are owned collectively and distributed according to their needs.

egeo, to need • **quotquot**, as many as • **vendo**, to sell • **pretium**, price

---

³²Multitudinis autem credentium erat cor et anima una, nec quisquam eorum quae possidebant aliquid suum esse dicebat, sed erant illis omnia communia. ³³Et virtute magnā reddebant Apostoli testimonium resurrectionis Iesu Christi Domini, et gratia magna erat in omnibus illis. ³⁴Neque enim quisquam egens erat. Inter illos quotquot enim possessores agrorum aut domorum erant, vendentes adferebant pretia eorum quae vendebant, ³⁵et ponebant ante pedes Apostolorum. Dividebantur autem singulis prout cuique opus erat. ³⁶Ioseph autem, qui cognominatus est Barnabas ab Apostolis—quod est interpretatum "Filius Consolationis"—Levites, Cyprius genere, ³⁷cum haberet agrum, vendidit illum et adtulit pretium et posuit ante pedes Apostolorum.

Multidudinis . . . : It's widely thought that verse 33 has been mis-located. The passage flows more naturally as 33, 32, 34-37. ***Anima una***: Luke repeatedly emphasizes the unity of spirit of the first Christ believers, to contrast this period with the dissent and divisions that were soon to break out. *Eorum*: partitive genitive, "none of them." ***Suum esse dicebat***: "said anything of the things he had to be his own." Essentially they've renounced the idea of private property. ***Erant illis omnia communia***: We read in Acts 12:12 that at least some held on to their private houses. ***Quotquot***: this is the subject of *erant*, "As many as were owners of land or houses (i.e., landlords)." ***Quae***: "for which." ***Singulis***: dative, "to each person." ***Prout cuique opus erat***: literally, "according as there was need to each one," or "to each according to his needs." ***Iosephus***: "Josephus" was a common name, so it makes sense that the disciples would give him a nickname to help keep him straight from others named Joseph. Barnabas is to become a key figure in Acts, serving as sponsor and early companion of Paul. The etymological explanation of the name "Barnabas," like many such etymologies in biblical literature, rests on similarity of sound and appropriateness of the moment rather than a true derivation. He name would seem more likely to mean "son of prophecy," from the Hebrew *bar-něbu'-āh*, rather than "son of consolation," which would be *bar-nahmā'*. *agrum*: The field he sold was surely in Judea, not back on Cyprus. He was one of the many distant landlords who'd inherited land in the homelands before he or his family migrated out into the Jewish diaspora.

ACTS
AD 30/33-35

A husband and wife are struck dead by God for having held back some of the money from the sale of their property. The Jesus movement continues to grow, and the Jewish authorities respond with more arrests. Their prisoners are miraculously released by an angel. They are taken into custody again and interrogated. Peter makes an eloquent defense. Gamaliel, a leading Pharisee, convinces the authorities that the movement will pass now that its leader has been executed. The prisoners are threatened, abused, and then released.

1–11: Two followers of Jesus try to hold back some of the money they made on the sale of their property.

---

uxor, wife • **conscius**, aware • **mentior**, to misrepresent • **venundatum**, profit • **cado**, to fall dow • **sepelio**, to bury • **quasi**, about • **ostium**, entrance • **confestim**, immediately

---

V̄ir autem quidam, nomine Ananias, cum Saffirā, uxore suā, vendidit agrum, ²et fraudavit de pretio agri, consciā uxore suā, et adferens partem quandam ad pedes Apostolorum, posuit. ³Dixit autem Petrus, "Anania, cur temptavit Satanas cor tuum mentiri te Spiritui Sancto et fraudare de pretio agri? ⁴Nonne manens tibi manebat? Et venundatum in tuā erat potestate? Quare posuisti in corde tuo hanc rem? Non es mentitus hominibus, sed Deo." ⁵Audiens autem Ananias haec verba cecidit et exspiravit. Et factus est timor magnus in omnes qui audierant. ⁶Surgentes autem iuvenes amoverunt eum et efferentes

Fraudavit de pretio: "He lied about the price" he got for the land. Ananias's fault will amount to blasphemy against the Holy Spirit, the only sin that cannot be forgiven (Luke 12:10). His offense is pretending to be filled with the Holy Spirit. *Consciā uxore suā*: This ablative absolute provides the basis for her punishment as well. If she had been unaware of her husband's fraud, she would have been innocent of the blasphemy. *Adferens*: Ananias mimics the pattern of giving followed by the true believers. This underscores his intention to pass himself off as a true convert. *Mentiri te*: The grammar isn't easy at this point. Most translations take *te* as the subject of the infinitive *mentiri*, "that you lie to the Holy Spirit." It's possible, however, that *mentiri* means "to make a false image of" and *te* is the object: "to make a false image of yourself to the Holy Spirit." This is exactly what Ananias he's doing. *Nonne [ager] manens tibi manebat*: "Wasn't the field yours when it belonged to you?" That is, Ananias was under no obligation to sell it. *Venundatum*: "the proceeds from the sale." Again, Ananias could have stopped the fraud before he committed it. He didn't have to sell the property, and when he had the money he could have done anything he liked with it. *Quare*: It's best to imagine Peter delivering his comments to Ananias in great sorrow, rather than rage, since he knows what the punishment will be. *Factum est autem quasi horarum trium spatium*: literally, "There came an interval of about three hours," or more idiomatically, "About three hours went by." *Tanti*: genitive of price, "for such an amount?"

33

sepelierunt. ⁷Factum est autem quasi horarum trium spatium, et uxor ipsius, nesciens quod factum fuerat, introiit. ⁸Respondit autem ei Petrus, "Dic mihi, mulier, si tanti agrum vendidistis?" At illa dixit, "Etiam tanti." ⁹Petrus autem ad eam, "Quid utique convēnit vobis temptare Spiritum Domini? Ecce: pedes eorum qui sepelierunt virum tuum ad ostium, et efferent te." ¹⁰Confestim cecidit ante pedes eius, et exspiravit. Intrantes autem iuvenes invenerunt illam mortuam, et extulerunt et sepelierunt ad virum suum. ¹¹Et factus est timor magnus in universā ecclesiā, et in omnes qui audierunt haec.

Quid utique convēnit vobis: *quid* isn't "what" here, but "why"; *utique* emphasizes the question, and *convēnit* is impersonal: "Just why did it occur to you . . ." **Ad ostium**: because burials weren't allowed in the city. **Efferent te**: "and who will carry you out [once you've died]." **Ecclesiā**: This is the first time the body of Christ believers is referred to as a whole. It's usually translated "church," but inasmuch as this implies both a structured system and a fixed, purpose-specific building, this can be misleading. The Greek word *ekklēsia* literally means a "calling out," like a "gathering," or "collective." It was used for the grand assembly of Athenian citizens meeting to consider state policy, and for smaller trade organizations. My notes will translate *ecclesiā* as "body of believers" to avoid any anachronistic associations with our word "church."

12–16: More and more people flock to the disciples.

platea, broad street • **lectulum**, cot • **grabattum** • stretcher, **saltim**, at any event • **vicinus**, neighboring • **aeger**, sick • **vexo**, to torment • **inmundus**, impure

---

¹²Per manūs autem Apostolorum, fiebant signa et prodigia multa in plebe. Et erant unianimiter omnes in porticu Salomonis. ¹³Ceterorum autem nemo audebat coniungere se illis, sed magnificabat eos populus. ¹⁴Magis autem augebatur credentium in Domino multitudo virorum ac mulierum, ¹⁵ita ut in plateas eicerent infirmos et ponerent in lectulis et grabattis, ut veniente Petro saltim umbra illius obumbraret quemquam eorum. ¹⁶Concurrebat autem et multitudo vicinarum civitatum Hierusalem adferentes aegros et vexatos ab spiritibus inmundis, qui curabantur omnes.

Fiebant: *signa et prodigia multa* are the subjects of the verb, not its objects. ***In porticu Salomonis***: The Temple compound was enclosed by four walls, on the inside of which ran long colonnades, also called *stoas* or *porticos*. The *Stoa* or Portico of Solomon has been positively identified as the one that engages with the eastern wall. ***Nemo audebat***: We can imagine what people thought of a relatively large number of people gathered at the Gate of Solomon praying in unison. It would have been as frightening as it was novel. ***Credentium***: present active participle used as a substantive, "of believers." What do these believers believe? Do they believe that the disciples have been given divine powers to heal, or do they believe that Jesus has been resurrected from the dead and is the living Messiah? Luke's reference only to *Domino* doesn't clear up the matter, for it could refer to Jesus as Lord or to God himself. In any case, we can see the emergence of different levels of commitment to and understanding of Jesus in the throngs of people attracted to the movement: those who believe the good news, and those who are merely seeking cures. ***Ita ut***: We have a result clause followed shortly by a purpose clause, "such that they . . . . so that Peter's shadow . . ." ***Umbra***: We're not told whether the ill whom Peter's shadow passes over were cured, only that this is what the people expected. It may say something about just how powerful Peter's gift is, or it may show only the superstition of the people. ***Omnes***: the position of the adjective, agreeing with *qui*, is emphatic, "who were cured, all of them."

17–21: The Jewish authorities arrest and imprison some of the apostles, but an angel frees them.

heresis, sect • **aperio**, to open • **ianua**, door • **carcer**, prison • **diluculum**, dawn

¹⁷Exsurgens autem princeps sacerdotum et omnes qui cum illo erant—quae est, heresis Sadducaeorum—repleti sunt zelo, ¹⁸et iniecerunt manūs in Apostolos et posuerunt illos in custodiā publicā. ¹⁹Angelus autem Domini per noctem aperiens ianuas carceris, et educens eos dixit, ²⁰"Ite et stantes, loquimini in Templo plebi omnia verba vitae huius." ²¹Qui cum audissent, intraverunt diluculo in Templum et docebant.

Princeps sacerdotum: As this disturbance is happening within the Temple compound, it's natural that the authorities would take action. ***Heresis Sadducaeorum***: The Sadducees comprised the party closely associated with the office of the high priest and other leading officials of the Temple. Hence it's entirely fitting that the Sadducees are the ones who first object to the commotion in the Temple compound. ***In custodiā publicā***: As of yet the Romans are not involved. This "public prison" is almost certainly not the Roman prison that was attached to the Temple. ***Omnia verba vitae huius***: This may be nothing more than a shorthand way of referring to what the disciples have been preaching all along: that salvation comes from repentance and baptism in Jesus' name. It's an unusual formulation repeated only one other time in Acts and nowhere else in the New Testament.

CHAPTER 5

21–28: Astonished to find the prisoners had escaped, the authorities round them up again and demand to know why they are still preaching to the crowds.

sacerdos, priest • **minister**, assistant • **revertor**, to return, • **intus**, within • **ambigo**, to debate about • **quidnam**, what(ever) • **lapido**, to stone • **vultis** < **volo**, to want

Adveniens autem princeps sacerdotum et qui cum eo erant convocaverunt concilium et omnes seniores filiorum Israhel, et miserunt in carcerem ut adducerentur. ²²Cum venissent autem ministri et aperto carcere non invenissent illos, reversi nuntiaverunt, ²³dicentes, "Carcerem quidem invēnimus clausum, cum omni diligentiā et custodes stantes ad ianuas. Aperientes autem neminem intus invēnimus. ²⁴Ut audierunt autem hos sermones, magistratŭs Templi et principes sacerdotum, ambigebant de illis, quidnam fieret. ²⁵Adveniens autem quidam nuntiavit eis quia "Ecce: viri quos posuistis in carcere sunt in Templo stantes et docentes populum." ²⁶Tunc abiit magistratŭs cum ministris et adduxit illos sine vi, timebant enim populum ne lapidarentur. ²⁷Et cum adduxissent illos, statuerunt in concilio et interrogavit eos princeps sacerdotum, ²⁸dicens, "Praecipiendo praecepimus vobis ne doceretis in nomine isto, et ecce: replestis Hierusalem doctrinā vestrā, et vultis inducere super nos sanguinem hominis istius."

Ut adducerentur: indirect command. ***Aperto carcere***: ablative absolute. ***Aperientes***: *sc. ianuas* as the object. ***Quidnam fieret***: indirect question. ***Magistratŭs***: the captain of the Jewish guard. ***Sine vi***: He handled the disciples delicately so as not to enrage the crowd. ***Timebant***: The change from singular to plural can be expected; surely the captain of the guard wasn't acting alone but giving orders to a squad of officers. ***Ne lapidarentur***: object clause after a verb of fearing. Note that it is negated, which reverses our normal English sense, "that they would be stoned." ***Praecipiendo***: gerund expressing means, "By ordering, we ordered you." The repetitive use of the root verb *praecipio* in different forms (a literary device called "polyptoton" or "*adnominatio*") gives the phrase an air of legal formality.

ACTS OF THE APOSTLES

29–32: Peter replies that they are obeying God's will to carry the news of Jesus' resurrection.

oboedio, to be obedient to • **lignum**, wood

²⁹Respondens autem Petrus et Apostoli dixerunt, "Oboedire oportet Deo magis quam hominibus. ³⁰Deus patrum nostrorum suscitavit Iesum, quem vos interemistis, suspendentes in ligno. ³¹Hunc Deus principem et salvatorem exaltavit dexterā suā, ad dandam paenitentiam Israhel et remissionem peccatorum. ³²Et nos sumus testes horum verborum et Spiritŭs Sanctus, quem dedit Deus omnibus oboedientibus sibi."

Suspendentes in ligno: The participle agrees with *vos* from the preceding clause. Strictly speaking the Jewish authorities didn't crucify Jesus; the Romans did on their insistence. Luke makes it clear that the ultimate responsibility lies with the Jews, not with the Romans. ***Salvatorem***: As familiar as this designation is in Christian worship and liturgy, this is the only time Jesus is called "Savior" in Acts, a title previously used in Jewish Scripture only for God himself (Isaiah 43:3, 11.) It could be indicative of a growing understanding by Peter and the other disciples of the reality of who Jesus was. It's also interesting that Jesus is called the savior only twice in the Gospels, once at John 3:42 and the only other time at Luke 2:11. ***Dexterā suā***: "on his right hand." To sit at the right side of the king indicated honor and authority. ***Israhel***: dative, "to grant repentance and forgiveness of sins to Israel." This means that the people of Israel have the right to repent and to have their sins forgiven because of Jesus, not that Jesus has repented on their behalf. ***Horum verborum et Spiritŭs Sanctus***: That is, we bear testimony of the words and so does the Holy Spirit, since it is visibly and tangibly acting through us.

33–39: Gamaliel, a widely respected member of the Sanhedrin, encourages patience with the new cult that has grown up around the figure of Jesus.

disseco, to be cut to the heart • **exto**, to rise up • **aliquis**, somebody • **consentio**, to agree with • **circiter**, approximately • **quadringenti**, four hundred • **occīdo**, to kill • **dissipo**, to disperse • **pereo**, to perish • **sino**, to allow • **forte**, perhaps • **repugno**, to fight against

³³Haec cum audissent dissecabantur, et cogitabant interficere illos. ³⁴Surgens autem quidam in concilio Pharisaeus, nomine Gamalihel, Legis doctor honorabilis universae plebi, iussit foras ad breve homines fieri, ³⁵dixitque ad illos, "Viri Israhelitae, attendite vobis super hominibus istis quid acturi sitis. ³⁶Ante hos enim dies extitit Theodas, dicens esse se aliquem, cui consensit virorum numerus, circiter quadringentorum. Qui occīsus est et omnes quicumque credebant ei dissipati sunt et redactus est ad nihilum. ³⁷Post hunc, extitit Iudas Galilaeus in diebus professionis et avertit populum post se. Et ipse periit et omnes, quotquot consenserunt ei, dispersi sunt. ³⁸Et nunc itaque dico vobis: discedite ab hominibus istis, et sinite illos, quoniam si est ex hominibus consilium hoc aut opus, dissolvetur. ³⁹Si vero ex Deo est, non poteritis dissolvere eos, ne forte et Deo repugnare inveniamini."

Interficere illos: It's probable that Jews could execute someone by stoning, but not by crucifixion, which was a strictly Roman method. ***Pharisaeus***: Gamaliel, only one of three named Pharisees—the other two being Paul and Nicodemus—in the New Testament, is a thoroughly sympathetic figure. ***Quid acturi sitis***: indirect question with the periphrastic future, "what you are going to do." ***Theodas . . . Iudas Galilaeus***: Gamaliel names two revolutionaries whose movements died out when they were executed. Judas the Galilean was executed in 6 AD by the Romans, but Theudas, at least the one we know anything about, led his movement in 46-48 AD, a full decade after the setting of this scene in Acts, which is dated to no later than 37 AD. It's also clear from *post hunc* that Luke puts Theuda's revolt before Judas the Galilean's, when in fact it came forty years later. What accounts for these errors? There are many possibilities. Maybe there was another Judas or Theudas we don't know anything about. Or maybe Luke or Gamaliel made an honest mistake. Another is that Luke or Gamaliel deliberately inverted the chronology to give prominence to Judas, a Galilean just as Jesus was. ***Si vero ex Deo est***: Gamaliel's argument is twofold. (1) Leave them alone, for their movement will die away. (2) But if it doesn't, then maybe Jesus is really who his followers say he is. If it's true he's from God, then there's no sense in trying to oppose them. ***Inveniamini***: "lest by chance we be found to be fighting against God too."

ACTS OF THE APOSTLES

39–42: They threaten and abuse the apostles they've arrested, and release them, with the order that they stop their preaching.

caedo, to beat • **dimitto**, to release • **gaudeo**, to rejoice • **dignus**, worthy • **contumelia**, abuse • **patior**, to suffer

Consenserunt autem illi. ⁴⁰Et convocantes Apostolos, caesis denuntiaverunt ne loquerentur in nomine Iesu, et dimiserunt eos. ⁴¹Et illi quidem ibant gaudentes a conspectu concilii quoniam digni habiti sunt pro nomine Iesu contumeliam pati. ⁴²Omni autem die in Templo et circa domos non cessabant docentes et evangelizantes Christum Iesum.

Caesis: dative after *denuntiaverunt*, "they commanded them (once they had been flogged)."
Gaudentes: They rejoiced because they were found worthy enough to be abused for Jesus' name.

ACTS

AD 30/33-35

As the number of Jesus' followers grows, there is increasing dissatisfaction among the Greek-speaking believers over the distribution of food. In response, the disciples appoint seven Greek-speaking assistants to free them from this task so that they can dedicate more time to prayer and preaching. Among the seven is Stephen, who shortly finds himself in a conflict with some Jews, who have him arraigned before the Sanhedrin.

1–5: The disciples call for the appointment of a board of seven assistants.

cresco, to grow • **murmur**, grumbling • **dispicio**, to neglect • **vidua**, widow • **duodecim**, twelve • **mensa**, table • **opus**, task • **instans**, be devoted to • **placeo**, to be pleasing to

In diebus autem illis, crescente numero discipulorum, factus est murmur Graecorum adversus Hebraeos, eo quod dispicerentur in ministerio cotidiano viduae eorum. ²Convocantes autem duodecim multitudinem discipulorum dixerunt, "Non est aequum nos derelinquere verbum Dei et ministrare mensis. ³Considerate ergo, fratres, viros ex vobis boni testimonii septem, plenos Spiritu et sapientiā, quos constituamus super hoc opus. ⁴Nos vero orationi et ministerio verbi instantes erimus. ⁵Et placuit sermo coram omni multitudine.

Graecorum adversus Hebraeos: By Greeks, Luke means ethnic Jews who spoke Greek as their first and perhaps only language, by Hebrews, he means ethnic Jews whose first and perhaps only language was Aramaic. Hebrew itself was dying out as a living language and was spoken by a small upper class associated with the Temple priesthood in Jerusalem. This is the first salvo in the battle between local, Aramaic followers of Jesus and the Greek-speaking Jews from abroad. It will be a major theme throughout Acts. ***Ministerio***: The Greek word here translated is *diakonia*, from which English gets "deacon," and "deaconate." ***Cotidiano***: The "daily" ministry appears to mean no more than providing them with regular meals. ***Viduae eorum***: This is one place among many others in Acts where Luke is agonizingly brief. We can only speculate what the full story is behind this complaint. It could be that these Greek-speaking Jews from abroad still have family living in Jerusalem and expect them to be taken care of by the disciples. The disciples, for their part, understandably might be looking after their own widows first, leaving the others to be supported by their own families. What's at issue is the evolving nature of this new community of believers. The exact boundaries dividing who's in a who's out are still being negotiated. It's also possible that the local Jews sensed the visitors were merely taking financial advantage of the movement by unloading the care of their widows on to them. The care of widows was a particular concern of the Jewish system of social support, but it was capable of being abused by its intended beneficiaries. Paul goes to great lengths in 1 Timothy 5: 3-16 to distinguish the true widows from those who are merely scamming the system. ***Considerate***: Unlike the selection of Matthias to replace Judas, the appointment of the seven will be left to the disciples themselves (not just the apostles), and we're not told how the decision was made (by vote, acclamation, or lot, for example). ***Septem***: There is no apparent significance to the number seven. ***Constituamus***: relative clause of characteristic.

ACTS OF THE APOSTLES

5–7: One of the seven selected, Stephen, is particularly noted for his gifts and constancy.

advena, visitor • **valde**, really

⁵Et elegerunt Stephanum, virum plenum fide et Spiritu Sancto, et Philippum et Prochorum et Nicanorem et Timonem et Parmenam et Nicolaum, advenam Antiochenum. ⁶Hos statuerunt ante conspectum Apostolorum, et orantes inposuerunt eis manūs. ⁷Et verbum Dei crescebat, et multiplicabatur numerus discipulorum in Hierusalem. Valde multa etiam turba sacerdotum oboediebat fidei.

Et elegerunt Stephanum: Only Stephen and Philip are mentioned again. Since they were appointed to address a "Greek" problem, it would make sense that they would at least speak Greek. ***Inposuerunt eis manūs***: The gesture that passes on the power of the Holy Spirit is repeated often in Acts (8:16-17; 13:3; 19:6). ***Turba sacerdotum***: This isn't terribly surprising that there would be a *turba* of priests, given that there were many low-level priests overseeing the daily operation in the Temple—serving as guards, gatekeepers, etc. At this point, Christ believers hadn't formally distinguished themselves from the larger body of Judaism, so there would have been no consequences for a "priest" to declare himself a follower of Jesus.

8–15: Members of the various synagogues from outside Jerusalem have problems with Stephen, and a plot with Jewish leaders to get him out of the way develops.

submitto, to bring as evidence • **cesso**, to cease • **tamquam**, like

⁸Stephanus autem, plenus gratiā et fortitudine, faciebat prodigia et signa magna in populo. ⁹Surrexerunt autem quidam de synagogā quae appellatur Libertinorum et Cyrenensium et Alexandrinorum et eorum qui erant a Ciliciā et Asiā, disputantes cum Stephano. ¹⁰Et non poterant resistere sapientiae et Spiritui quo loquebatur. ¹¹Tunc submiserunt viros qui dicerent se audisse eum dicentem verba blasphemiae in Mosen et Deum. ¹²Commoverunt itaque plebem et seniores et scribas, et concurrentes rapuerunt eum et adduxerunt in concilium. ¹³Et statuerunt testes falsos, dicentes, "Homo iste non cessat loqui verba adversus locum sanctum et Legem. ¹⁴Audivimus enim eum dicentem quoniam Iesus Nazarenus hĭc destruet locum istum et mutabit traditiones quas tradidit nobis Moses." ¹⁵Et intuentes eum omnes qui sedebant in concilio viderunt faciem eius tamquam faciem angeli.

Faciebat prodigia: Stephen, at least, was not merely a waiter at the tables, but he might have been an exception. ***De synagogā . . . Asiā***: These were local synagogues for Greek-speaking Jews visiting Jerusalem from the diaspora. ***Disputantes cum Stephano***: What were they arguing about? The specific charge they will make before the Sanhedrin is blasphemy, though we can only guess what in particular they accused him of having said. ***Qui dicerent***: a relative clause of purpose, "who would say," or "to say." ***Contra Mosen et Deum***: In the minds of his accusers, Stephen attacks Moses when he challenges the Laws he gave the Jews, and he attacks God himself by attacking the Temple. Both charges are arguably true. Jesus' understanding of the Law isn't altogether clear. His first followers argue among themselves about it. Even the Gospel writers have different takes on the question. If Stephen is repeating any of this in his sermons, his accusers need not have spoken falsely about him to get the attention of the Sanhedrin. ***Tamquam faciem angeli***: thus indicating that the Holy Spirit is inspiring him.

ACTS

AD 30/33-35

Stephen responds to the authorities with an account of the history of the Jewish people down to the moment of the Messiah's appearance. They are enraged when he reminds them that the Jewish authorities have a record of executing prophets sent by God, with a clear implication that they had just killed another. They have him dragged out of the city, where he is stoned to death. A young man, named Saul (later renamed Paul), witnesses the murder.

1–5: Stephen begins: "God delivered Abraham to Canaan, and promised him that it would be his land and the land of his descendants."

appareo, to appear • **priusquam**, before • **moror**, to stay • **exi** < **exeo**, to leave • **cognatio**, kindred • **transtulit** < **transfero** • **hereditas**, inheritance

Dixit autem princeps sacerdotum, "Si haec ita se habent?" ²Qui ait, "Viri, fratres, et patres, audite. Deus gloriae apparuit patri nostro Abraham cum esset in Mesopotamiam, priusquam moraretur in Charram, ³et dixit ad illum, 'Exi de terrā tuā et de cognatione tuā, et věni in terram quam tibi monstravero. ⁴Tunc exiit de terrā Chaldeorum, et habitavit in Charram. Et inde postquam mortuus est pater eius, transtulit illum in terram istam in quā nunc vos habitatis. ⁵Et non dedit illi hereditatem in eā, nec passum pedis, et repromisit dare illi eam in possessionem et semini eius post ipsum, cum non haberet filium."

Princeps sacerdotum: It's difficult to believe that the high priest would be presiding. Perhaps Luke means the one who was in charge of the inquiry. ***Si haec ita se habent***: *Si* can often be used to introduce a question, implying a leading verbal expression, such as *dic nobis*, in this case. Literally "If these things hold themselves thus?" = "Is this the way things are?" ***Qui ait***: The modern reader may well be puzzled by Stephen's speech. It's a retelling of the early history of the Jewish people down to Moses, something Jews of all ages know by heart, and he never directly addresses the specific charges. But it is precisely because the story is so well-known that Stephen can make his point by subtle emphases in his version that would have been noticed by his audience. Seen this way, his speech, far from being a dull rehash of the obvious and irrelevant, is a masterpiece of innuendo and veiled, and not so veiled, accusations. Stephen's purpose is to show that God is active in Jewish history but is continually opposed by his ignorant and stubborn people. That's well-known, but making a point of it in this setting is definitely provocative. He also says that the Temple itself is a kind of idolatry. None of this is missed by the Sanhedrin. They don't find his speech tedious; they find it insulting and blasphemous. ***Nec passum pedis***: "not even a footstep," = "not a bit of it." ***Cum non haberet filium***: *concessive*, "even though he didn't have a son."

6–8: "But the Jewish nation had to serve another before claiming the land God promised them."

accola, resident of a nearby country • **tracto**, to treat • **quadringenti**, forty • **gigno**, to give birth to • **circumcido**, to circumcise • **octavus**, eighth

⁶"Locutus est autem Deus quia erit semen eius accola in terrā alienā, et servituti eos subicient et male tractabunt eos annis quadringentis, ⁷et 'gentem cui servierint iudicabo ego,' dixit Deus. 'Et post haec exibunt et deservient mihi in loco isto.' ⁸Et dedit illi testamentum circumcisionis, et sic genuit Isaac, et circumcidit eum die octavā. Et Isaac Iacob, et Iacob duodecim patriarchas [genuit].''

Locutus est autem Deus: God's plan for Abraham's descendants will be achieved through the base envy of Joseph's brothers (*aemulantes* at verse 9). An implication is that God's will for Jesus will be fulfilled through the wicked intentions of the Sanhedrin.

9–16: "God brought his people into Egypt."

aemulor, to be envious of • **vendo**, to sell • **praepositus**, fames • **cibus**, food • **accerso**, to summon • **septuaginta**, seventy • **defungor**, to die • **emo**, to buy

⁹"Et patriarchae aemulantes Ioseph vendiderunt in Aegyptum. Et erat Deus cum eo, ¹⁰et eripuit eum ex omnibus tribulationibus eius, et dedit ei gratiam et sapientiam in conspectu Pharaonis, regis Aegypti, et constituit eum praepositum super Aegyptum et super omnem domum suam. ¹¹Vēnit autem fames in universam Aegyptum et Chanaan et tribulatio magna, et non inveniebant cibos patres nostri. ¹²Cum audisset autem Iacob esse frumentum in Aegypto, misit patres nostros primum, ¹³et in secundo [tempore] cognitus est Ioseph a fratribus suis, et manifestatum est Pharaoni genus eius. ¹⁴Mittens autem Ioseph accersivit Iacob patrem suum et omnem cognationem, in animabus septuaginta quinque. ¹⁵et descendit Iacob in Aegyptum, et defunctus est ipse et patres nostri. ¹⁶Et translati sunt in Sychem et positi sunt in sepulchro quod emit Abraham pretio argenti a filiis Emmor filii Sychem.

Patriarchae duodecim: The twelve sons of Jacob are the eponymous founders of the twelve tribes of Israel. This could conceivably be an implicit parallel to the twelve apostles in the current age, but its effectiveness would depend on whether the members of the Sanhedrin knew of how the Christ believers were organized.

17–24: "Moses was born and raised in Egypt at the height of their oppression."

adpropinquo, to approach • **repromissio**, a promise • **quoadusque**, up until • **circumvenio**, to exploit • **vivifico**, to live • **nutrio**, to raise • **mensis**, month • **erudo**, to instruct

---

¹⁷"Cum adpropinquaret autem tempus repromissionis quam confessus erat Deus Abrahae, crevit populus et multiplicatus est in Aegypto, ¹⁸quoadusque surrexit rex alius in Aegypto, qui non sciebat Ioseph. ¹⁹Hĭc circumveniens genus nostrum adflixit patres, ut exponerent infantes suos, ne vivificarentur. ²⁰Eodem tempore natus est Moses, et fuit gratus Deo, qui nutritus est tribus mensibus in domo patris sui. ²¹Exposito autem illo, sustulit eum filia Pharaonis et enutrivit eum sibi in filium. ²²Et eruditus est Moses omni sapientiā Aegyptiorum, et erat potens in verbis et in operibus suis. ²³Cum autem impleretur ei quadraginta annorum tempus, ascendit in cor eius ut visitaret fratres suos, filios Israhel.

Gentem cui servierint: This will of course be Egypt. *In secundo* [*tempore*]: "in the following time," or "after that." *Hĭc circumveniens genus*: *hic* is the new king of Egypt; *genus* is the object of *circumveniens*, "getting around," or "dealing craftily with." *Sibi in filium*: *sibi* is dative of possession, "as a son to herself," or "as her own son."

25–29: "Moses fled Egypt, fearing that his murder of an Egyptian would be discovered."

patior, to suffer • **vindico**, to avenge • **ultio**, revenge • **sequor**, to follow • **litigo**, to quarrel • **alteruter**, one another • **proximus**, a neighbor • **iudex**, judge • **vis** < **volo** • **quemadmodum**, just as • **interficio**, to kill • **heri**, yesterday • **advena**, migrant

²⁴Et cum vidisset quendam iniuriam patientem, vindicavit illum et fecit ultionem ei qui iniuriam sustinebat, percusso Aegyptio. ²⁵"Existimabat autem intellegere fratres quoniam Deus per manum ipsius daret salutem illis. At illi non intellexerunt. ²⁶Sequenti vero die apparuit illis litigantibus et reconciliabat eos in pacem, dicens, 'Viri, fratres estis. Ut quid nocetis alterutrum?' ²⁷Qui autem iniuriam faciebat proximo reppulit eum, dicens, 'Quis te constituit principem et iudicem super nos? ²⁸Numquid interficere me tu vis quemadmodum interfecisti heri Aegyptium?' ²⁹Fugit autem Moses in verbo isto, et factus est advena in terrā Madiam ubi generavit filios duos.

Quendam iniuriam patientem: *Quendam* doesn't agree with *iniuriam*, despite its appearance: "someone enduring injury." *Ei*: dative, "for the one who was enduring the abuse." *Existimabat*: The subject is Moses. Moses thought the Hebrews would understand that God had sent him to rescue them. Stephen begins one of the central themes of his defense. As the patriarchs didn't recognize their savior, so the present day authorities don't understand who Jesus is and why he was sent. *Ut quid*: *Ut* emphasizes the question: "So why . . . ?" *Alterutrum*: In Classical Latin this would be dative, not accusative, *nocetis alterutri*. *Proximo*: substantive, "to the one nearby."

ACTS OF THE APOSTLES

30–35: "After forty years, God told Moses to return to free his people from Egypt."

expleo, to complete • **rubus**, bush, **visus**, a vision • **calciamentum**, shoe • **pes**, foot • **sto**, to stand • **gemitus**, sigh

³⁰"Et expletis annis quadraginta, apparuit illi in deserto montis Sina angelus in igne flammae rubi. ³¹Moses autem videns admiratus est visum, et accedente illo ut consideraret, facta est vox Domini, ³²'Ego Deus patrum tuorum, Deus Abraham et Deus Isaac et Deus Iacob.' Tremefactus autem Moses non audebat considerare. ³³Dixit autem illi Dominus, 'Solve calciamentum pedum tuorum, locus enim in quo stas terra sancta est. ³⁴Videns vidi adflictionem populi mei qui est in Aegypto, et gemitum eorum audivi et descendi liberare eos. Et nunc veni, et mittam te in Aegyptum.' ³⁵"Hunc Mosen quem negaverunt, dicentes, 'Quis te constituit principem et iudicem?' Hunc [hominem] Deus principem et redemptorem misit cum manu angeli, qui apparuit illi in rubo."

36–41: "Moses led them out of Egypt, but soon they lost faith and asked Aaron to make idols of the old gods."

---

ruber, red • **tamquam**, like • **eccelesia**, meeting • **nolo**, not to want • **praecedo**, to lead the way • **vitulus**, male calf • **aetor**, to be joyful

---

³⁶"Hĭc eduxit illos, faciens prodigia et signa in terrā Aegypti et in Rubro Mari et in deserto annis quadraginta. ³⁷Hĭc est Moses qui dixit filiis Israhel, 'Prophetam vobis suscitabit Deus de fratribus vestris tamquam me.' ³⁸Hĭc est qui fuit in ecclesiā in solitudine cum angelo, qui loquebatur ei in monte Sina, et cum patribus nostris, qui accepit verba vitae dare nobis, ³⁹cui noluerunt oboedire patres nostri sed reppulerunt et aversi sunt cordibus suis in Aegyptum, ⁴⁰dicentes ad Aaron, 'Fac nobis deos qui praecedant nos. Moses enim hĭc qui eduxit nos de terrā Aegypti, nescimus quid factum sit ei.' ⁴¹Et vitulum fecerunt in illis diebus et obtulerunt hostiam simulacro et laetabantur in operibus manuum suarum."

Annis quadraginta: "for forty years." ***Israhel***: genitive. ***Tamquam me***: "just like me." ***Cui***: dative ofter *oboedire*. ***Praecedant***: relative clause of purpose.

42–43: "God punished them for their disobedience by delaying their arrival into Canaan."

militia, service • **hostia**, sacrificial animal • **sidus**, star

⁴²"Convertit autem Deus et tradidit eos servire militiae caeli, sicut scriptum est in libro Prophetarum: 'Numquid victimas aut hostias obtulistis mihi annis quadraginta in deserto, domus Israhel? ⁴³Et suscepistis tabernaculum Moloch et sidus dei vestri Rempham, figuras quas fecistis adorare eas. Et transferam vos trans Babylonem.'"

Militiae caeli: "The service of heaven" is another way of saying the idolatrous worship of the heavenly bodies such as was practiced by the peoples around them. ***Prophetarum***: Jews divided, and still do divide, their Scripture into three sections: the Torah, the Prophets, and the Writings. From the first letter of the Hebrew word of these sections, they derive the acronym *TANAKH*, which is shorthand for the library of all their sacred texts. By using the plural *prophetarum*, therefore, Stephen doesn't mean all the prophets, but from the section of Scripture that includes the prophets. The specific reference is to Amos 5:25-27. But Stephen quotes from the Septuagint, the third century BC Greek translation, which differs significantly from the original Hebrew: "you have carried Sikkut, your king, [not the tent of Moloch] and Kijjun [not Rompha], your idol, the star of your god that you made for yourselves; and I shall send you into exile beyond Damascus [not Babylon]" (New American Standard Bible). It's at least possible that the furious reaction of the Sanhedrin to his speech is fueled in part by his use of the Greek, which corrupts the passage they all knew from Hebrew. But this assumes a memory so prodigious and accurate that it strains credulity, even granting that the ancients often displayed astonishing feats of memory. ***Trans Babylonem***: The Septuagint accurately translates the Hebrew "across Damascus," but Stephen changes it to Babylon. The Babylonian Exile (597 to 536 BC) would have driven home the point more forcefully that God punished the Jews for their idolatry than a vague reference to some place "beyond Damascus."

44–50: "Moses' tabernacle was holy; the Temple of Solomon is not."

possessio, land • **excelsus**, exhalted one • **sedis**, throne • **requietio**, repose

⁴⁴"Tabernaculum testimonii fuit patribus nostris in deserto, sicut disposuit loquens ad Mosen ut faceret illud secundum formam quam viderat ⁴⁵quod et induxerunt suscipientes patres nostri cum Iesu in possessionem Gentium, quas expulit Deus a facie patrum nostrorum, usque in diebus David, ⁴⁶qui invēnit gratiam ante Deum et petiit ut inveniret tabernaculum Deo Iacob. ⁴⁷Salomon autem aedificavit illi domum. ⁴⁸Sed non Excelsus in manufactis habitat, sicut propheta dicit, ⁴⁹'Caelum mihi sedis est, terra autem scabillum pedum meorum. Quam domum aedificabitis mihi? dicit Dominus, aut quis locus requietionis meae est? ⁵⁰Nonne manus mea fecit haec omnia?'"

Tabernaculum testimonii: Stephen's speech now pivots from Moses to his views on the Temple. Comparing it, even obliquely, to the idolatry of Moloch could only have inflamed the Sanhedrin. Stephen's argument is that the original Mosaic tabernacle, even though complex, was by design not a permanent *domus* for God. It could be disassembled, moved, and reassembled wherever his people were. The Temple, by contrast, is *de facto* idolatrous because it was not built according to God's exact specifications, as given to Moses in Exodus 36:8-39:43, and is a fixed structure. It's also not surprising that a Greek-speaking Jew, and others from the diaspora, would have less reverence for the Temple than those living in and around Jerusalem. **Cum Iesu**: "with Joshua" of the Old Testament, not "with Jesus." The name "Jesus" is a Greek approximation of the Hebrew name "Joshua." **Possessionem Gentium**: He means the land of the Canaanites. Since the Canaanites were not Jewish, they could be called Gentiles, which is the word for the entire non-Jewish world. **Iacob**: genitive. **Sicut propheta**: Isaiah 66: 1-2. **Sed non Excelsus in manufactis habitat**: *Excelsus* = "the Heavenly One." There could be no more stinging rebuke to the Sanhedrin than to say that God neither approves of nor resides in the Temple.

51–53: "And now you have disobeyed the Holy Spirit, just as your fathers had disregarded the prophets."

cervix, neck • **incirumcisus**, uncircumcised • **auris**, ear • **iustus**, just • **proditor**, traitor • **homicida**, murderer • **dispositio**, arrangement

⁵¹"Durā cervice et incircumcisi cordibus et auribus vos semper Spiritui Sancto resistitis, sicut patres vestri et vos. ⁵²Quem prophetarum non sunt persecuti patres vestri? et occīderunt eos qui praenuntiabant de adventu Iusti, cuius vos nunc proditores et homicidae fuistis, ⁵³qui accepistis Legem in dispositionem angelorum et non custodistis."

Durā cervice: Stephen's narrative breaks down at this point, and he resorts to direct accusations and insults. We might imagine that the Sanhedrin had already erupted in outrage and the inquiry had devolved into a shouting match. *Incircumcisi*: i.e., "disobedient" because they don't really follow the laws in their heart. *Patres vestri*: It's interesting that Stephen doesn't refer to *patres nostri* here. Earlier he used the first person possessive to refer to Abraham: *patri nostro*. By walling off the Sanhedrin like this and distinguishing "your fathers" as the cause of the problem, he has divided the true from the false Jews, who'd even failed to be circumcised in their minds and hearts. They are perverters of the faith and stand outside of it.

54–55: Stephen claims to see Jesus sitting at God's right hand.

disseco, to cut to the heart • **strideo**, to hiss • **intendo**, to stare at • **aperio**, to open

⁵⁴Audientes autem haec dissecabantur cordibus suis, et stridebant dentibus in eum. ⁵⁵Cum autem esset plenus Spiritu Sancto, intendens in caelum vidit gloriam Dei et Iesum stantem a dextris Dei, et ait, "Ecce: video caelos apertos et Filium hominis a dextris stantem Dei."

56–59: His address enrages the Sanhedrin, who take him out of the city and have him stoned.

contineo, to close up • **peccatum**, a sin • **obdormio**, to fall asleep • **consentio**, to agree with • **nex**, murder

⁵⁶Exclamantes autem voce magnā continuerunt aures suas et impetum fecerunt unianimiter in eum. ⁵⁷Et eicientes eum extra civitatem lapidabant, et testes deposuerunt vestimenta sua secus pedes adulescentis qui vocabatur Saulus. ⁵⁸Et lapidabant Stephanum invocantem et dicentem, "Domine Iesu, suscipe spiritum meum. ⁵⁹Positis autem genibus clamavit voce magnā, "Domine, ne statuas illis hoc peccatum." Et cum hoc dixisset, obdormivit. Saulus autem erat consentiens neci eius.

Eicientes eum extra civitatem: Stephen is murdered by an extra juridical mob action, inasmuch as the Sanhedrin never pronounces a sentence. **Obdormivit**: Despite the stoning, God gave Stephen a peaceful death. **Consentiens neci eius**: "assented to his death." Luke will start calling Saul "Paul" without explanation at 13:9. These notes will refer to Saul/Paul as "Paul" throughout to avoid confusion.

The Stoning of Stephen

The Stoning of St. Stephen by Rembrandt, 1635 (The Met)

ACTS

 AD 30/33-35

There follows a selective persecution of the Christ believers in Jerusalem, in which Paul is particularly active. Many leave the city. A Greek-speaking Christ believer, Philip, converts Simon, a sorcerer in Samaria, but Simon is rebuked when he tries to buy some of the power of the Holy Spirit. Philip is sent by the Holy Spirit to encounter a servant of the queen of Ethiopia. He helps him understand the meaning of a passage in the Old Testament and the servant is converted.

1–3: Many of the Christ believers leave Jerusalem when a persecution begins.

praeter, except for • **timoratus**, reverent • **planctum**, grieving • **mulier**, woman • **custodia**, watch

---

Facta est autem in illā die persecutio magna in ecclesiā quae erat Hierosolymis, et omnes dispersi sunt per regiones Iudaeae et Samariae, praeter Apostolos. ²Curaverunt autem Stephanum viri timorati, et fecerunt planctum magnum super illum. ³Saulus vero devastabat ecclesiam. Per domos intrans et trahens viros ac mulieres tradebat in custodiam.

Omnes . . . praeter Apostolos: The persecution targeted the Greek-speaking Jews only, and the original apostles, representing the local, Aramaic-speaking Christ believers, were allowed to stay in Jerusalem. The Jerusalem believers might even have cooperated with the Jewish authorities to be rid of these "grumbling" outsiders. ***Curaverunt . . . viri timorati***: Ethnic Greeks who were sympathetic to the Jewish religion were called "God-fearers." The degree of their involvement in Jewish practices would vary by individual and by individual synagogues. It makes perfect sense that they, and not the local Jewish Christ believers, would tend to Stephen's body. Stoning was a sign that the victim was outcast and abhorred. From a later source, we learn the corpse of one stoned was to be hung up and then buried only when it started to decompose. It's also revealing that the local Christ believers were absent from this act. Perhaps they feared punishment if they had buried him. Or perhaps they weren't entirely opposed to his execution and the expulsion of Greek-speaking converts that followed. ***Devastabat***: Obviously Paul wasn't alone. He must have been in charge of a detachment of officers empowered with some kind of legal authority by the Sanhedrin to do this. What was the charge against these people? If they were associated with a cult that attacked the legitimacy of the Temple and the religious systems that shaped Jewish life, then a charge of sedition would be the likely choice. We have to remember that all this is happening under the watchful eyes of the Romans. They'd proven before the kind of repression they were capable of if a local population got out of hand. Over time, the Jewish authorities had managed a kind of truce with them, and having this arrangement threatened by a new breed of revolutionaries from within wasn't something they could afford to take lightly. ***Per domos***: Though technically a fourth declension noun, *domus* can slip over to the second declension for some of its endings. ***Viros ac mulieres***: We're not told the extent of Paul's persecution, but it's reasonable to assume that it was limited for now to Jerusalem itself and perhaps the immediate environs. This may have been part of a deal struck with the Aramaic-speaking Christ believers, represented by the observant apostles, to cast out the more extreme, Greek-speaking members of their movement.

ACTS OF THE APOSTLES

4–8: Philip evangelizes in Samaria and performs many wonders.

inmundus, unclean • **claudus**, crippled • **gaudium**, joy

⁴Igitur qui dispersi erant pertransiebant evangelizantes verbum. ⁵Philippus autem descendens in civitatem Samariae praedicabat illis Christum. ⁶Intendebant autem turbae his quae a Philippo dicebantur unianimiter, audientes et videntes signa quae faciebat. ⁷Multi enim eorum qui habebant spiritūs inmundos, clamantes voce magnā, exiebant. Multi autem paralytici et claudi curati sunt. ⁸Factum est ergo magnum gaudium in illā civitate.

Evangelizantes verbum: The Sanhedrin thought it had eliminated the threat by expelling some of the Christ believers from Jerusalem, when in fact it had only spread it. Ironically, Christianity spread as rapidly and as widely as it did not in spite of the fact that it was persecuted, but because it was. **Philippus**: not the disciple Philip, but one of the seven Greek-speaking deacons appointed at 6:5. He is often called "Philip the Evangelist" to distinguish him from Philip the apostle. ***Descendens***: "going down," because Jerusalem is on a fairly substantial hill in Judea, 2500 feet above sea level, whereas Samaria is at sea level at many points. ***Civitatem Samariae***: "the state (district) of Samaria." There is no city named Samaria in the district of Samaria. Its largest city is Sebaste. ***Magnum gaudium***: It's significant that the first new converts to the Jesus movement outside of Jerusalem were from Samaria, a region devout Jews avoided because of its reputation for its festering idolatry. It would be almost as much of a challenge for the disciples to accept Samaritans as their baptized followers as it would be to accept non-Jews. The major theme of Acts, the offer of salvation to the world, has begun.

9–13: He converts a local miracle worker, Simon, who had been mesmerizing the people of Samaria.

magus, sorcerer • **ausculto**, to listen to attentively • **demento**, to drive mad • **adhaereo**, to adhere to • **stupeo**, to be astonished

⁹Vir autem quidam, nomine Simon, qui ante fuerat in civitate magus, seducens gentem Samariae, dicens esse se aliquem magnum, ¹⁰cui auscultabant omnes a minimo usque ad maximum, dicentes, "Hic est virtus Dei, quae vocatur Magna." ¹¹Attendebant autem eum propter quod multo tempore magicis suis dementasset eos. ¹²Cum vero credidissent Philippo evangelizanti de regno Dei et nomine Iesu Christi, baptizabantur, viri ac mulieres. ¹³Tunc Simon et ipse credidit, et cum baptizatus esset adherebat Philippo, videns etiam signa et virtutes maximas fieri, stupens admirabatur.

Nomine Simon: Simon the Magician has a lively history in later Christian lore, though it's all fanciful. Suffice it to say that he was a wizard of sorts with a gullible following in Samaria. *Magus*: appositive, "as a magician." This initiates a series of plays on words that work in the Greek as well. *Hic est virtus*: "this man is the power of God," not "this is the power of God." *Dementasset*: dementavisset. *Vero*: "but."

14–17: The apostles send Peter and John to Samaria to confer the power of the Holy Spirit on the new converts.

nondum, not yet • **quisquam**, anyone • **tantum**, only

¹⁴Cum autem audissent Apostoli qui erant Hierosolymis quia recepit Samaria verbum Dei, miserunt ad illos Petrum et Iohannem, ¹⁵qui cum venissent oraverunt pro ipsis, ut acciperent Spiritum Sanctum. ¹⁶Nondum enim in quemquam illorum venerat, sed baptizati tantum erant in nomine Domini Iesu. ¹⁷Tunc inponebant manūs super illos et accipiebant Spiritum Sanctum.

Quia recepit Samaria verbum Dei: The Samaritans were hardly considered to be Jews at all by the orthodox Jews. Having them baptized by Philip, who'd been expelled from Jerusalem with other Greek-speaking Christ believers, must have greatly concerned the Aramaic-speaking, Christ believing Jews back in Jerusalem. Peter and John's visit is as much an investigation as a celebration. *Sed baptizati tantum erant*: "but they had only been baptized." The people had converted and had been baptized by the deacon Philip, but only the apostles could confer on them the gift of the Holy Spirit. This they accomplish by the ritual of the laying on of hands, thus providing a physical conduit for the Holy Spirit's power that had been first given to the apostles.

18–25: Simon is sternly rebuked for trying to buy the power of the Holy Spirit from the two apostles.

obtulit < **offero**, to offer • **quicumque**, whosoever • **sors**, lot • **coram**, before • **fellis**, gall • **amaritudo**, bitterness • **paenitentia**, repentance

¹⁸Cum vidisset autem Simon quia per inpositionem manūs Apostolorum daretur Spiritus Sanctus, obtulit eis pecuniam, ¹⁹dicens, "Date et mihi hanc potestatem, ut cuicumque inposuero manūs, accipiat Spiritum Sanctum." Petrus autem dixit ad eum, ²⁰"Pecunia tua tecum sit in perditionem quoniam donum Dei existimasti pecuniā possideri. ²¹Non est tibi pars neque sors in sermone isto, cor enim tuum non est rectum coram Deo. ²²Paenitentiam itaque age ab hāc nequitiā tuā et roga Deum si forte remittatur tibi haec cogitatio cordis tui. ²³In felle enim amaritudinis et obligatione iniquitatis video te esse." ²⁴Respondens autem Simon dixit, "Precamini vos pro me ad Dominum ut nihil veniat super me horum quae dixistis." ²⁵Et illi quidem testificati et locuti verbum Domini rediebant Hierosolymam, et multis regionibus Samaritanorum evangelizabant.

Obtulit eis pecuniam: The buying and selling of church offices is called "Simony" after this scene. *Existimasti*: existimavisti. ***Date et mihi hanc potestatem***: Why was Simon excluded from this? He offered money only after he'd seen others receiving the Holy Spirit? One explanation is that Peter and John withheld the ritual because they knew his heart was not yet right with God. This illustrates the point that whereas confession and baptism may be formulaic and external only, the final confirmation of the inward conversion, manifested by the presence of the Holy Spirit, also requires pure intentions. ***Precamini vos pro me***: Simon expresses an entirely understandable fear of punishment, but was his heart truly turned? The text is silent on this, and Simon the Magician is heard of no more. It's hard not to have some sympathy for him. Peter accurately describes him as being imprisoned by his own iniquity, which makes it impossible for him truly to repent of his ways. Simon doesn't dispute Peter's analysis and begs only that God not deal with him harshly for his failings. *Evangelizabant*: There's an unresolvable ambiguity here. Do we have a change of subject? Did Peter and John (*illi*) preach for a while in Samaria before returning to Jerusalem, leaving Philip and others to continue the evangelizing there? Or are we to understand that Peter and John returned to their home base in Jerusalem and that they visited Samaria occasionally to evangelize there themselves?

ACTS OF THE APOSTLES

25–29: Philip is directed to Gaza by a backroad, where he meets a servant of the Queen of Ethiopia.

contra meridianum, southward • **gaza**, treasury

²⁶Angelus autem Domini locutus est ad Philippum, dicens, "Surge et vade contra meridianum ad viam quae descendit ab Hierusalem in Gazam. Haec est deserta." ²⁷Et surgens abiit et ecce: vir Aethiops, eunuchus potens Candacis, reginae Aethiopum, qui erat super omnes gazas eius, venerat adorare in Hierusalem. ²⁸Et revertebatur, sedens super currum suum legensque prophetam, Esaiam. ²⁹Dixit autem Spiritus Philippo, "Accede et adiunge te ad currum istum."

Haec est deserta: The angel has instructed Philip not to take the main road from Samaria to Gaza but to return to Jerusalem first and from there take a back road (*deserta*) to Gaza. *Vir Aethiops*: We know nothing about this man. We don't know whether he was reading the text himself (either in Greek or Hebrew/Aramaic) or whether it was being read to him; we don't know whether he was Ethiopian or a slave of another nationality serving in Ethiopia; we don't know whether he was Jewish by birth or a convert; we don't know why he was traveling by himself in Judea or what had drawn him to Jerusalem at this particular time. It would appear that Luke has something specific in mind by including the details he does, but what that is isn't knowable. *Candacis*: "Candice." This isn't a proper name but a title, like "President," "Pharaoh," or "Caesar." *Gazas*: The pun with "Gaza" suggests that the geography of the story is entirely fanciful. *Eunuchus potens*: There's no significance to the fact that the servant was a eunuch. Court officials were regularly eunuchs for a variety of reasons. *Adiunge te ad currum istum*: "join yourself to that chariot," or "get in his chariot."

CHAPTER 8

30–35: Philip helps him see that a passage from Isaiah he was trying to understand is referring to Jesus.

quomodo, how • **obsecro**, to beg

---

³⁰Adcurrens autem Philippus audivit illum legentem Esaiam prophetam, et dixit, "Putasne intellegis quae legis?" ³¹Qui ait, "Et quomodo possum si non aliquis ostenderit mihi?" Rogavitque Philippum ut ascenderet et sederet secum. ³²Locus autem Scripturae quam legebat erat hĭc: "Tamquam ovis ad occisionem ductus est, et sicut agnus coram tondente se sine voce, sic non aperuit os suum. ³³In humilitate iudicium eius sublatum est. Generationem illius quis enarrabit, quoniam tollitur de terrā vita eius." ³⁴Respondens autem eunuchus Philippo dixit, "Obsecro te, de quo propheta dicit hoc? De se an de alio aliquo? ³⁵Aperiens autem Philippus os suum, et incipiens ab scripturā istā evangelizavit illi Iesum.

Illum legentem: Reading aloud was the normal custom. This is how Philip knows what the man was reading, or being read to. ***Esaiam***: The passage is Isaiah 53: 7-8. The entire narrative of the servant conversion is a doublet of the failed conversion of Simon that preceded it. In this passage, we have step-by-step instructions for salvation: a personal search of Scripture, a teacher with the proper authority to elucidate Scripture, baptism, and the arrival of the Holy Spirit. None of this happened with Simon. ***Putasne intellegis***: This is colloquial: "Think you understand . . ." Formal Latin would have been *putasne intellegasne . . ."* ***Locus***: "passage." ***In humilitate . . . tollitur de terrā vita eius***: = "In humiliation, his judgment was taken away. But who will proclaim his generation, since his life was taken from this land." The servant's uncertainty is justified, as this passage both in the Greek and original Hebrew isn't at all clear and has spawned an enormous body of modern commentary. Whatever its original sense, the early Christ believers had no doubt that Isaiah was talking about the abuse and execution of the Messiah.

ACTS OF THE APOSTLES

36–38: He asks Philip to baptize him.

quidam, a certain • **uterque**, each one

³⁶Et dum irent per viam, venerunt ad quandam aquam, et ait eunuchus, "Ecce: aqua. Quid prohibet me baptizari?" ³⁷Dixi autem Philippus, "Si credis ex toto corde, licet." Et respondens ait, "Credo Filium Dei esse Iesum Christum." ³⁸Et iussit stare currum, et descenderunt uterque in aquam, Philippus et eunuchus, et baptizavit eum.

Ad quandam aquam: Luke's vague description hasn't prevented a fruitless effort to identify this creek or small pond. Traditionally, it has been identified as Ain-Dirue, near modern-day Hebron.
Si credis ex toto corde: yet another contrast with Simon's entirely utilitarian wish to be converted.
In aquam: As this is the first Christian baptism recorded in any detail, the expression *in aquam* has received a great deal of attention. Was the servant immersed in water or merely sprinkled with it? To the disappointment of everyone involved in the debate, this passage doesn't make it clear.

CHAPTER 8

39-40: After the baptism, the Holy Spirit takes Philip through Azotus to Caesarea.

amplius, anymore • **pertranseo**, to pass through • **cunctus**, all • **donec**, until

³⁹Cum autem ascendissent de aquā Spiritus Domini rapuit Philippum, et amplius non vidit eum eunuchus. Ibat enim per viam suam, gaudens. ⁴⁰Philippus autem inventus est in Azoto, et pertransiens evangelizabat civitatibus cunctis donec veniret Caesaream.

Spiritus Domini: the Holy Spirit? *per viam suam*: Nothing more is said of the servant of Candace. Later traditions claim he became an evangelist in Ethiopia and eventually an *episkopos* (bishop) of Abyssinia. **Inventus est in Azoto**: Azotus (modern-day Ashdod) is on the coast, about thirty miles north of Gaza City. Hence Philip is completing a circle that took him from Samaria south to Jerusalem, east to Gaza, and then north again along the coast to Caesarea in Samaria.

ACTS

AD 35-36

On his way to Damascus in pursuit of more of Jesus' followers, Paul is overcome and blinded by a flash of light. His traveling companions escort him into Damascus. Meanwhile, Ananias, a follower of Jesus living in Damascus, receives a vision that he is to find Paul. He is reluctant at first, because he knows him to be a persecutor of Jesus' followers, but God tells him that Paul has been chosen to deliver the good news to the Gentiles. Ananias goes to Paul and heals him of his blindness. Straightaway, Paul represents himself as a preacher of the word. The people are suspicious and hatch a plot to kill him. Paul is led out of the city and goes to Jerusalem to meet the apostles. They are also suspicious of his intentions, but Barnabas speaks up for him. He is sent back to his hometown of Tarsus to preach there. Peter cures several people on his missionary trip, and even brings a young girl back from the dead.

1–2: Paul seeks authority from the high priest to arrest any Christ believers he finds in Damascus and to bring them back to Jerusalem.

---

mina, a threat • **caedes**, destruction • **vincio**, to bind up

---

Saulus autem, adhuc inspirans minarum et caedis in discipulos Domini, accessit ad principem sacerdotum, ²et petiit ab eo epistulas in Damascum ad synagogas, ut si quos invenisset huius viae viros ac mulieres vinctos perduceret in Hierusalem.

Saulus: Luke now begins to shift his focus from Peter to Paul, whose missions will completely dominate Acts from Chapter 13 on. *In Damascum*: Damascus was the largest of the scattering of ten cities to the west and north of Judea, collectively referred to as Decapolis. Culturally, these cities were a fusion of Greek and Semitic cultures and enjoyed some degree of autonomy from Rome. Perhaps Paul and the Sanhedrin were responding to requests for help from the synagogues in Damascus to do something about the rising presence of Greek-speaking Christ believers in their midst. Paul, being fluent in Greek, would have been well qualified to head up the team sent to Damascus. *Huius viae*: the first instance of what will become a shorthand way of referring to the beliefs of the Jesus movement: "the way." The Greek word is *hodos*. A "meth<u>od</u>ist," therefore, is etymologically one who goes along (*meta*) the way.

ACTS OF THE APOSTLES

3–9: As he approaches Damascus, he is blinded by a brilliant light from the sky.

contigit, it came about • **stupeo**, to be astonished • **ingredior**, to enter into • **comitor**, to accompany • **manduco**, to eat • **bibo**, to drink

³Et cum iter faceret, contigit ut adpropinquaret Damasco. Et subito circumfulsit eum lux de caelo. ⁴Et cadens in terram audivit vocem, dicentem sibi, "Saule, Saule! Quid me persequĕris?" ⁵Qui dixit, "Quis es, Domine?" Et ille [dixit], "Ego sum Iesus, quem tu persequĕris." ⁶Et tremens ac stupens dixit, "Domine, quid me vis facere?" ⁷"Sed surge et ingredere civitatem, et dicetur tibi quid te oporteat facere." Viri autem illi qui comitabantur cum eo stabant stupefacti, audientes quidem vocem, neminem autem videntes. ⁸Surrexit autem Saulus de terrā apertisque oculis nihil videbat. Ad manūs autem illum trahentes introduxerunt Damascum. ⁹Et erat tribus diebus non videns, et non manducavit neque bibit.

Contigit ut: "it happened that," or "it came about that." *Circumfulsit eum lux de caelo*: Paul relates this event two more times in his own voice in Acts (22: 3-20; 26: 12-18), each time with different emphases and minor discrepancies. Appendix A, "Three Accounts of Paul's Conversion," displays them side-by-side in a table for comparison. *Cadens in terram*: perhaps from his mount on a horse. Paul's vision has been the subject of innumerable interpretations, from an hallucination resulting from a knock on the head when he fell off his horse, to a nearby lightening strike, epilepsy, and a guilty conscience for having done nothing to stop the stoning of Stephen. The English expression "the road to Damascus" signifies a sudden and complete reversal of ideas or beliefs. *Persequĕris*: present tense; *persequēris* would be the future. *Domine*: Paul is overwhelmed by the "magisty" of the experience and addresses whomever he thinks he sees as "Lord." This shouldn't be taken to mean he recognized Jesus and recognized that Jesus was God, as it sometimes is. *Apertisque oculis*: ablative absolute with an adversative sense, "even though his eyes were open." *Ad manūs*: "hand-in-hand," by the hand." *Introduxerunt Damascum*: Paul was taken to the house of Judas (verse 11), presumably an orthodox Jew in the city with whom he originally was to stay while in the city to arrest the Christ believers.

10–16: Ananias is sent out of Damascus to cure Paul of his blindness.

visus, a vision • **vado**, to go • **vicum**, district • **quaero**, to ask for • **sanctus**, holy • **alligo**, to tie up • **vas**, vessel • **ostendo**, to show

¹⁰Erat autem quidam discipulus Damasci, nomine Ananias, et dixit ad illum in visu Dominus, "Anania?" At ille ait, "Ecce: ego, Domine." ¹¹Et Dominus ad illum, "Surgens, vade in vicum qui vocatur Rectus, et quaere in domo Iudae Saulum nomine, Tarsensem. Ecce enim: orat. ¹²Et vidit virum, Ananiam nomine, introeuntem et inponentem sibi manūs ut visum recipiat." ¹³Respondit autem Ananias, "Domine, audivi a multis de viro hōc quanta mala sanctis tuis fecerit in Hierusalem, ¹⁴et hĭc habet potestatem a principibus sacerdotum alligandi omnes qui invocant nomen tuum." ¹⁵Dixit autem ad eum Dominus, "Vade, quoniam vas electionis est mihi iste, ut portet nomen meum coram gentibus et regibus et filiis Israhel. ¹⁶Ego enim ostendam illi quanta oporteat eum pro nomine meo pati."

Damasci: locative, "at" or "in Damascus." *in visu*: "in a vision." *Tarsensem*: "the Tarsene" or "of Tarsus." It was common practice for one to have a nickname to distinguish him from others with the same name. *Ecce enim: orat*: The subject of the verb is Paul. Ananias is given a remote vision of Paul praying: "For behold, he is praying." Further, Ananias is told that Paul had a vision of a man named "Ananias" curing his blindness. *Sanctis tuis*: See note at 11:19-26 for the first instance of the adjective/pronoun *Christianu*s. *Alligandi*: gerund in the genitive, "of putting into chains," or "of arresting." *Vas electionis*: "a vessel of election" or "of choice." This is a literal rendering of an Aramaic idiom that means "chosen vessel" or "chosen instrument."

17–20: Paul, cured of his blindness and baptized with the Holy Spirit, begins preaching that Jesus is the son of God in the local synagogues.

squama, scale • **aliquot**, some • **continuo**, immediately

---

¹⁷Et abiit Ananias, et introivit in domum, et inponens ei manūs dixit, "Saule, frater, Dominus misit me Iesus qui apparuit tibi in viā quā veniebas, ut videas et implearis Spiritu Sancto. ¹⁸Et confestim ceciderunt ab oculis eius tamquam squamae, et visum recepit. Et surgens baptizatus est. ¹⁹Et cum accepisset cibum, confortatus est. Fuit autem cum discipulis qui erant Damasci per dies aliquot. ²⁰Et continuo in synagogis praedicabat Iesum, quoniam hĭc est Filius Dei.

Ananias: One of the mysteries of this passage is Ananias. Where did he get the authority to lay hands on a convert and confer the Holy Spirit? Previously this power was limited to the original apostles in Jerusalem. ***Et surgens baptizatus est***: How was he baptized and by whom? It's possible that when Paul rose, the two went to where water could be found and Paul was baptized there. But the expression "and getting up he was baptized" suggests that he was baptized by Ananias the moment he stood up. ***Praedicabat***: Despite its appearance it doesn't mean to "predict." It means to stand before and declare something. "Profess" would be an etymologically close translation, or "preach," which is based on the Old French *prechier < praedicare*. ***Iesum, quoniam hĭc est Filius Dei***: This construction is a mild *anacoluthon* (break in grammar) to create a rhetorical effect: "He professed Jesus . . . that this man is the son of God," instead of "He professed that Jesus is the son of God."

21–25: The followers of Jesus in Damascus are suspicious that their former tormenter is claiming to be one of them, and they plot against him.

huc, to this place • **convalesco**, to get better • **confundo**, to put into an uproar • **insidiae**, plot • **murus**, city wall • **sporta**, basket

²¹Stupebant autem omnes qui audiebant, et dicebant, "Nonne hĭc est qui expugnabat in Hierusalem eos qui invocabant nomen istud, et huc ad hoc vēnit, ut vinctos illos duceret ad principes sacerdotum?" ²²Saulus autem magis convalescebat et confundebat Iudaeos qui habitabant Damasci, adfirmans quoniam hĭc est Christus. ²³Cum implerentur autem dies multi, consilium fecerunt Iudaei, ut eum interficerent. ²⁴Notae autem factae sunt Saulo insidiae eorum. Custodiebant autem et portas die ac nocte, ut eum interficerent. ²⁵Accipientes autem discipuli eius nocte per murum dimiserunt eum, submittentes in sportā.

Stupebant: Understandably, the Jews in the synagogues would have been shocked. They thought Paul had come to help rid them of the growing number of Christ believers, only to find him professing their beliefs. *Saulus autem magis convalescebat*: I.e., he grew stronger in his faith and understanding. *Iudaei*: Are these non-believing Jews only or the Christ believers themselves? Given the context, it could be both. *In sportā*: This isn't as ingenious or unique a solution as it may seem to a modern reader. Heavy loads could be hoisted to openings along the upper floors of the city wall by means of a block and tackle pulley system, thus eliminating the need to travel around the walls to the nearest gate.

26–31: Paul is received in Jerusalem through the intercession of Barnabas. The apostles send him out of the city to his hometown of Tarsus.

iungo, to join • **quomodo**, how • **quia**, that • **fiducialiter**, earnestly • **egerit** < **ago**, to act • **ambulo**, to walk

²⁶Cum autem venisset in Hierusalem, temptabat iungere se discipulis, et omnes timebant eum, non credentes quia esset discipulus. ²⁷Barnabas autem adprehensum illum duxit ad Apostolos, et narravit illis quomodo in viā vidisset Dominum, et quia locutus est ei, et quomodo in Damasco fiducialiter egerit in nomine Iesu. ²⁸Et erat cum illis intrans et exiens in Hierusalem, et fiducialiter agens in nomine Domini. ²⁹Loquebatur quoque et disputabat cum Graecis. Illi autem quaerebant occīdere eum. ³⁰Quod cum cognovissent fratres, deduxerunt eum Caesaream, et dimiserunt Tarsum. ³¹Ecclesia quidem per totam Iudaeam et Galilaeam et Samariam habebat pacem, et aedificabatur, ambulans in timore Domini et consolatione Sancti Spiritūs replebatur.

Barnabas: This is presumably the same Barnabas noted for his generous piety at 4:36. Like Paul, Barnabas is a Greek-speaking Jew who was born in the diaspora. He's from Cyprus, just off the coast of Asia Minor from Turkey. He is able to vouch for Paul's sincerity, and Paul is permitted to join the Christ believers in Jerusalem for a time. ***Cum illis intrans et exiens in Hierusalem***: "with them going in and out of Jerusalem." This is just an idiom for "he associated with them." ***Fiducialiter agens***: The adverb is significant. It might be that the Aramaic-speaking Christ believers were allowed to stay in Jerusalem after the first persecution (8:1-3) on the condition that they keep to themselves. Paul's enthusiastic (*fiducialiter*) proselytizing among Greek-speaking Jews would have been a problem, similar to the disturbance and brief persecution Stephen had caused earlier. ***Disputabat cum Graecis***: I.e., with Greek-speaking Jews in the city. ***Deduxerunt eum Caesaream***: Even Barnabas is unable to intercede on Paul's behalf this time. Paul is send away to Caesarea, and from there he is sent to Taurus. ***Habebat pacem***: I.e., now that the trouble maker Paul is out of the way, they can return to the accord they'd struck earlier with the Jewish leadership.

32–35: In Judea, Peter heals a paralytic named Aeneas in the town of Lydda, a miracle that brings about the conversion of everyone in Lydda and nearby Sarona.

quendam < **quidam**, a certain one • **iaceo**, to be lying down • **grabattum**, stretcher • **sano**, to heal • **sterno**, to roll up

³²Factum est autem Petrum, dum pertransiret [videns] universos, devenire et ad sanctos qui habitabant Lyddae. ³³Invēnit autem ibi hominem quendam, nomine Aeneam, ab annis octo iacentem in grabatto, qui erat paralyticus. ³⁴Et ait illi Petrus, "Aeneas, sanat te Iesus Christus. Surge et sterne tibi." Et continuo surrexit. ³⁵Et viderunt illum omnes qui habitant Lyddae et Saronae, qui conversi sunt ad Dominum.

Factum est autem Petrum: These will be the last two miracles performed by Peter. He begins to drop out as the central figure in the narrative as Paul's role increases. After this, Peter will be reduced to responding to Paul's actions. **Dum pertransiret [videns] universos**: He was making a tour of all the new communities of Christ believers. *Lyddae*: locative. *Lydda* (modern day Lod) was a small but prosperous town about thirty-five miles from Jerusalem on the road to Joffa (modern-day Tel Aviv). **Sterne tibi**: "make your bed." *Saronae*: the district that extends along the coast from Joppa northward into Galilee.

ACTS OF THE APOSTLES

36–42: In Joppa, Peter restores a woman to life, with the result that large numbers of people there are converted.

interpretor, to be translated • **opus**, a work • **morior**, to die • **lavo**, to wash • **prope**, nearby • **pigrito**, to be slow • **advenio**, to arrive • **circumsto**, to stand around • **tunica**, shirt • **vestis**, clothing • **eicio**, to dismiss • **foras**, outside • **genu**, knee • **resideo**, to sit up • **adsigno**, to point out • **moror**, to remain • **coriarius**, leather worker

³⁶In Ioppe autem fuit quaedam discipula, nomine Tabitas, quae interpretata dicitur Dorcas. Haec erat plena operibus bonis et elemosynis, quas faciebat. ³⁷Factum est autem in diebus illis ut infirmata moreretur. Quam cum lavissent, posuerunt eam in cenaculo. ³⁸Cum autem prope esset Lydda, ab Ioppe discipuli audientes quia Petrus esset in eā, miserunt duos viros ad eum, rogantes, "Ne pigriteris venire usque ad nos." ³⁹Exsurgens autem Petrus venit cum illis, et cum advenisset, duxerunt illum in cenaculum. Et circumsteterunt illum omnes viduae, flentes et ostendentes tunicas et vestes quas faciebat illis Dorcas. ⁴⁰Eiectis autem omnibus foras, Petrus ponens genua oravit et conversus ad corpus dixit, "Tabita, surge!" At

Tabitas: the first named female Christ believer. Her Aramaic name means "gazelle," *dorkas* in Greek. ***Lavissent . . . in cenaculum***: that is, they have prepared her body for burial and for lying in state to receive visitors. She has been dead for some time. ***Cum vocasset sanctos et viduas***: *Viduae* are a distinct class of *sancti*. They are supported by the community of *sancti* and in return provide the kind of services that are described in this scene: preparation of dead bodies for burial, weaving, etc. ***Resedit***: "sat up." ***Coriarium***: There was no ritual taboo against associating with tanners per se. Still, a tanner's house wasn't a pleasant place to stay because of the smell of chemicals and animal carcasses. Yet Peter remained *multos dies*.

illa aperuit oculos suos, et viso Petro resedit. ⁴¹Dans autem illi manum erexit eam. Et cum vocasset sanctos et viduas, adsignavit eam vivam. ⁴²Notum autem factum est per universam Ioppen, et crediderunt multi in Domino. ⁴³Factum est autem ut dies multos moraretur in Ioppe apud quendam Simonem, coriarium.

The Conversion of Saul

The conversion of Saul, who lies on the ground surrounded by horses and soldiers as Christ appears above him by Pieter Perret 1583 (The Met)

ACTS 10

AD 37-41

A Roman soldier named Cornelius in Caesarea is visited by an angel, who instructs him to send representatives to Joppa to find Peter. In Joppa, meanwhile, Peter has a vision that signifies God has ended the old designations of clean and unclean. Cornelius's representatives find Peter. Urged on by God, he accompanies them to Caesarea. Peter tells Cornelius that previously Jews would not associate with Gentiles but now the prohibition has been lifted. He briefly tells him and other Gentiles who have gathered the story of Jesus. Cornelius, along with an astonishingly large number of Gentiles, is converted. The power of the Holy Spirit is poured out on them.

1–8: Cornelius, a Gentile living in Caesarea, is told to send for Peter in Joppa by an angel.

centurio, a centurian • **cohors**, a battalion • **quasi**, about • **corripio**, to seize • **accersio**, to summon • **hospitor**, to be a guest • **metuo**, to respect • **pareo**, to be obedient to

Vir autem quidam erat in Caesareā, nomine Cornelius, centurio cohortis quae dicitur Italica, ²religiosus et timens Deum cum omni domo suā, faciens elemosynas multas plebi et deprecans Deum semper. ³Vidit in visu manifeste quasi horā nonā diei angelum Dei introeuntem ad se et dicentem sibi, "Corneli." ⁴At ille intuens eum, timore correptus dixit, "Quid est, Domine." Dixit autem illi, "Orationes tuae et elemosynae tuae ascenderunt in memoriam in conspectu Dei. ⁵Et nunc mitte viros in Ioppen, et accersi Simonem quendam, qui cognominatur Petrus. ⁶Hic hospitatur apud Simonem quendam, coriarium, cuius est domus iuxta mare." ⁷Et

In Caesareā: There are two Caesareas, which are often distinguished from one another with an adjective. Caesarea Maritima, the one in this story, is on the Mediterranean coast, about forty-five miles north of Joppa. It was the imperial capital of the Roman Province of Judea. Caesarea Philippi is twenty-five miles inland at a major spring that feeds the Jordan River north of the Sea of Galilee. ***Centurio cohortis quae dicitur Italica***: A commander of a "cohort" (about six hundred soldiers) would have been a Roman citizen, and the name of his cohort suggests it was comprised entirely or in part of Romans from Italy. This is the first time a Roman authority appears in Acts. Consistent with Luke's generally sympathetic portrayal of them, Cornelius is an admirable figure. ***Religiosus et timens Deum***: For "God-fearers" see 8:1-3. Cornelius maintained some kind of household cult, gave alms, and prayed to the God of the Jews. ***Quasi horā nonā***: "about the ninth hour," = "about three o'clock," the time for midday prayers. ***Dicentem sibi***: There is a noticeable change in tone as Acts continues. The narratives become more detailed in their descriptions and almost novelistic. This suggest that Luke had access to better source materials than he did for the first years of the Christ movement, and/or that he is giving more attention to the elements in the story that would have most interested Theophilus, his Roman patron. ***Qui cognominatur Petrus***: Distinguishing Simon Peter from Simon the leatherworker in Joppa is

cum discessisset angelus qui loquebatur illi, vocavit duos domesticos suos et militem metuentem Dominum, ex his qui illi parebant. ⁸Quibus cum narrasset omnia, misit illos in Ioppen.

an understandible necessity. ***Cuius est domus iuxta mare***: A leatherworking shop would need an abundant source of water for tanning and for carrying away waste chemicals.

9–16: Peter is overcome by a vision of an elaborate meal being lowered from heaven on a cloth.

esurio, to be hungry • **gusto**, to eat • **excessus**, a departure • **linteum**, table cloth • **initium**, corner • **quadrupedius**, four-footed • **volatilis**, flying • **absum**, to be away from • **numquam**, never • **inmundus**, unclean • **iterum**, again • **statim**, immediately

⁹Posterā autem die, iter illis facientibus et adpropinquantibus civitati, ascendit Petrus in superiora ut oraret, circa horam sextam. ¹⁰Et cum esuriret, voluit gustare. Parantibus autem eis cecidit super eum mentis excessus. ¹¹Et videt caelum apertum et descendens vas quoddam, velut linteum magnum, quattuor initiis submitti de caelo in terram, ¹²in quo erant omnia quadrupedia et serpentia terrae et volatilia caeli. ¹³Et facta est vox ad eum, "Surge, Petre, et occide et manduca." ¹⁴Ait autem Petrus, "Absit, Domine, quia numquam manducavi omne commune et inmundum." ¹⁵Et vox

Iter illis facientibus et adpropinquantibus civitati: two ablative absolute constructions. Iter is the direct object of *facientibus*; *civitati* is the dative complement of *adpropinquantibus*, "with them making their journey and coming close to the city." ***In superiora***: I.e., to the roof top, not to a mountain or hilltop. ***Circa horam sextam***: Both Peter, a Jew, and Cornelius, a pagan, pray at about the same time of the day. Thus Cornelius is no less observant than Peter, even though he is only a "God-fearer." ***Parantibus autem eis cecidit super eum mentis excessus***: literally, "While they were preparing for him [something to eat], there fell upon him a departure of mind," or "While they were preparing his meal, he fell into a trance." ***Vas quoddam***: "a kind of a vessel" or "bundle." The image Peter saw is a large bundle being unfurled into a tablecloth loaded with food of all kinds and being lowered to the ground. ***Quattuor initiis***: "by its four beginning points" or "corners." ***Occide***: "lie down," since formal meals were taken while reclining on the left arm. ***Absit***: "Let it be gone," or perhaps "Perish the thought." The vision is of a religious banquet, not of a regular noontime meal. Hence Peter's dismay at the prohibited food on the cloth is all the more pointed. The list of ritually impure animals is impressive (Leviticus 11:1-47), but Jews were not just forbidden to eat them. Even touching their carcasses would make someone unclean. ***Iterum secundo***: "for a second time."

iterum secundo ad eum, "Quae Deus purificavit, ne tu 'commune' dixeris." ¹⁶Hoc autem factum est per ter, et statim receptum est vas in caelum.

Commune: neuter singular, as if enumerating the individual food items contained in the collect plural *quae*. ***Dixeris***: The perfect subjunctive often used for the negative imperative.

17–23: The men from Caesarea arrive at the house in Joppa where Peter is staying.

---

¹⁷Et dum intra se haesitaret Petrus quidnam esset visio quam vidisset, ecce: viri qui missi erant a Cornelio inquirentes domum Simonis adstiterunt ad ianuam. ¹⁸Et cum vocassent, interrogabant si Simon, qui cognominatur Petrus, illic haberet hospitium. ¹⁹Petro autem cogitante de visione, dixit Spiritus ei, "Ecce: viri tres quaerunt te. ²⁰Surge itaque, et descende, et vade cum eis, nihil dubitans quia ego misi illos." ²¹Descendens autem Petrus ad viros dixit, "Ecce: ego sum quem quaeritis. Quae causa est propter quam venistis?" ²²Qui dixerunt, "Cornelius centurio, vir iustus et timens Deum et testimonium habens ab universā gente Iudaeorum, responsum accepit ab angelo sancto accersire te in domum suam et audire verba abs te." ²³Introducens igitur eos recepit hospitio. Sequenti autem die surgens profectus est cum eis, et quidam ex fratribus ab Ioppe comitati sunt eum.

Illic haberet hospitium: "was a guest there." ***Nihil***: as an adverb, "not doubting at all," or "for a minute." ***Hospitio***: "hospitably." This may seem a simple act of civility to a modern reader, but at the time allowing Gentiles into a Jewish home was forbidden. It's a sign that big changes are on their way. ***Ab universā gente Iudaeorum***: Even though he was nominally part of the Roman occupation of the province of Judea, he must have been recognized as having performed his duty with notable fairness to the local Jews. The fact that there is no independent evidence for him is unfortunate but not surprising. The vast majority of the officials who populated the imperial bureaucracy left no trace behind them. Some later Christian traditions maintain that he became the first bishop of Caesarea or of Scepsis in Mysia.

24–29: In Caesarea, Peter asks Cornelius why he summoned him.

necessarius, a relative • **levo**, to lift up • **alienigena**, a foreigner

²⁴Alterā autem die introivit Caesaream. Cornelius vero expectabat illos, convocatis cognatis suis et necessariis amicis. ²⁵Et factum est cum introisset Petrus, obvius [vēnit] ei Cornelius et procidens ad pedes adoravit. ²⁶Petrus vero levavit eum, dicens, "Surge. Et ego ipse homo sum." ²⁷Et loquens cum illo intravit et invēnit multos qui convenerant ²⁸Dixitque ad illos, "Vos scitis quomodo abominatum sit viro Iudaeo coniungi aut accedere ad alienigenam. Et mihi ostendit Deus neminem communem aut inmundum dicere hominem, ²⁹propter quod sine dubitatione veni accersitus. Interrogo ergo quam ob causam accersistis me?"

Alterā autem die: "On the next day." Joppa is about thirty miles south of Caesarea Maritima on the coast, a long but doable one-day journey. ***Necessariis amicis***: "close friends." ***Cum introisset***: It's easy for modern readers to miss the significance of this moment. Simon Peter, one of Jesus' original and closest followers, steps into a pagan's house, manifestly violating the restrictions against it. ***Obvius [vēnit] ei Cornelius***: Cornelius surely knew of the taboo Peter had violated just by coming into his house. Out of respect for this practice, he tries to block his way into the house.

CHAPTER 10

30–33: Cornelius says he and his friends have gathered to listen to Peter's teachings.

nudius, just barely

---

³⁰Et Cornelius ait, "A nudius quartanā die usque in hanc horam orans eram horā nonā in domo meā, et ecce: vir stetit ante me in veste candidā, et ait, ³¹"Corneli, exaudita est oratio tua, et elemosynae tuae commemoratae sunt in conspectu Dei. ³²Mitte ergo in Ioppen, et accersi Simonem, qui cognominatur Petrus. Hīc hospitatur in domo Simonis, coriarii, iuxta mare." ³³Confestim igitur misi ad te, et tu bene fecisti veniendo. Nunc ergo omnes nos in conspectu tuo adsumus audire omnia quaecumque tibi praecepta sunt a Domino."

A nudius . . . in domo meā: This very odd expression is difficult to unpack grammatically. This isn't the only difficult reading in this section, which raises an interesting possibility. Cornelius might have known just enough Greek to do his job satisfactorily. Peter's first language was surely Aramaic, but he also might have possessed enough Greek to get by. Thus it's possible that the grammatical oddities of this section have their source in a near accurate transcription of a conversation between two non-native Greek speakers trying to communicate with each other in a second language as best they could. The imperfections in the Greek are visible even in the Latin translation. ***Quartanā die***: Cornelius includes the first day in his counting. From "the fourth day back" would be our equivalent of "three days ago." *Usque in hanc horam*: "up until this very hour." He means that he had the vision three days ago at the same time of day that Peter has now entered his house. Cornelius will specify the time as the ninth hour (*horā nonā*). Altogether the expression appears to mean, "Three days ago at this exact time of day I was praying in my house at the ninth hour." ***Vir stetit ante me in veste candidā***: Cornelius appropriately gives only a literal description of the visitor, which Luke had identified in verse 3 as an angel. Like a dutiful soldier, he passes on the information without trying to interpret it. ***Confestim igitur misi ad te***: Again, like a good soldier, Cornelius obeys the order without understanding what it will lead to. ***Veniendo***: gerund, "by coming." This sounds entirely like a staff sergeant commending a subordinate for obeying orders. ***Audire***: infinitive showing purpose. ***Quaecumque***: "whatever," or just "what." Cornelius might not have known about Jesus or the Jesus movement from his dealings with other Jews in Caesarea. It was still a small sect within Judaism. If he had heard about it, it probably wouldn't have struck him as out of the ordinary for a religion known for its many factions.

34–43: Peter tells them of Jesus.

conperio, to find • **acceptor** + **personarum**, one who plays favorites • **ungo**, to annoint • **constituo**, to decide upon

³⁴Aperiens autem Petrus os dixit, "In veritate conperi quoniam non est personarum acceptor Deus, ³⁵sed in omni gente qui timet eum et operatur iustitiam acceptus est illi. ³⁶Verbum misit filiis Israhel, adnuntians pacem per Iesum Christum. Hĭc est omnium Dominus. ³⁷Vos scitis quod factum est verbum per universam Iudaeam, incipiens enim a Galilaeā post baptismum quod praedicavit Iohannes, ³⁸Iesum a Nazareth quomodo unxit eum Deus Spiritu Sancto et virtute, qui pertransivit benefaciendo et sanando omnes oppressos a diabolo, quoniam Deus erat cum illo. ³⁹Et nos testes sumus omnium quae fecit in regione Iudaeorum et Hierusalem, quem et occīderunt, suspendentes in ligno. ⁴⁰Hunc Deus suscitavit tertiā die et dedit eum manifestum fieri, ⁴¹non omni populo sed testibus praeordinatis a Deo—nobis qui manducavimus et

Personarum acceptor: This is often translated literally as "a respecter of persons," which is almost meaningless. The two Latin words are the direct rendering of the Greek word *prosōpolēmptēs*, "one who shows favoritism," which is very clear. *In omni gente*: Thus Peter specifies his understanding. People of all nations, not just the Jews, can be acceptable to God, provided they behave righteously. *Illi*: dative complement after *acceptus est*, "is acceptable to him." *Israhel*: dative. *Adnuntians*: Peter's opening sentence is a short preface and summary of his speech: God sent Jesus first to the sons of Israel to announce the coming of a worldwide kingdom. *Non omni populo*: Peter may be answering a charge that had begun to emerge against the apostles: If Jesus had come back from the dead, why is it that others didn't see him too? a legitimate question, which Peter answers by saying it wasn't God's will that everyone should see him, but only his elect. *Remissionem . . . in eum*: This is indirect statement implied after *testimonium*: "for this fact, all the prophets offer *testimonium* that *omnes qui credunt in eum* will receive [*accipere*] *remissionem peccatorum per nomen eius*.

bibimus cum illo postquam resurrexit a mortuis. ⁴²Et praecepit nobis praedicare populo et testificari quia ipse est qui constitutus est a Deo, iudex vivorum et mortuorum. ⁴³Huic omnes prophetae testimonium perhibent remissionem peccatorum accipere per nomen eius omnes qui credunt in eum."

44–48: They are converted, and Peter's companions are amazed to see the Holy Spirit poured out on a crowd of Gentiles.

obstupesco, to be astonished • **effundo**, to pour out • **lingua**, language

⁴⁴Adhuc loquente Petro verba haec, cecidit Spiritus Sanctus super omnes qui audiebant verbum. ⁴⁵Et obstipuerunt ex circumcisione fideles, qui venerant cum Petro, quia et in nationes gratia Spiritūs Sancti effusa est. ⁴⁶Audiebant enim illos loquentes linguis et magnificantes Deum. ⁴⁷Tunc respondit Petrus, "Numquid aquam quis prohibere potest ut non baptizentur hi qui Spiritum Sanctum acceperunt sicut et nos?" ⁴⁸Et iussit eos in nomine Iesu Christi baptizari. Tunc rogaverunt eum ut maneret aliquot diebus.

Ex circumcisione fideles: I.e., ethnic Jews. *Numquid aquam quis prohibere potest*: Peter recognizes that this is an unusual conversion event. The normal procedure is repentance and confession, baptism, and conferral of the gifts of the Holy Spirit. Here it seems the converts don't have the opportunity to repent because the Holy Spirit arrives while Peter is finishing his sermon (*Adhuc loquente Petro verba haec*). This is followed by the ritual of baptism, which usually is a precondition for receiving the powers of the Holy Spirit.

ACTS

AD 41-43

News that Peter has been baptizing Gentiles reaches the apostles and disciples in Jerusalem. When he returns, he tells them that a vision sent to him from God signifies non-Jews must be considered clean and worthy of receiving the Holy Spirit. Nevertheless, some of Jesus' followers preach only to other Jews. The believers in Jerusalem dispatch Barnabas to Antioch, where there is a large concentration of Gentile converts. He approves of what he sees, and exhorts them to continue in the ways of God. Barnabas goes to Tarsus to bring Paul back to Antioch, where they stay for a year and help get the new converts organized. The followers of Jesus are called Christians for the first time in Antioch. The Christ believers there collect aid for brethren in Jerusalem during a food shortage. Paul and Barnabas deliver the aid.

1–10: Questioned by the other apostles in Jerusalem, Peter tells them of his vision.

quoniam, that • **discepto**, to make an investigation • **adversus**, against • **praeputium**, foreskin • **nequaquam**, not at all • **os**, mouth • **secundo**, a second time • **mundo**, to make clean • **per ter**, a third time • **rursum**, again

Audierunt autem Apostoli et fratres qui erant in Iudaeā quoniam et gentes receperunt verbum Dei. ²Cum ascendisset autem Petrus in Hierosolymam, disceptabant adversus illum, qui erant ex circumcisione, ³dicentes, "Quare introisti ad viros praeputium habentes et manducasti cum illis?" ⁴Incipiens autem Petrus exponebat illis ordinem, dicens, ⁵"Ego eram in civitate Ioppe orans, et vidi in excessu mentis visionem: descendens vas quoddam, velut linteum magnum quattuor initiis submitti de caelo, et vēnit usque ad me. ⁶In quod intuens considerabam, et vidi

Apostoli et fratres: The clause *qui erant in Iudaeā* suggests, but doesn't prove, that they are the local Aramaic speaking members of the Jesus movement, and not the Hellenists (Greek-speaking Jews). It would make sense that the traditional core of Christ believers would be anxious about the conversion of large numbers of Gentiles. *Qui erant ex circumcisione*: This extra qualification explains their suspicion of converting Gentiles to their movement. *Manducasti*: *manducavisti*. See note at 2: 29-36. *Exponebat illis ordinem*: "explaining to them in order." We might say, "explaining to them from the beginning what happened." *Visionem*: This bears repeating. One of the principal themes of Acts is how a Jewish sect broke out into the non-Jewish population around them and in the whole of the Mediterranean area.

quadrupedia terrae et bestias et reptilia et volatilia caeli. ⁷Audivi autem et vocem dicentem mihi, 'Surgens, Petre, occide et manduca.' ⁸Dixi autem, 'Nequaquam, Domine, quia commune aut inmundum numquam introivit in os meum.' ⁹Respondit autem vox secundo de caelo, 'Quae Deus mundavit, tu ne 'commune' dixeris.' ¹⁰Hŏc autem factum est per ter, et recepta sunt rursum omnia in caelum.

11–18: Peter tells them of the conversion of Cornelius and the outpouring of the Holy Spirit on the non-Jewish converts in Caesarea.

confestim, immediately • **haesito**, to hesitate • **coepi**, to begin • **decado, recordor**, to remember • **taceo**, to be silent

¹¹"Et ecce: confestim tres viri adstiterunt in domo in quā eram, missi a Caesareā ad me. ¹²Dixit autem Spiritus mihi ut irem cum illis, nihil haesitans. Venerunt autem mecum et sex fratres isti, et ingressi sumus in domum viri. ¹³Narravit autem nobis quomodo vidisset angelum in domo suā stantem et dicentem sibi, 'Mitte

Sex fratres isti: isti = "your six brethren." This emphasizes that they needn't take only Peter's word for it. There were witnesses. *Ego quis eram qui*: "Who am I to . . ." *Tacuerunt*: It's understandable and significant that the disciples don't raise any of the questions that will soon trouble them. After they've been converted, what rules and rituals of Judaism should these new Gentiles converts observe? Are they bound to observe the Laws of the Torah? What about circumcision? Another issue has to do with the wider Jewish community. Are these new converts fully Jewish with the right to enter the areas of the Temple restricted to Jews, or will they be merely honorary, or half-Jews? *Ad vitam*: Ad can often show purpose, "repentance for life."

in Ioppen, et accersi Simonem, qui cognominatur Petrus, ¹⁴qui loquetur tibi verba in quibus salvus eris tu et universa domus tua.' ¹⁵Cum autem coepissem loqui, decidit Spiritus Sanctus super eos, sicut et in nos in initio. ¹⁶Recordatus sum autem verbi Domini, sicut dicebat, 'Iohannes quidem baptizavit aquā. Vos autem baptizabimini Spiritu Sancto.' ¹⁷Si ergo eandem gratiam dedit illis Deus, sicut et nobis qui credidimus in Dominum Iesum Christum, ego quis eram qui possem prohibere Deum?" ¹⁸His auditis tacuerunt et glorificaverunt Deum, dicentes, "Ergo et gentibus Deus paenitentiam ad vitam dedit."

19–26: Some begin preaching to Greek pagans in Antioch, resulting in massive numbers of converts. Barnabas is sent from Jerusalem to investigate. He sends for Paul in Tarsus to help with the instruction of the new Christ believers, who are called Christians for the first time.

perambulo, to journey • **nemo**, no one • **solus**, alone • **pervenio**, to arrive • **gavisus est** < **gaudeo** • **propositum**, purpose • **quia**, since • **adpono**, to add to • **proficiscor**, to set out • **conversor**, to stay

---

¹⁹Et illi quidem qui dispersi fuerant a tribulatione quae facta fuerat sub Stephano perambulaverunt usque Foenicen et Cyprum et Antiochiam, nemini loquentes verbum nisi solis Iudaeis. ²⁰Erant autem quidam ex eis viri Cyprii et Cyrenei, qui, cum introissent Antiochiam, loquebantur et ad Graecos, adnuntiantes Dominum Iesum. ²¹Et erat manus Domini cum eis, multusque numerus credentium conversus est ad Dominum. ²²Pervenit autem sermo ad aures ecclesiae quae erat Hierosolymis super istis et miserunt Barnaban usque Antiochiam, ²³qui cum pervenisset et vidisset gratiam Dei, gavisus est et hortabatur omnes proposito cordis permanere in Domino, ²⁴quia erat vir bonus et plenus Spiritu Sancto et fide. Et adposita est turba multa Domino. ²⁵Profectus est autem Tarsum ut quaereret

A tribulatione: This is the persecution that drove Greek-speaking Christ believers out of Jerusalem after the stoning of Stephen (8:1). ***Loquebantur et ad Graecos***: "even to Greeks." Whereas *Graeci* before meant Greek-speaking Jews, here it means ethnic Greeks. Many Greek-speaking Jews who'd left Jerusalem were limiting their preaching to Jewish Greek speakers, but this changes when "some men from Cyprus and Cyrene" begin to preach to Gentiles. These believers from Cyrene and Cyprus appear out of nowhere. Who are they, who was preaching to them, how and by whom were they converted and baptized, and most importantly, are they preaching the same thing about Jesus that the Jerusalem brethren were? After the conversion of Cornelius, it was inevitable that non-Jewish Greek speakers would be preached to and converted, but the older, Aramaic speaking core of the movement is losing control of events and even the language (Greek, and not Aramaic) in which their beliefs are being conveyed. ***Quia erat vir bonus . . .***: This compliment might indicate that Barnabas was sent to put an end to the widespread dissemination of the Gospel to Gentiles. Cornelius could be seen as a one-off exception because of the extraordinary message to Peter and his unquestionable authority as one of the first followers of Jesus. ***Ut quaereret Saulum***: It's altogether fitting that Barnabas should seek out Paul's help. He spoke on behalf of Paul at Jerusalem (9:26-31), and Paul was noted for preaching to Greek-speaking Jews outside of Jerusalem. ***Christiani***: This neologism almost certainly was created by their detractors as a kind of slur: "Kingsters," "Christizers," or "Messiahists." The one other time it's used in Acts is by King Agrippa II (26:28) during one of Paul's trials, where clearly it's meant as a kind of joke. The only other instance of the term in the New Testament is 1 Peter 4:16, where Peter says it should cause no one shame to be martyred as a Christian. It's never used in Acts

Saulum, quem cum invenisset, perduxit Antiochiam ²⁶et annum totum conversati sunt in ecclesiā. Et docuerunt turbam multam ita ut cognominarentur primum Antiochiae discipuli Christiani.

by the Christ believers themselves. Instead they refer to themselves as the "Holy Ones," "Brethren," followers of "The Way," "Nazarenes," or "Prophets." The word itself has a Greek root (*christos*) and a Latin suffix (-*ianus*). As in English, neologisms can fuse two words from different languages together, as in "capitalize," where "capital" is from Latin and "ize" is a Greek verbal suffix.

27–30: The Christ believers in Antioch send help to the Jerusalem believers during a famine in Judea.

supervenio, to come to • **fames**, famine • **futurus**, coming • **orbis terrarum**, world • **seniores**, elders

²⁷In his autem diebus supervenerunt ab Hierosolymis prophetae Antiochiam. ²⁸Et surgens unus ex eis, nomine Agabus, significabat per Spiritum famem magnam futuram in universo orbe terrarum, quae facta est sub Claudio. ²⁹Discipuli autem prout quis habebat proposuerunt singuli eorum in ministerium mittere habitantibus in Iudaeā fratribus, ³⁰quod et fecerunt, mittentes ad seniores per manūs Barnabae et Sauli.

Prophetae: I.e., important Christ believers. ***Nomine Agabus***: He is traditionally considered to be one of the seventy (or seventy-two) disciples commissioned to go out and preach by Jesus (Luke 10:1-24). He may be the same Agabus who meets Paul later in Acts (21: 10-12) in Caesarea Maritima. ***Quae facta est sub Claudio***: Claudius became emperor in AD 44, so it would have to have occurred no earlier than that. There are no reports of wide spread food shortages that would fit this chronology. It's probably best to take *in universo orbe terrarum* as an exaggeration and assume that there was only a local crisis that was not significant enough to be mentioned by any contemporary sources. ***Habitantibus in Iudaeā fratribus***: Thus the Aramaic-speaking Christ believers in Jerusalem are not only losing their control over their movement, they've even become dependent on the growing numbers of non-Jewish converts. ***Seniores***: Luke for the first time refers to the leaders of the Christ believers as *seniores* (*presbyteroi* in the Greek), a term hitherto used only for part of the Sanhedrin. We can't expect a precise definition for what he means by *seniores*, as he doesn't show much interest in the emerging organization of Christ believers in Jerusalem or anywhere else. His point is to demonstrate to Theophilus how the Jesus movement made its way to Rome, not to give him an exhaustive account of all the details. ***Per manūs Barnabae et Sauli***: Paul's appearance at the head of an aid mission couldn't have sat well with the Jerusalem brethren. They'd expelled him only a few years before for having stirred up trouble with the Jewish authorities (see the note on *fiduciter* at 9:28), and instructed him to go back to his home in Tarsus.

ACTS 12 AD 43-45

A second persecution of the Christ believers in Jerusalem begins when Herod Agrippa I (aka Agrippa) executes James and arrests Peter. Peter is miraculously released from his cell by an angel. He arrives at the house of Mary, where others had gathered. In her excitement and disbelief, the slave girl Rhoda, who answers the door, leaves him standing there, while she runs off to tell the brethren inside that Peter has been returned to them. Agrippa has the guards at the jail executed. Later he is struck down by God. Barnabas and Paul, joined by John Mark, return to Antioch, their mission to deliver aid to Jerusalem having been completed.

1–5: Agrippa persecutes the Christ believers with the approval of the Jews.

adfligo, to strike • **occīdo**, to kill • **gladius**, sword • **quia**, that • **adpono**, to add • **adprehendo**, to arrest • **azyma**, Feast of the Unleavened Bread • **quaternio**, body of four soldiers • **miles**, soldier • **custodio**, to guard • **Pascha**, Passover season • **produco**, to put on display • **servo**, to keep • **carcer**, prison

Eodem autem tempore misit Herodes rex manūs ut adfligeret quosdam de ecclesiā. ²Occīdit autem Iacobum, fratrem Iohannis, gladio. ³Videns autem quia placeret Iudaeis, adposuit adprehendere et Petrum. Erant autem dies azymorum. ⁴Quem cum adprehendisset misit in carcerem, tradens quattuor quaternionibus militum custodire eum, volens post Pascha producere eum populo. ⁵Et Petrus quidem servabatur in carcere. Oratio autem fiebat sine intermissione ab ecclesiā ad Deum pro eo.

Herodes: This Herod has the epithet Agrippa I, and is often referred simply as Agrippa to distinguish him from several other Herods. The first is Herod the Great, who ruled as the "King" of the Jews for Rome over much of the area from 36 to 4 BC. Two years after his death, his lands were organized into the province of Roman Judea, which was carved up into three districts, each ruled by one of his sons. Herod Archelaus, sometimes called just Archelaus, ruled over Jerusalem and the area around it. Herod Philip I ruled over the northeast region of the old kingdom, and Herod Antipas ruled over the area that included Galilee. Agrippa, the one mentioned here in Acts, was well liked by the Roman emperor Caligula, and when Herod Philip I died in 37, he was awarded his territory. To this was added the lands of Herod Antipas in 39 CE. Finally in 41 the new emperor Claudius granted him the lands around Judaea, too. Thus Agrippa for a while ruled alone over the full extent of Herod the Great's original, unified kingdom. Until his death in 44, he was one of the most powerful kings ruling for Rome in the east. *Eo tempore*: This would have to be 44 to fit the chronology set in Chapter 11 (*sub Claudio*). *Occidit . . . gladio*: Agrippa would naturally want to send a message to the Jerusalem Christ believers that they were on his list as potential subversives, the previous arrangements with the local authorities notwithstanding (8:1). By a swift act of cruelty, Agrippa would have been hoping to establish the

Continued

tone of his new reign. Agrippa, not coincidentally, would become familiar with real revolutionaries. He was often to find himself caught between the increasingly irrational Roman emperor Caligula and the religious intransigence of the Jews. Luke specifies the method of execution to show that this was an official state sentence and not, as in the case of Stephen, the result of a mob action instigated by the Sanhedrin. ***Dies azymorum***: The Azymes, the Days of Unleavened Bread, were the seven days after the Passover day. ***Tradens quattuor quaternionibus militum custodire eum***: "assigned [to] four squads of four soldiers to guard him." There were four detachments of four soldiers on guard throughout the night to cover each of the four night watches. Two of the soldiers were stationed outside of the cell and two were inside the cell with Peter. Finally, Peter was chained to one of the two guards inside the cell. ***Post Pascha***: meaning the entire Passover celebration, including the seven days of Azymes after the actual Passover day. ***Producere***: suggests a very visible, public trial and execution.

6–11: Peter is freed from prison by an angel.

catena, chain • **custos**, guard • **adsto**, to stand near • **lumen**, light • **refulgeo**, to shine • **habitaculum**, cell • **latus**, side • **suscito**, to awaken • **velociter**, swiftly • **praecingo**, to bind up • **calcium**, sandal • **gallica**, boot • **circumdo**, to put on • **vestimentum**, clothes • **custodia**, guard house • **ferreus**, iron • **ultro**, on its own

---

⁶Cum autem producturus eum esset Herodes, in ipsā nocte erat Petrus dormiens inter duos milites, vinctus catenis duabus et custodes ante ostium custodiebant carcerem. ⁷Et ecce: angelus Domini adstitit, et lumen refulsit in habitaculo, percussoque latere Petri suscitavit eum, dicens, "Surge velociter." Et ceciderunt catenae de manibus eius. ⁸Dixit autem angelus ad eum, "Praecingere et calcia te gallicas tuas." Et fecit sic. Et dixit illi, "Circumda tibi vestimentum tuum et sequere me." ⁹Et exiens sequebatur, et nesciebat quia verum est quod fiebat per angelum, aestimabat autem se visum videre. ¹⁰Transeuntes autem primam et secundam custodiam venerunt ad portam ferream quae ducit ad civitatem, quae ultro aperta est eis. Et exeuntes processerunt vicum unum, et continuo discessit angelus ab eo. ¹¹Et Petrus ad se reversus dixit, "Nunc scio vere quia misit Dominus angelum suum et eripuit me de manu Herodis et de omni expectatione plebis Iudaeorum."

Verum est quod fiebat per angelum: "what was being done by the angel was real." The details of his escape suggest the source for this ultimately is Peter himself, who would have been asked to tell his story so many times to his brethren that it became fixed in their memories. *Vicum unum*: that is, the point from which Peter would be able to find his own way. *De omni expectatione*: The word had probably gotten around that Peter was going to be executed just as James had been. The crowd was anticipating Peter's public execution.

12–19: To the astonishment of all, Peter arrives at the house of Mary, the mother of John Mark.

pulso, to pound • **ut**, when • **intro**, within • **insanio**, to be crazy • **persevero**, to persevere • **annuo**, to nod approval • **parvus**, small • **turbatio**, distrubance • **requiro**, to ask for

¹²Consideransque vēnit ad domum Mariae, matris Iohannis, qui cognominatus est Marcus, ubi erant multi congregati et orantes. ¹³Pulsante autem eo ostium ianuae, processit puella ad audiendum, nomine Rhode. ¹⁴Et ut cognovit vocem Petri, prae gaudio non aperuit ianuam, sed intro currens nuntiavit stare Petrum ante ianuam. ¹⁵At illi dixerunt ad eam, "Insanis." Illa autem adfirmabat sic se habere. Illi autem dicebant, "Angelus eius est." ¹⁶Petrus autem perseverabat pulsans, cum autem aperuissent, viderunt eum et obstipuerunt. ¹⁷Annuens autem eis manu ut tacerent enarravit quomodo Dominus eduxisset eum de carcere, dixitque, "Nuntiate Iacobo et fratribus haec." Et egressus abiit in alium locum. ¹⁸Factā autem die, erat non parva turbatio inter milites: "Quidnam de Petro factum esset?" ¹⁹Herodes autem cum requisisset eum et non invenisset, inquisitione factā de custodibus, iussit eos duci [ad mortem]. Descendensque a Iudaeā in Caesaream ibi commoratus est.

Qui cognominatus est Marcus: This is quite possibly John Mark, who later traditions say was Peter's companion and the author the second Gospel. *Angelus eius est*: since they assumed he'd been executed. *Iacobo*: I.e., James "the Less," not James "the Greater," a son of Zebedee and one of the original disciples. The latter James had just been executed. *Et egressus abiit in alium locum*: for safe keeping, since Agrippa would likely search for him in his friend's house. *Ut tacerent*: so they could see he wasn't just a ghost.

20–23: Agrippa is struck dead.

unianimis, of one mind • **cubiculum**, cabinet [of officials] • **postulo**, to seek • **alo**, to feed • **statuo**, to set, **vestitus**, dressed • **regius**, royal • **contionor**, to convene with • **vermis**, worm • **exspiro**, to die

²⁰Erat autem iratus Tyriis et Sidoniis. At illi unianimes venerunt ad eum, et persuaso Blasto, qui erat super cubiculum regis, postulabant pacem, eo quod alerentur regiones eorum ab illo. ²¹Statuto autem die, Herodes vestitus veste regiā sedit pro tribunali et contionabatur ad eos. ²²Populus autem acclamabat, "[Audimus] Dei voces et non hominis!" ²³Confestim autem percussit eum angelus Domini, eo quod non dedisset honorem Deo, et consumptus a vermibus exspiravit.

Iratus Tyriis et Sidoniis: Tyre and Sidon are both coastal cities in the Roman province of Syria. We aren't told why Agrippa is angry with them, but the fact that he is explains why representatives from the two cities were in Caesarea Maritima. They were meeting to work out a resolution to whatever problem had come up. *Persuaso Blasto*: "with the support of Blastus." The representatives of Tyre and Sidon first approached Agrippa's chief of staff, who was *super cubiculum regis*, to arrange a meeting to negotiate a truce. Nothing else is known of Blastus. We would like to know, however, why Luke mentions him by name. Perhaps he was known for some reason to Theophilus. *Eo quod alerentur regiones eorum ab illo*: The two coastal cities relied on Agrippa's lands to the east for food. Agrippa might have blockaded trade, and Blastus was in the city to negotiate an end to an embargo. A disruption of trade could also account for the local food shortage reported in at 11:27-30. *Statuto autem die*: This could very well be the day of the provincial celebration for Claudius' victories in Britain in 44, a good time to take up other business, since all the notables from the provinces of Judaea and Syria would have been present. *Dei voces et non hominis*: In the original Greek, the expression has the rhythm of a chant that could be shouted out repeatedly: *theOU phoNEH, kai OUK anTHROpou*. *Non dedisset honorem Deo*: Agrippa, as a Jew, should have turned back their excessive flattery and given thanks to God. With some differences, the contemporary historian Josephus also says Agrippa was struck with a sudden illness in Caesarea (*Jewish Antiquities*, 19:8.2, 343-361).

ACTS OF THE APOSTLES

24–25: Barnabas and Paul return from their mission and John Mark joins them.

cresco, to grow • **expleo**, to complete

²⁴Verbum autem Domini crescebat et multiplicabatur. ²⁵Barnabas autem et Saulus reversi sunt ab Hierosolymis expleto ministerio, adsumpto Iohanne, qui cognominatus est Marcus.

Expleto ministerio: the service of delivering the aid (11:30).

St. Peter

St. Peter by Bernardo Strozzi 1581-1644 (The Met)

ACTS 13

AD 46-47

Paul and Barnabas, accompanied by John Mark, are sent out on a mission from Antioch. They confront a false Jewish prophet, Bar-Jesus, on Cyprus. In the presence of Paul, Bar-Jesus is struck blind. The Roman governor, Sergius Paulus, who witnessed the event, thereupon converts. The mission moves from Cyprus to Asia Minor, but John Mark returns to Jerusalem. After passing through the port city of Perge, Paul speaks at a synagogue in Pisidian Antioch. The local Jews are disturbed to see many of their number going over to this new cult. Nearly the entire city comes out to hear Paul preach. He says that the offer of salvation was at first a gift to the Jewish people, but since they rejected it, just as they had rejected their prophets in the past, God instructed him and Barnabas to deliver the word to outsiders. They are forced to leave town.

1–3: The Holy Spirit orders Paul and Barnabas to go on a mission.

Erant autem in ecclesiā quae erat Antiochiae prophetae et doctores, in quibus Barnabas et Symeon, qui vocabatur Niger, et Lucius Cyrenensis et Manaen, qui erat Herodis tetrarchae conlactaneus, et Saulus. ²Ministrantibus autem illis Domino et ieiunantibus dixit Spiritus Sanctus, "Separate mihi Barnaban et Saulum in opus quod adsumpsi eos." ³Tunc ieiunantes et orantes inponentesque eis manūs dimiserunt illos.

Antiochiae: locative. ***Prophetae et doctores***: This doesn't mean the recognized clergy as will develop later. It means holy ones and people developing in the faith intellectually. ***Barnabas . . . Manean***: Only Barnabas is more than a name to us in this list. ***Herodis tetrarchae***: This is Herod Antipas (circa 20 BC to AD 39), the ruler of the region of Galilee and Pera during Jesus' life. ***Conlactaneus***: literally, "milk mate." In the Greek, it's *syntrophos* ("messmate"). It means that he was Herod Antipas's childhood friend, thus indicating that the Jesus movement is spreading to the highest levels of Jewish society. ***In opus quod adsumpsi eos***: "the work I have taken them for."

4–8: On Cyprus, he visits the court of the Roman proconsul Sergius Paulus, where a local guru named Bar-Jesus is plying his trade.

magus, sorcerer • **accio**, to summon • **desidero**, to wish • **averto**, to turn away

⁴Et ipsi quidem missi ab Spiritu Sancto abierunt Seleuciam, et inde navigaverunt Cyprum. ⁵Et cum venissent Salamina, praedicabant verbum Dei in synagogis Iudaeorum. Habebant autem et Iohannem in ministerio. ⁶Et cum perambulassent universam insulam usque Paphum, invenerunt quendam virum, magum, pseudoprophetam, Iudaeum, cui nomen erat Bariesu, ⁷qui erat cum proconsule, Sergio Paulo, viro prudente. Hĭc, accitis Barnabā et Saulo, desiderabat audire verbum Dei. ⁸Resistebat autem illis Elymas, magus (sic enim interpretatur nomen eius), quaerens avertere proconsulem a fide.

Seleuciam: "to Seleucia," the port city for Antioch. Antioch itself is fifteen miles inland. *Salamina*: the largest city on the island's eastern coast. The seat of Roman administration is at Paphos, on the other side of the island. *Iohannem*: I.e., John Mark, mentioned at 12:12. ***Magum, pseudoprophetam, Iudaeum***: We shouldn't think of a *magus* as primarily a sorcerer performing magic tricks. He was more like a modern-day guru, imparting mystic doctrines to his followers, usually for pay or influence, using a hodgepodge of allegorical methods to coax out the "deeper" meanings of passages from sacred texts. Though denounced by the official authorities, they could nevertheless (and still do) attract a large and energetic following, as Bar-Jesus had in Cyprus. Jesus was a fairly common name. There's no connection between Bar-Jesus and Jesus. ***Proconsule, Sergio Paulo***: A governor that was sensible and well-intentioned, such as Sergius Paulus, was a noteworthy exception to the rule. The governors of these provinces were more often than not massively corrupt and incompetent. Historians unanimously agree that the failure of the Senate or the emperor to rein them in crippled the policies of imperial Rome. ***Elymas***: There is no recognizable etymology of this word. Given the nature of his profession, however, it's entirely possible that Bar-Jesus made up this mystic sounding name himself out of whole cloth to baffle and impress his potential clients. ***Avertere proconsulem a fide***: Bar-Jesus must have known that losing the governor to the Jesus movement would be a serious blow to his status and income.

9–12: Paul confronts the guru, whom God strikes blind.

dolus, trick • **fallacia**, deceit • **inimicus**, enemy • **iustitia**, justice • **desino**, to cease • **caecus**, blind • **sol**, sun • **usque ad tempus**, for a while • **caligo**, fog • **tenebra**, darkness

⁹Paulus autem, qui et Paulus, repletus Spiritu Sancto intuens in eum ¹⁰dixit, "O plene omni dolo et omni fallaciā, fili diaboli, inimice omnis iustitiae, non desinis subvertere vias Domini rectas? ¹¹Et nunc ecce: manūs Domini [sunt] super te et eris caecus, non videns solem usque ad tempus." Et confestim cecidit in eum caligo et tenebrae, et circumiens quaerebat qui ei manum daret. ¹²Tunc proconsul cum vidisset factum, credidit, admirans super doctrinam Domini.

Qui et Paulus: "who was also a Paul," like Sergius "Paulus." Henceforth, Luke will use "Paul" instead of the more Semitic name "Saul." The fact that Luke makes this change without any editorial or explanatory comment means he found nothing usual about it. It could be that Paul himself made the change to fit in better with the largely Gentile world of his missions, just as in our time someone with the Greek name "Ioannis" will be called "John." *Fili diaboli*: Paul accuses Bar-Jesus, whose name means "son of Jesus," of actually being *Bar-Satana*. **Vias Domini rectas**: By the "straight ways" Paul may mean the obvious significance of the words in the text, and the not bizarre conjectures imputed to them by Bar-Jesus. *Cecidit*: Grammatically the verb should be plural, but it is attracted to *caligo*, with *tenebrae* serving almost as an apposition, as in "Upon him a mist descends, shadows." **Credidit, admirans super doctrinam Domini**: Even though Sergius Paulus is considered to be among the first pagan converts, it's not clear from Acts that he actually became a Christ believer. There's no baptism and the power of the Holy Spirit isn't conferred on him. The most we can say is that he acquired a respect for the Gospel of Jesus.

ACTS OF THE APOSTLES

13–15: Instead of continuing on to Asia Minor with them after Cyprus, John Mark returns to Jerusalem. Paul speaks in a synogogue in Pisidian Antioch.

discedo, to leave • **lectio**, a reading • **si quis** = **si aliquis** • **exhortatio**, encouragement

¹³Et cum a Papho navigassent Paulus et qui cum eo, venerunt Pergen Pamphiliae. Iohannes autem discedens ab eis reversus est Hierosolymam. ¹⁴Illi vero pertranseuntes Pergen venerunt Antiochiam Pisidiae, et ingressi synagogam die Sabbatorum sederunt. ¹⁵Post lectionem autem Legis et prophetarum miserunt principes synagogae ad eos, dicentes, "Viri, fratres, si quis est in vobis sermo exhortationis ad plebem, dicite."

Venerunt Pergen Pamphiliae: Perge, in the district of Pamphilia in the south of modern-day Turkey, is about 175 miles across open sea from Paphos in Cyprus. *Iohannes autem discedens ab eis*: The silence about what caused this split is agonizing. He might simply have feared the region's well deserved reputation of being overrun by thieves. On the other hand, the split might have been over substantial doctrinal disagreements. As one whose family was close to the original apostles (12:12), he might have been dismayed at Paul's direct appeal to pagans and/or by what he was telling them. *Antiochiam Pisidiae*: The qualification "of Pisidia" distinguishes it from the larger Antioch in Syria. *Post lectionem autem Legis et prophetarum*: A typical synagogue service would include a reading from Scripture followed by an invitation to anyone who wished to address the congregation about it. Having someone announce the arrival of the Messiah is not what would have been expected. *Si quis est in vobis sermo*: Take *[ali]quis* with **Sermo**: literally, "If there is any speech among you . . ." We might say, "If any of you has anything he'd like to say . . ."

16–20: Paul begins the traditional story of the Jewish people.

eligo, to choose • **exalto**, to raise up • **incola**, inhabitant • **brachium**, arm • **excelsus**, heavenly • **destruo**, to destroy

¹⁶Surgens autem Paulus et manu silentium indicens ait, "Viri Israhelitae et qui timetis Deum, audite. ¹⁷Deus plebis Israhel elegit patres nostros et plebem exaltavit cum essent incolae in terrā Aegypti, et in brachio excelso eduxit eos ex eā, ¹⁸et per quadraginta annorum tempus mores eorum sustinuit in deserto, ¹⁹et destruens gentes septem in terrā Chanaan sorte distribuit eis terram eorum ²⁰quasi post quadringentos et quinquaginta annos. Et post haec dedit iudices usque ad Samuhel, prophetam."

Et qui timetis Deum: Again this indicates that "god-fearing" pagans were invited to the worship services. *Cum essent incolae in terrā Aegypti*: Jews never tired of hearing their sacred history. This explains why sections of it acquired such stability. Presumably, however, it would be expected that each time it was retold there would be some unique emphases that would have bearing on the present moment. In Paul's case, he shapes Jewish history into a prelude to the arrival of Jesus. *In brachio excelso*: "heavenly" or "exalted" or "uplifted." It's hard to know why Paul alters the image of the pillar of smoke from Exodus that guided the Hebrews out of Egypt. He might have been referring to some local artifact—a statue or painting—that is lost to us in order to give the beginning of his discourse some local poignancy. *Destruens gentes septem*: When the Jews were led into the promised land of Canaan after the exodus, they were commanded to kill all the people already living there and cleanse the land of traces of paganism. The seven tribes they were to exterminate are those listed at Deuteronomy 7:1. *Iudices*: The Jews first lived in twelve semi-autonomous tribes in Canaan, and came together occasionally for shared rituals or to unite against a common enemy. A "judge" was the military leader of such a temporary coalition. Once the threat was overcome, the judge would step down. After Samuel, the Jews chose to have a permanent leader.

ACTS OF THE APOSTLES

21–25: "God gives Israel kings, and from King David's lineage Jesus eventually comes as its savior."

exinde, next • **postulo**, to ask for • **tribus**, tribe • **amoveo**, to pass on • **perhibeo**, to hold forth • **secundum**, according to • **voluntas**, will • **semen**, seed • **salvator**, savior • **facies**, presence • **adventus**, arrival • **impleo**, to fulfill • **cursus**, journey • **calciamentum**, shoe • **solvo**, to untie

---

²¹"Et exinde postulaverunt regem et dedit illis Deus Saul, filium Cis, virum de tribu Beniamin annis quadraginta. ²²Et amoto illo, suscitavit illis David regem, cui et testimonium perhibens dixit, 'Inveni David, filium Iesse, virum secundum cor meum, qui faciet omnes voluntates meas.' ²³Huius Deus ex semine secundum promissionem eduxit Israhel salvatorem, Iesum, ²⁴raedicante Iohanne ante faciem adventūs eius baptismum paenitentiae omni populo Israhel. ²⁵Cum impleret autem Iohannes cursum suum, dicebat, 'Quem me arbitramini esse non sum ego, sed ecce: vĕnit post me cuius non sum dignus calciamenta pedum solvere.'"

Postulaverunt regem: The Jews asked God for a king to meet the specific existential threat from the Philistines. Saul was their first king. *Regem*: apposition to David, "as king." *Secundum promissionem*: The promise that the Messiah would come from the house of David is a composite of texts, one from an oracle of Nathan, a prophet in the time of David's kingship, (2 Sam. 7: 12—16), and the other David's final words (2 Sam. 22:51). *Eduxit Israhel salvatorem*: "for Israel" (dative). *Ante faciem adventūs eius*: "before the presence of his arrival," which we might translate simply as "before his arrival." *Omni populo Israhel*, "for the entire nation of Israel" (genitive). *Impleret... cursum*: a euphemism for "he died." *Quem me arbitramini esse non sum ego*: "Whom you think me to be I am not" = "I am not who you think I am." The Gospels all report that there were many who thought John the Baptist was a great prophet if not the Messiah himself. *Vĕnit post me...*: This comment by John is repeated in all four Gospels (Matt. 3:11, Mark 1:7, Luke 3:16, John 1:20, 27).

26–31: "The Jewish people in Jerusalem ignored the words of their own prophets and had Jesus crucified."

genus, race • **peto**, to seek • **interficio**, to kill • **consummo**, to accomplish • **depono**, to take down • **monumentum**, grave • **simul**, at the same time

²⁶"Viri, fratres, filii generis Abraham et qui in vobis timent Deum, vobis verbum salutis huius missum est. ²⁷Qui enim habitabant Hierusalem et principes eius, hunc ignorantes et voces prophetarum, quae per omne Sabbatum leguntur, iudicantes impleverunt, ²⁸et nullam causam mortis invenientes in eum petierunt a Pilato ut interficerent eum. ²⁹Cumque consummassent omnia quae de eo scripta erant, deponentes eum de ligno posuerunt in monumento. ³⁰Deus vero suscitavit eum a mortuis [tertiā die], qui visus est per dies multos his ³¹qui simul ascenderant cum eo de Galilaeā in Hierusalem, qui usque nunc sunt testes eius ad plebem."

In vobis: including the non-Jewish God-fearers, as indicated in the clause before, *et qui in vobis timent Deum*. **Hunc...impleverunt**: literally, "not knowing this man and the voices of the prophets, which are read every Sabbath, judging [him] they fulfilled [the words of the prophets]." ***De ligno***: Paul uses the shortened expression *de ligno* for the cross as a reference to Deuteronomy (21:22-23). ***His***: dative, "was visible to those who."

ACTS OF THE APOSTLES

32–37: "God is offering you forgiveness and justification."

---

adimpleo, to complete • **gigno**, to give birth to • **amplius iam**, ever more • **ideo**, wherefore • **administro**, to serve • **vero**, but

---

³²"Et nos vobis adnuntiamus eam [promissam] quae ad patres nostros repromissio facta est, ³³quoniam hanc Deus adimplevit filiis nostris, resuscitans Iesum, sicut et in psalmo secundo scriptum est: 'Filius meus es tu. Ego hodie genui te.' ³⁴Quod autem suscitaverit eum a mortuis amplius iam non reversurum in corruptionem, ita dixit, quia 'Dabo vobis sancta David fidelia.' ³⁵Ideoque et alias dicit, 'Non dabis Sanctum tuum videre corruptionem.' ³⁶David enim, [in] suā generatione cum administrasset voluntati Dei, dormivit et adpositus est ad patres suos et vidit corruptionem. ³⁷Quem vero Deus suscitavit non vidit corruptionem."

Nos: The Jerusalem disciples are empirical witnesses of the resurrection, which Paul interprets as the fulfillment of the prophecies. ***Secundo***: The precision of the citation establishes Paul status as a scholar of Scripture. It's one thing to be able to quote a line, but it's an entirely different order of knowledge to be able to cite its chapter and verse as well. ***Filius meus es tu. Ego hodie genui te***: Paul's argument is constructed from a sequence of the three passages from Scripture. He has to establish the fact that the promises God made to David apply in fact to Jesus. The first (Ps. 2:7) proves that the king of Israel is a son of God. The second (Isa. 55:3) affirms that the king of Israel will have all the blessings God conferred to David. The third (Ps. 16:10) demonstrates the king will not die. But since it's known that David did in fact die and that his body did decompose—his tomb is visible to everyone—these promises must have been made not to David but to someone in his dynasty, That would be Jesus. Thus Jesus' bodily resurrection ties together this nexus of prophecies. ***Quem vero Deus suscitavit***: This is almost a rhetorical question. Paul has said that he whom God raises up does not see corruption, but David did see corruption. Now he repeats the point that what God raises up doesn't see corruption.

CHAPTER 13

38–41: "In Jesus, all who believe are justified."

supervenio, to come upon • **contemptor**, a despiser • **disperdo**, to perish • **operor**, to perform

---

³⁸"Notum igitur sit vobis, viri, fratres, quia per hunc vobis remissio peccatorum adnuntiatur ab omnibus quibus non potuistis in Lege Mosi iustificari. ³⁹In hōc omnis qui credit iustificatur. ⁴⁰Videte ergo ne superveniat quod dictum est in prophetis: ⁴¹'Videte, contemptores, et admiramini, et disperdimini, quia opus operor ego in diebus vestris, opus quod non credetis si quis enarraverit vobis." ⁴²Exeuntibus autem illis, rogabant ut sequenti Sabbato loquerentur sibi verba haec. ⁴³Cumque dimissa esset synagoga, secuti sunt multi Iudaeorum et colentium advenarum Paulum et Barnaban, qui loquentes suadebant eis ut permanerent in gratiā Dei."

Per hunc: This is the critical point. So far Paul has made the argument that Jesus' resurrection was a prediction about the "anointed" one, but how do we get from that to the promise of forgiveness and resurrection for rank-and-file Jews and the rest of humanity? For this we need to circle back to Paul's reference to John the Baptist. John brought the promise of redemption. This was necessary, for no one can be justified by obedience to laws they cannot obey. ***Ab omnibus quibus non potuistis in Lege Mosi iustificari***: forgiveness "from all of the sins for which you can't be justified in the Law of Moses." The only purpose of the Law was to bring an awareness of failure and sin, thus making repentance possible. One cannot truly repent or apologize unless there's a genuine sense of wrongdoing. ***Ne superveniat***: negative jussive clause, "lest that which was proclaimed in the prophets come upon [you]." ***Quod dictum est in prophetis***: The quotation is from Hababkuk (1:5), one of the twelve minor prophets. He was thought to have predicted the Babylonian exile of the sixth century as God's punishment for Israel's disobedience to the Law. The warning is that God will punish those who don't believe now, just as he punished the nation of Israel with the exile before. ***Opus quod***: This is an appositional restart of *opus* in the previous clause, literally, "I am working a work in your time, a work which . . ." This *opus* is the Babylonian Exile. ***Exeuntibus autem illis, rogabant***: "While they [Paul and Barnabas] were leaving, they [Jews and God-fearers] asked them." ***Colentium advenarum***: "Of worshiping visitors" refers to the "God-fearers." They are "visitors" to the synagogue. Paul covered a lot of ground in his speech. It's possible that this was the first time any of them had heard of Jesus, so it not unexpected that the people in the synagogue would ask him back.

44–49: The following week, Paul and Barnabas address a much larger crowd, and many Jews are offended by their message.

paene, almost • **zelus**, passion • **constanter**, steadily • **repello**, to reject • **indignus**, unworthy • **lumen**, light • **praeordino**, to preordain • **dissemino**, to spread around

⁴⁴Sequenti vero Sabbato paene universa civitas convēnit audire verbum Domini. ⁴⁵Videntes autem turbas Iudaei repleti sunt zelo et contradicebant his quae a Paulo dicebantur, blasphemantes. ⁴⁶Tunc constanter Paulus et Barnabas dixerunt, "Vobis oportebat primum loqui verbum Dei, sed quoniam repellitis illud et indignos vos iudicastis aeternae vitae, ecce: convertimur ad Gentes. ⁴⁷Sic enim praecepit nobis Dominus, 'Posui te in lumen Gentibus, ut sis in salutem usque ad extremum terrae.'" ⁴⁸Audientes autem Gentes gavisae sunt et glorificabant verbum Domini et crediderunt quotquot erant praeordinati ad vitam aeternam. ⁴⁹Disseminabatur autem verbum Domini per universam regionem.

Paene universa civitas: Word of Paul's teachings has gotten out and attracted a huge crowd to the synagogue on the next Sabbath. ***Vobis***: this is the dative indirect object of the expression, *loqui verbum*, not the dative complement of *oportebat*. ***Praecepit nobis Dominus***: The reference is to Isaiah 49:6. There God is talking not to Israel as a whole but to the Messiah in particular. By extrapolation, though, Paul interprets this to mean that all who are doing the work of the Messiah are to be a light to the Gentiles. ***In lumen***: "as a light." ***In salutem:*** "as a means of salvation." ***Quotquot erant praeordinati***: "as many as were preordained." The notion that everlasting life is only for those pre-ordained to receive it is one of the cornerstones of Paul's theology (See Rom. 9:1—29, for example).

50–52: The Jews of the city stir up opposition to them. They leave for Iconium.

religiosus, devout • **honestus**, well placed • **excutio**, to shake off • **pulvis**, dust • **gaudium**, joy

⁵⁰Iudaei autem concitaverunt religiosas mulieres et honestas et primos civitatis, et excitaverunt persecutionem in Paulum et Barnaban, et eiecerunt eos de finibus suis. ⁵¹At illi, excusso pulvere pedum in eos, venerunt Iconium. ⁵²Discipuli quoque replebantur gaudio et Spiritu Sancto.

Iudaei: Noticeable by their absence in this are the God-fearers. The devout Jews (*religiosas*) and those content with the status quo (*honestas*) would understandably be suspicious of anyone telling them their understanding of Scripture is incomplete and that the God-fearers are more than just kindly disposed friends and neighbors of the Jews, but in some way are part of the Jewish world itself. We can only speculate why the Jewish women were among the most hostile to Paul's message. *Primos*: Who were these city leaders? Were they God-fearers or just men interested in keeping the peace and expelling agitators, whatever their cause may be? At the very least it shows the considerable influence the local Jewish population had with the civil authorities. *Gaudio*: perhaps because they have kicked the dust off their shoes as they leave, just as Jesus had told his original apostles to do to insult any city that doesn't accept them (Matt. 10:14; Mark 6:11; Luke 10:11).

Map 3: Paul's First Journey

Paul's first missionary journey, from AD 46-48, is described in chapters 13-14. Initially Paul is accompanied by Barnabas and John Mark, but John Mark returns to Jerusalem shortly after the mission began.

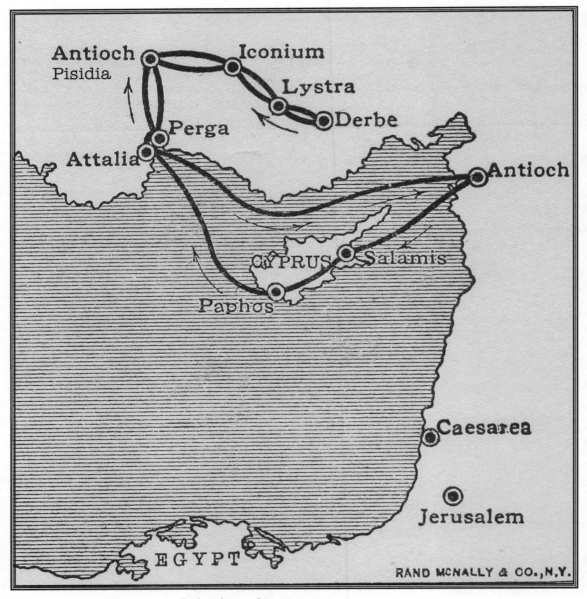

Paul's Campaigns by David James Burrell, The Library of Congress 1918.

AD 48

Paul and Barnabas are driven out of Iconium after converting large numbers. They continue their mission by visiting several nearby towns. In Lystra, they heal a man who was lame from birth, which leads many to mistake them for Olympian gods. At the instigation of local Jews, Paul is stoned by a crowd and is left for dead outside of the city. He is rescued by his companions. Paul and Barnabas then leave for nearby Derbe, where they continue their preaching. They return to the towns of Lystra, Iconium, and Pisidian Antioch, winning new converts. They proceed to the regions of Pamphylia and then to the port of Attalia, from which they sail back to Antioch in Syria. They tell the people there about the success they had and how God has opened the promise of the kingdom to Gentiles.

1–6: Paul and Barnabas are driven from the city of Iconium by an alliance of Jews and Greeks.

iracundia, anger • **impetus**, attack • **contumelia**, abuse

Factum est autem Iconii ut simul introirent synagogam Iudaeorum, et loquerentur ita ut crederet Iudaeorum et Graecorum copiosa multitudo. ²Qui vero increduli fuerunt Iudaei suscitaverunt et ad iracundiam concitaverunt animas Gentium adversus fratres. ³Multo igitur tempore demorati sunt, fiducialiter agentes in Domino, testimonium perhibente verbo gratiae suae, dante signa et prodigia fieri per manūs eorum. ⁴Divisa est autem multitudo civitatis, et quidam quidem erant cum Iudaeis, quidam vero cum Apostolis. ⁵Cum autem factus esset impetus Gentilium et Iudaeorum cum

Agentes in Domino: Take the participle as intransitive: "working for the Lord." This by the way is a curious way to translate the Greek original which has a participle that means "speaking openly" (παρρησιαζόμενοι). ***Perhibente . . . dante***: both participles agree with *Domino*. It's God who's providing witness of his favor through their words and God who's giving them the power to perform miracles. ***Quidam quidem erant cum Iudaeis***: We can well imagine that the God-fearers with longstanding cordial relations with the Jews of the synagogue could be pressured by their Jewish friends to oppose and even to rise up against what they were told was an heretical sect. ***Ut . . . lapidarent eos***: This was their intention, though it didn't actually happen.

principibus suis ut contumeliis adficerent et lapidarent eos. ⁶Intellegentes confugerunt ad civitates Lycaoniae, Lystram et Derben, et universam in circuitu regionem, et ibi evangelizantes erant.

7–12: When they heal a crippled man in Lystra the crowd hails them as Zeus and Mercury.

exilio, to jump up • **Lycaonice**, in Lycaonian • **similis**, similar to • **taurus**, bull • **corona**, garland

⁷Et quidam vir in Lystris infirmus pedibus sedebat, claudus ex utero matris suae qui numquam ambulaverat. ⁸Hīc audivit Paulum loquentem, qui intuitus eum et videns quia haberet fidem ut salvus fieret, ⁹dixit magnā voce, "Surge super pedes tuos rectus!" Et exilivit et ambulabat. ¹⁰Turbae autem cum vidissent quod fecerat Paulus levaverunt vocem suam, Lycaonice dicentes, "Dii similes facti hominibus descenderunt ad nos!" ¹¹Et vocabant Barnaban Iovem, Paulum vero Mercurium, quoniam ipse erat dux verbi. ¹²Sacerdos quoque Iovis qui erat ante civitatem, tauros et coronas ante ianuas adferens, cum populus volebat sacrificare.

In Lystris: There appears to have been no visit to a synagogue in Lystra, perhaps because there was a very small number of Jews in the city, maybe none at all. If that's so, this would be the first time that a pagan crowd was evangelized directly without having first been God-fearers. **Videns quia haberet fidem**: This doesn't mean that the man was persuaded by Paul's message about Jesus, but only that he knew Paul could heal him. Why would he think that? It could be that among the *signa* and *prodigia* mentioned in 14:3 there were miraculous cures and the man had heard the rumors. This will be the first documented healing by Paul. After this, he will acquire such power that even objects he'd touched could heal (19:12). **Lycaonice dicentes**: There are a few extant inscriptions in the local Lycaonian language. This explains why Paul and Barnabas didn't recoil sooner when they're called Zeus and Mercury. They didn't understand what the people were saying. ***Dii similes facti hominibus***: "Gods having become like men." Greek myth is filled with stories of gods coming to earth disguised at humans for various reasons. The famous myth of Philemon and Baucis, who were rewarded for hospitably receiving Zeus in their modest home, is often set in nearby Tyana. **Mercurium**: because Mercury was, among other things, the god of eloquence, and Paul was the one who gave the sermons. **Ante ianuas**: This may be a hint to the setting for this miracle. Pagan sacrifices to their gods took place in front of their temples. This likely means that the priests are bringing their offerings to the front of a temple where Paul's sermon and the cure took place. Hence *ante ianuas* would mean the gates of a temple.

CHAPTER 14

13–17: They object to the crowd's adoration and explain that it was God who healed the man.

conscindo, to tear apart • **vanus**, vain • **praeteritus**, previous • **ingredior**, to walk in • **semet** = se • **pluvia**, rain • **fructiferus**, fruit bearing • **laetitia**, joy • **sedo**, to calm • **immolo**, to slay as a sacrifice

---

¹³Quod ubi audierunt Apostoli Barnabas et Paulus, conscissis tunicis suis, exilierunt in turbas, clamantes ¹⁴et dicentes, "Viri! Quid haec facitis? Et nos mortales sumus similes vobis homines, adnuntiantes vobis ab his vanis converti ad Deum vivum, qui fecit caelum et terram et mare et omnia quae in eis sunt, ¹⁵qui in praeteritis generationibus dimisit omnes gentes ingredi in vias suas. ¹⁶Et quidem non sine testimonio semet ipsum reliquit, benefaciens de caelo dans pluvias et tempora fructifera, implens cibo et laetitiā corda vestra." ¹⁷Et haec dicentes vix sedaverunt turbas ne sibi immolarent.

Quod ubi audierunt: when someone explained to them what was going on. ***Conscissis tunicis suis***: This odd gesture was a traditional way Jewish leaders showed great dismay and agitation. ***Ab his vanis***: The people wouldn't have appreciated having their gifts called vanities. ***Semet ipsum reliquit***: That is, he didn't just create the world and then walk away. He continues to bless it with rain and harvest for the sake of humankind. ***Cibo et laetitiā corda vestra***: This is a clear reference to the celebration of a pagan festival, where there was feasting and merry-making, the very things these people were about to engage in to honor of their supposed divine visitors. ***Ne sibi immolarent***: Paul and Barnabas barely escape being offered as a sacrifice themselves by the mob. Though the threat of being lynched was real, human sacrifice was not a part of pagan ritual. This should be taken as a kind of sardonic joke.

ACTS OF THE APOSTLES

18–22: Paul is stoned by a hostile crowd in Lystra, but recovers and is able to continue his preaching in the area.

posterus, next • **proficiscor**, to set out • **doceo**, to teach • **constituo**, to establish • **ieiunatio**, fasting • **commendo**, to entrust

---

¹⁸Supervenerunt autem quidam ab Antiochiā et Iconio Iudaei, et persuasis turbis lapidantesque Paulum traxerunt extra civitatem, aestimantes eum mortuum esse. ¹⁹Circumdantibus autem eum discipulis, surgens intravit civitatem. Et posterā die profectus est cum Barnabā in Derben. ²⁰Cumque evangelizassent civitati illi et docuissent multos, reversi sunt Lystram et Iconium et Antiochiam, ²¹confirmantes animas discipulorum, exhortantes ut permanerent in fide et quoniam per multas tribulationes oportet nos intrare in regnum Dei. ²²Et cum constituissent illis per singulas ecclesias presbyteros et orassent cum ieiunationibus, commendaverunt eos Domino in quem crediderunt.

Supervenerunt autem quidam: Paul and Barnabas are being shadowed by Jewish authorities who are trying to stamp out the spread of what they see as heresy. This is going to continue throughout Acts. *Et persuasis turbis lapidantesque*: This somewhat clumsy expression combines an ablative absolute and an active participle in the nominative to agree with the subject of *traxerunt*. Literally, "and with the people having been persuaded and stoning [him] they dragged him out of the city." Stoning was not a means of execution used by the Greeks or Romans, but it's not unthinkable that the pagans in Lystra were shown how to participate in one by the Jews from Iconium and Pisidian Antioch. *Aestimantes eum mortuum esse*: This is a botched stoning. The sanctioned procedure for stoning would have precluded any mistake that the victim was dead. *Et posterā die*: It's not credible that a man who'd nearly been stoned to death would be ready to travel on the next day. Perhaps the implication is that God restored him. *Reversi sunt*: retracing their steps along the same road they took from Pisidian Antioch to Derbe. *Quoniam*: "that" after the implied speech in the verb *exhortantes*. *Presbyteros*: This is merely a transliteration of the Greek word for "elders." At this point a *presbyterus* is not the technical term it will soon become. It is significant, however, that Christ believers need guidance not provided by the local synagogues. This is a first step on the gradual diverging paths of Judaism and Christianity.

CHAPTER 14

23–27: Paul and Barnabas return to Antioch and tell them of their success at converting Gentiles.

congrego, to assemble together with • **rettulerunt** < **refero**, to report • **modicus**, little

²³Transeuntesque Pisidiam venerunt Pamphiliam, ²⁴et loquentes in Pergen verbum Domini descenderunt in Attaliam. ²⁵Et inde navigaverunt Antiochiam, unde erant traditi gratiae Dei in opus quod conpleverunt. ²⁶Cum autem venissent et congregassent ecclesiam, rettulerunt quanta fecisset Deus cum illis, quia aperuisset gentibus ostium fidei. ²⁷Morati sunt autem tempus non modicum cum discipulis.

Quanta fecisset Deus cum illis: indirect question.
Tempus non modicum: "for a time not a little" = "for a good long time."

ACTS

 AD 49/50

Representatives from Jerusalem arrive in Antioch and insist that the pagan converts must be circumcised. Paul and Barnabas go to Jerusalem to make a case against this requirement. Peter sides with Paul, and Paul carries the day. A short list of expectations for the new converts is drawn up. Paul and Barnabas return to Antioch with a letter explaining the decision, adding that the people of Antioch should listen only to those authorized to speak about such matters. As they prepare for their next mission, Paul and Barnabas disagree over whether John Mark should join them. Paul contends that he shouldn't. The two split and go their separate ways.

1–6: Paul and Barnabas go to Jerusalem to settle the question of whether circumcision is a requirement for the Gentile converts.

mos, custom • **statuo**, to determine

Et quidam descendentes de Iudaeā docebant fratres quia "Nisi circumcidamini secundum morem Mosi, non potestis salvi fieri." ²Factā ergo seditione non minimā Paulo et Barnabae adversum illos, statuerunt ut ascenderent Paulus et Barnabas et quidam alii ex illis ad Apostolos et presbyteros in Hierusalem super hāc quaestione. ³Illi igitur deducti ab ecclesiā pertransiebant Foenicen et Samariam, narrantes conversionem Gentium, et faciebant gaudium magnum omnibus fratribus. ⁴Cum autem venissent Hierosolymam suscepti sunt ab ecclesiā et ab Apostolis et senioribus, adnuntiantes quanta Deus fecisset cum illis. ⁵Surrexerunt autem quidam de heresi

Quidam ... docebant fratres: We can't tell whether these brethren are representing a consensus back in Jerusalem or whether they're speaking only on their own behalf. When Peter and the other disciples accepted the conversion of Gentiles in Chapter 10, they left some important details unaddressed. Luke doesn't say whether these numerous Gentile converts were circumcised or expected to follow the Law, like any other good Jew. Now at least some of the Jerusalem disciples are trying to correct this previous oversight. ***Paulo et Barnabae***: *Barnabae* is ablative, part of another ablative absolute with *Paulo*: "with a not small disagreement happening [and] with Paul and Barnabas being against them." ***Presbyteros***: The organization of the Jerusalem *ecclesia* must have been evolving since the first days. It's now about 50 CE, twenty some-years after the death of Jesus, and the ranks of the apostles would be thinning out. Others are stepping up into leadership positions. ***Foenicen et Samariam***: These are the two districts where the first non-Jewish or semi-Jewish conversions occurred. Paul and Barnabas are surely whipping up support for their cause among these converts as they progress to Jerusalem for the meeting. ***Quidam de heresi Pharisaeorum***: Converted Pharisees would naturally argue that the new pagan believers should be required to observe the full spread of Jewish law. ***Circumcidi eos praecipere***: "instruct them to be circumcised and to keep the Law of Moses."

117

Pharisaeorum qui crediderant, dicentes quia "Oportet circumcidi eos praecipere quoque servare Legem Mosi."

⁶Conveneruntque Apostoli et seniores videre de verbo hōc.

7–12: Peter argues that by giving the Gentile converts the gift of the Holy Spirit, God has already signaled that circumcision is not required of them.

---

conquisitio, a quarrel • **scio**, scio • **discerno**, to distinguish • **inpono**, to place on • **iugum**, a yoke

---

⁷Cum autem magna conquisitio fieret, surgens Petrus dixit ad eos, "Viri, fratres, vos scitis quoniam ab antiquis diebus in nobis elegit Deus per os meum audire Gentes verbum evangelii et credere. ⁸Et qui novit corda Deus testimonium perhibuit, dans illis Spiritum Sanctum, sicut et nobis, ⁹et nihil discrevit inter nos et illos, fide purificans corda eorum. ¹⁰Nunc ergo quid temptatis Deum inponere iugum super cervicem discipulorum quod neque patres nostri neque nos portare potuimus? ¹¹Sed per gratiam Domini Iesu credimus salvari quemadmodum et illi." ¹²Tacuit autem omnis multitudo et audiebant Barnaban et Paulum narrantes quanta fecisset Deus signa et prodigia in Gentibus per eos.

Ab antiquis diebus in nobis: Peter means the first days of the Jesus movement, not the early days of Jewish history. We have to remember that some ten to fifteen years would have passed from when Peter converted the first Gentiles in Caesarea (Chapter 11) and explained how God had sanctioned it. ***Per os meum . . . credere***: This is indirect statement implied by *elegit*: God decided [that the] *Gentes audire verbum evangelii per os meum et credere*. ***Corda***: object of *novit*, "God who knows their hearts." ***Quod:*** antecedent is *iugum*. ***Credimus salvari quemadmodum et illi***: "We believe that we are saved, just as they are, too."

13–18: James adds that expanding the call has been God's plan all along, as is seen in the Old Testament.

Iacobus = James • **sumo**, to take up • **concordo**, to agree with • **decido**, to fall down • **aedifico**, to to build • **diruta**, ruins • **erigo**, to set back up • **saeculum**, age

---

¹³Et postquam tacuerunt, respondit Iacobus, dicens, "Viri, fratres, audite me. ¹⁴Simeon narravit quemadmodum primum Deus visitavit sumere ex Gentibus populum nomini suo. ¹⁵Et huic concordant verba prophetarum, sicut scriptum est: ¹⁶'Post haec revertar et aedificabo tabernaculum David, quod decidit, et diruta eius reaedificabo, et erigam illud, ¹⁷ut requirant ceteri hominum Dominum et omnes Gentes super quas invocatum est nomen meum, dicit Dominus,' faciens haec. ¹⁸Notum a saeculo est Domino opus suum."

Iacobus: This James is a brother of Jesus, not James the son of Zebedee and brother of John, one of the original twelve disciples, who was executed by Agrippa at 12: 2. This James was not one of the first among the first apostles, but became a convert somewhat later (we don't know when or under what circumstances). We can see the diminished role of Peter in the *ecclesia* at Jerusalem. Once the leader of the movement, Peter now is just one other voice in the discussion. It's James the brother of Jesus who fashions the compromise that carries the day. **Simeon**: This meeting would have been conducted in Aramaic, so it's natural that James should use Peter's original name. **Visitavit**: "how God first came to take a people from the Gentiles to his name," = "brought Gentiles to be one of his people." **Post haec revertar**: Amos 9:11-12. James quotes this text to confirm what Peter knows by experience: A renewed kingdom of David will be extended over all the nations of the world. **Domino**: dative after *notum*, "Known to God was his own work from beginning of time," which we might paraphrase as "God knew what he was doing all along."

ACTS OF THE APOSTLES

19–20: He continues that though circumcision should not be required of them, the Gentile converts need to observe a small handful of other restrictions.

inquieto, to disturb • **abstineo**, to keep away from • **simulacrum**, idol • **suffoco**, to strangle • **sanguis**, blood

[19]"Propter quod ego iudico non inquietari eos qui ex gentibus convertuntur ad Deum, [20]sed scribere ad eos ut abstineant se a contaminationibus simulacrorum et fornicatione et suffocatis et sanguine. [21]Moses enim a temporibus antiquis habet in singulis civitatibus qui eum praedicent in synagogis, ubi per omne Sabbatum legitur."

Iudico: translate as "it is my judgment" to set up the indirect statement that follows, "that those from the nations who . . . not be troubled . . ." *Ut abstineant se*: The four prohibitions that follow are specific to the God-fearers. In their pagan lives, they would have been accustomed to sacred idols, meat meals at sacrifices of unclean animals improperly prepared, and relaxed sexual mores. *Suffocatis*: Supply *animalibus, victimis, corporibus, vel sim*. The meat from animals that had been killed by strangling would be saturated with blood. The compromise thus reached by the council is known as "Dual Covenant Theology," which acknowledges a second tier of Jews, who must follow only a limited number of ritual prohibitions. Ethnic Jewish converts, however, are still required to observe all the Law as best as they are able. *In singulis civitatibus*: "in every single city." James reiterates that nothing is clearer to the practicing Jew everywhere that these prohibitions are fundamental to Judaism. *Qui*: supply *eos* as the object of *habet*, "Moses has [those] who profess him synagogues." I.e., Moses is read all the time by all kinds of people in the synagogues. *Praedicent*: subjunctive in a relative clause of characteristic.

22–29: The apostles send a letter to the Gentile Christ believers stating their decision about the Law.

ultra, beyond • **onus**, burden

²²Tunc placuit Apostolis et senioribus cum omni ecclesiā eligere viros ex eis et mittere Antiochiam cum Paulo et Barnabā Iudam, qui cognominatur Barsabban, et Silam, viros primos in fratribus, ²³scribentes per manūs eorum: "Apostoli et seniores, fratres, his qui sunt Antiochiae et Syriae et Ciliciae fratribus ex Gentibus salutem. ²⁴"Quoniam audivimus quia quidam ex nobis exeuntes turbaverunt vos verbis, evertentes animas vestras quibus non mandavimus, ²⁵placuit nobis collectis in unum eligere viros et mittere ad vos cum carissimis nostris Barnabā et Paulo ²⁶hominibus qui tradiderunt animas suas pro nomine Domini nostri, Iesu Christi. ²⁷Misimus ergo Iudam et Silam, qui et ipsi vobis verbis referent eadem. ²⁸Visum est enim Spiritui Sancto et nobis nihil ultra inponere vobis oneris quam haec necessario: ²⁹ut abstineatis vos ab immolatis simulacrorum et sanguine suffocato et fornicatione, a quibus custodientes vos bene agetis. Valete."

Iudam . . . Silam: Silas will play a minor role in Paul's second mission; Judas drops out of the story entirely after this. It's important that the brethren in Jerusalem send some of their own number with Paul and Barnabas to serve as witnesses that the letter is authentic. Paul and Barnabas's opinion on the matter was already well-known to the believers in Antioch. If these two had returned without independent verification, they might well have suspected that the letter was forged. **Quibus**: the antecedent could be *verbis*, "with words . . . by which we have issued instructions." **Quidam ex nobis**: That is, some representatives from the Jerusalem believers themselves have been falsely spreading the stricter form of the Jesus movement for pagan converts. Before the issues were settled by this council, rumors and self-appointed experts would have been making up the rules ad hoc. **Oneris**: partitive genitive after *nihil*. **Ut abstineatis vos**: indirect command explaining *necessario*. **Vos** accusative object of *abstineatis*, "keep yourselves from." **Suffocato**: "strangled blood," i.e., "blood from a strangled animal." **Sos**: accusative object of *custodientes*.

30–35: The message from the Jerusalem apostles is enthusiastically received.

consolatio, consolation

³⁰Illi igitur dimissi descenderunt Antiochiam et congregatā multitudine tradiderunt epistulam, ³¹quam cum legissent gavisi sunt super consolatione. ³²Iudas autem et Silas, et ipsi cum essent prophetae, verbo plurimo consolati sunt fratres et confirmaverunt. ³³Facto autem ibi tempore, dimissi sunt cum pace a fratribus ad eos qui miserant illos. [³⁴Visum est autem Silae ibi remanere, Iudas autem solus abiit Hierusalem.] ³⁵Paulus autem et Barnabas demorabantur Antiochiae, docentes et evangelizantes cum aliis pluribus verbum Domini.

Congregatā multitudine: This scene will be repeated numerous times in the first century: believers in different cities will receive instructions from various leaders in the form of a letter, which is read aloud to the congregation. *Prophetae*: In practical terms, this means simply that they could speak with authority about these matters. Theologically, it means that they too have received the Holy Spirit. *Fratres*: is the accusative object of the deponent verb *consolati sunt*. *Confirmaverunt*: "To confirm" to a modern Christian has a technical meaning. Here it conveys only its etymological sense of "to strengthen." The news that Gentiles could be full members of the new community of believers encouraged them and gave them a new sense of commitment. *Cum pace*: that is, they weren't expelled. They had successfully settled the conflict in Antioch and both sides were satisfied with the compromise. Soon, however, we're going to get evidence that this debate was far from over. *Visum est . . . Hierusalem*: The verb *video* used impersonally, as it is here, doesn't mean "it seemed," but "it seemed right." Verse 33 implies that both Silas and Judas returned to Jerusalem, but in verse 34, we're told that only Judas went back to Jerusalem. Silas, Paul, and Barnabas stayed in Antioch. It looks very much like an editorial comment to account for 40, where Paul and Silas leave Antioch together on another mission.

CHAPTER 15

36–41: Paul and Barnabas break with each other over whether John Mark should accompany them on their next mission.

praceptum, precept

³⁶Post aliquot autem dies dixit ad Barnaban Paulus, "Revertentes visitemus fratres per universas civitates in quibus praedicavimus verbum Domini, quomodo se habeant." ³⁷Barnabas autem volebat secum adsumere et Iohannem, qui cognominatur Marcus. ³⁸Paulus autem rogabat eum (ut qui discessisset ab eis a Pamphiliā et non isset cum eis in opus) non debere recipi eum. ³⁹Facta est autem dissensio, ita ut discederent ab invicem, et Barnabas quidem adsumpto Marco navigaret Cyprum. ⁴⁰Paulus vero electo Silā profectus est, traditus gratiae Domini a fratribus. ⁴¹Perambulabat autem Syriam et Ciliciam, confirmans ecclesias, praecipiens custodire praecepta Apostolorum et seniorum.

Quomodo se habeant: Add a leading verb for this clause, such as "to see how they are doing." ***Non debere recipi eum***: Take *eum* as the accusative subject of the infinitive *debere*: "he asked him [Barnabas] . . . that he [John Mark] should not be taken." The trailing *eum* at the end of this sentence serves as a reminder of sorts that John Mark is meant. *Ut qui discessisset*: "on the grounds that he is one who . . ." Paul hasn't forgotten John Mark's inconstancy on their first mission together (13:13-14). At least this is what Luke wants us to think. We need to remember that Luke didn't tell us why John Mark left. It could have been simply that he was afraid to be traveling in an area known to be filled with thieves and criminals, but it may be there was a serious rupture between the two over the nature of Paul's teachings to the Gentiles. Thus Paul's current objection to John Mark may not simply be that he lacks the courage to see things through; it's that he disapproves of the dual covenant accord reached in Jerusalem. *Ita ut discederent ab invicem*: It doesn't take much digging to suspect that the Jesus movement was in fact splitting into two hostile factions over the question of Gentile converts. In his letter to the Galatians (2:11-14), Paul says that he and Peter had a tough face-to-face confrontation in Antioch, which may have occurred at about this time. This is the so-called Incident at Antioch. As best as can be conjectured, Peter came to Antioch to join Paul after the Council at Jerusalem, and for a while he was eating with Gentiles as he had done previously in Caesarea at the house of Cornelius. But when a faction which opposed such a violation of the purity laws led by James arrived in Antioch from Jerusalem, Peter became afraid and stopped mingling with Gentiles. This led to a defection of a large number of Jews in the city back to the stricter interpretation of the Law. Paul berated Peter to his face for his lack of conviction. An important detail Paul adds in the letter is that Barnabas was one of the backsliders (Gal. 2:13). If we try to blend the

(Continued on following page.)

Incident at Antioch with what's in Acts, we arrive at much more complicated picture of how fragile the unity of the early believers was. The Council at Jerusalem doesn't seem to have produced the unanimity Luke wants us to think it did. Paul's more liberal approach to Gentile converts continued to be fiercely opposed by a faction led by James even after the council, and Peter was caught somewhere in the middle. Perhaps Paul and his followers stormed off from Jerusalem to Antioch. He was followed to Antioch by Peter, who tried to find some middle ground for compromise. James followed Peter to Antioch with his partisans and spread the word that Paul was not teaching the approved doctrines of Christ believers as determined by the council. He successfully convinced Barnabas, and this is what really caused Paul and Barnabas to go their separate ways, not some doubt over John Mark's reliability in hard times. **Praecipiens custodire praecepta**: That is, the *praecepta* as Paul and Silas understood them. This is far from over. Paul is going to be shadowed for the rest of Acts by disciples from Jerusalem whose mission is to undo his work.

ACTS

AD 50

In Lystra, Paul circumcises a young man named Timothy, who joins him on the mission. They [Timothy and Paul] travel farther north and west in Asia Minor, but they are forbidden to preach there by the Holy Spirit and by the "spirit of Jesus." While they're in Troas, Paul receives a vision of a "man from Macedonia," who pleads with him to come across the Bosphorus and into Greece. In the city of Philippi, they meet a wealthy woman named Lydia, whom they convert and baptize. They stay in her house while they are prosylitizing in the area. A young girl in the city with a gift of prophecy follows Paul and Silas wherever they go exclaiming that they are preaching the way of salvation. They are annoyed by this and order the spirit that possesses her to come out. Angered by the loss of their income, her handlers accuse Paul and Silas before the Roman magistrate of being Jewish troublemakers. The two are flogged and imprisoned. That night an earthquake opens the prison gates. When he sees the opened cell, the guard at first considers killing himself, knowing that he will be held responsible for their escape. But Paul and Silas show themselves. His family and he are converted, and Paul returns to the jail. The next day the Roman magistrates send word that the prisoners are to be released. Paul insists that the magistrates release them personally because they have unlawfully abused Roman citizens. Alarmed that they treated Roman citizens illegally, they come set them free. After a visit to Lydia, Paul and the others leave the city.

1–7: Paul circumcises Timothy, who joins him on the mission.

---

decerno, to decide upon • **veto**, to prevent

Pervenit autem in Derben et Lystram, et ecce: discipulus quidam erat ibi, nomine Timotheus, filius mulieris Iudaeae fidelis, patre Gentili. ²Huic testimonium reddebant qui in Lystris erant et Iconii fratres. ³Hunc voluit Paulus secum proficisci, et adsumens circumcidit eum propter Iudaeos qui erant in illis locis. Sciebant enim omnes quod pater eius Gentilis esset. ⁴Cum autem pertransirent civitates, tradebant eis custodire dogmata quae erant decreta

Pervenit autem in Derben et Lystram: Paul's second missionary journey, his longest, last until AD 52 (Chapter 18). ***Patre Gentili***: ablative absolute, "with the father [being] a Gentile." The fact that Luke doesn't comment on the marriage shows that exogamy had become tolerated, if not acceptable, for diasporic Jews. ***Circumcidit eum***: Timothy isn't fully a Gentile and hence Paul and others could argue that he wasn't covered by the exemption from circumcision. In any case, Luke implies that Paul performs the circumcision not out of conviction, but only to head off the objections of other Jews whom he would encounter during the rest of his mission. It is interesting, nonetheless, that Timothy had not been circumcised already as the son of a Jewish mother. It shows either an indifference on the part of his mother and her family about observing Jewish law or the opposition of his pagan father to the odd practice of his in-laws. ***Dogmata quae erant decreta***: probably the instructions to Gentile converts. This shows that Paul is faithfully implementing the agreements reached at the Council at Jerusalem. Later Paul will be accused of deviating from them.

ab Apostolis et senioribus qui essent Hierosolymis. ⁵Et ecclesiae quidem confirmabantur fide et abundabant numero cotidie. ⁶Transeuntes autem Frygiam et Galatiae regionem vetati sunt a Sancto Spiritu loqui verbum in Asiā. ⁷Cum venissent autem in Mysiam, temptabant ire Bithyniam et non permisit eos Spiritus Iesu.

Numero: ablative of specification, "in number." ***Vetati sunt a Sancto Spiritu in Asiā***: By this, Luke means the area to the north and east of the direction he eventually took to the coast. After he passed through Galatia, he proceeded west-northwest instead of continuing north, which would have taken him to the southern coast of the Black Sea. ***Temptabant ire***: Mysia is the region to the south and west of Bithynia. Going there would have taken Paul away from the western coast of Asia Minor and back east and into the interior. He is being directed though these divine prohibitions to go west. ***Spiritu Iesu***: *Iesu* is the genitive form. There's only one other time this remarkable expression is used in the New Testament (Phil. 1:19): *scio enim quia hoc mihi proveniet in salutem per vestram orationem et subministrationem Spiritūs Iesu Christi.*

8–12: Paul has a vision of a man, who encourages them to go to Macedonia.

ostendo, to show • **Macedo**, Macedonian • **adiuvo**, to help • **sequor**, to follow • **rectus**, straight

⁸Cum autem pertransissent Mysiam, descenderunt Troadem, ⁹et visio per noctem Paulo ostensa est: vir Macedo quidam erat stans et deprecans eum et dicens, "Transiens in Macedoniam adiuva nos." ¹⁰Ut autem visum vidit, statim quaesivimus proficisci in Macedoniam, certi facti quia vocasset nos Deus evangelizare eis. ¹¹Navigantes autem a Troade recto cursu vēnimus Samothraciam, et sequenti die Neapolim, ¹²et inde Philippis quae est prima partis Macedoniae civitas colonia. Eramus autem in hāc urbe diebus aliquot conferentes.

Troadem: In Paul's time, Troas, near the site of ancient Troy, was a major port for travel between northwestern Asia Minor and Europe. Only scattered ruins remain today. ***Quaesivimus***: The narrative point-of-view suddenly shifts to the first person plural. This is the first undisputed "we passage" in Acts. (The others are 20: 5–15, 21: 1–18, 27: 1–37, and 28: 1-16.) They are often taken to indicate Luke's actual presence on the journeys starting in Troas. ***Recto cursu***: There is a noticeable increase in detail in these "we-passages" that suggests a first-hand witness. We have a step-by-step retelling of the voyage: first the island of Samothrace, which was a direct, one-day voyage from Troas, followed by another day's sail to the port city of Neapolis (modern-day Kavalla). From there it's about ten miles inland to Philippi, a city on the major Roman trade road, the *Via Ignatia*, constructed in the second century BC. ***Prima partis Macedoniae civitas colonia***: "the first city in the district of Macedonia, a colony." There is some imprecision in this. The capital of this district, if this is what is meant by *prima*, was Amphipolis, not Philippi, which was about forty-five miles southwest of Neapolis.

13–15: Lydia becomes the first European Paul baptizes.

purpurarius, having to do with purple dye • **coago**, to force

---

¹³Die autem Sabbatorum egressi sumus foras portam iuxta flumen, ubi videbatur oratio esse. Et sedentes loquebamur mulieribus quae convenerant. ¹⁴Et quaedam mulier, nomine Lydia, purpuraria civitatis Thyatirenorum, colens Deum audivit, cuius Dominus aperuit cor intendere his quae dicebantur a Paulo. ¹⁵Cum autem baptizata esset et domus eius deprecata est, dicens, "Si iudicastis me fidelem Domino esse, introite in domum meam et manete." Et coegit nos.

Iuxta flumen: There is a small outdoor theater bordering a stream in the modern city of Philippi built to celebrate this event. Whether its location is historically accurate is another matter. ***Ubi videbatur oratio esse***: "where there was supposed to be a sermon." The service wasn't held as they had expected. We can infer that the local Jewish community wasn't large enough or organized enough to support a building dedicated to regular services on the Sabbath. ***Mulieribus quae convenerant***: The role of powerful, influential aristocratic women is one of the most striking features of the earliest days of the Christ movement in Greece. They could provide accommodatioins for the missionaries during their stay in a particular city, but their network of social ties with other well placed families throughout the Mediterranean area would have also been a source of important connections. ***Purpuraria civitatis Thyatirenorum***: Her hometown of Thyatira was famous for its manufacture of purple dye, and Lydia was probably a traveling salesperson of sorts. Whatever her specific background, which is unknowable, Lydia was a remarkable woman in many ways. She is away from her hometown, presumably unaccompanied by a husband or other male relatives, owns a large house in a foreign country and is involved in some way in a lucrative business. She exhibits a degree of autonomy that would have been unprecedented in the experience of Greeks and Greek-speaking people of the east, including Paul's. We may surmise that Lydia was Roman by ethnicity, or at least Roman by affiliation, for Roman women had much more power and independence than did women of the east. We can also infer that she was among the God-fearers. ***Et coegit nos***: "And she compelled us." We can imagine the surprise the Hellenized Paul and his colleagues must have felt at meeting such a powerful and confident woman. The fact that she insisted he stay with her clears Paul of any scandal of being in the house of an unattached, pagan female.

ACTS OF THE APOSTLES

16–24: Paul and Silas exorcise a demon and then are beaten and imprisoned.

python, prophetic • **obvio**, to impede • **quaestus**, livelihood • **divino**, to make predictions • **salus**, salvation • **doleo**, to be distressed • **spes**, expectation • **virga**, a rod • **caedo**, to beat • **plaga**, wound • **stringo**, to tie up

---

¹⁶Factum est autem euntibus nobis ad orationem puellam quandam habentem spiritum pythonem obviare nobis, quae quaestum magnum praestabat dominis suis divinando. ¹⁷Haec subsecuta Paulum et nos clamabat, dicens, "Isti homines servi Dei excelsi sunt qui adnuntiant vobis viam salutis!" ¹⁸Hŏc autem faciebat multis diebus. Dolens autem Paulus et conversus spiritui dixit, "Praecipio tibi in nomine Iesu Christi exire ab eā!" Et exiit eādem horā. ¹⁹Videntes autem domini eius quia exivit spes quaestūs eorum, adprehendentes Paulum et Silam perduxerunt in forum ad principes. ²⁰Et offerentes eos magistratibus dixerunt, "Hi homines conturbant civitatem nostram, cum sint Iudaei, ²¹et adnuntiant morem quem non licet nobis suscipere neque facere, cum simus Romani." ²²Et concurrit plebs adversus eos, et magistratus scissis

Euntibus nobis: The "we passage" started at verse 10 continues. *Spiritum pythonem*: direct object of *habentem*. The adjective *pythonem* means nothing more than a prophetic ability and necessitates no specific connection with Pythian Apollo. The girl is possessed by a demon or spirit that gives prophecies through the mouth of its medium. *Divinando*: The verbal root of the gerund suggests not just an ability but a profession. The girl's handlers might have set up private "readings" for paying customers. *Subsecuta*: *Paulum* is the object of this participle. *Excelsi*: "of heavenly God," not "of the heavenly servants." In Greek, the adjective unambiguously agrees with God: Οὗτοι οἱ ἄνθρωποι δοῦλοι τοῦ θεοῦ τοῦ ὑψίστου εἰσίν. *Ad principes... magistratibus*: As a Roman colony, Philippi would be under the supervision of two Roman rulers ("duumvirs"), elected by the assembly of the people. *Conturbant civitatem nostram*: This, of course, is not the true reason they are bringing them to the attention of the authorities. The mere mention of the word "Jews" might have been sufficient reason for the Roman magistrates to get involved because of the well-known, and ongoing troubles back in the Roman Province of Judaea. *Adnuntiant morem*: The second charge is that they are trying to convert Romans to an alien way of life. Roman practice was to be very tolerant of established religions, but suspicious of new ones. *Virgis*: The *duumvirs* have the right of being accompanied by *lictors* who carried the *fasces*, a bundle of rods tied together around an axe. A *fasces* was both the symbol of the duumvirs' authority over life and death as well as the actual means for scourging someone. The victim would be stripped and beaten with rods taken from the *fasces* bundle.

tunicis eorum iusserunt virgis caedi. ²³ Et cum multas plagas eis inposuissent, miserunt eos in carcerem, praecipientes custodi ut diligenter custodiret eos. ²⁴ Qui cum tale praeceptum accepisset, misit eos in interiorem carcerem et pedes eorum strinxit in ligno.

25–28: In the middle of the night, an earthquake loosens their shackles and opens their cell door, but they do not escape.

terraemotus, earthquake • **solvo**, to untie • **expergeficio**, to arouse • **evagino**, to unsheathe

²⁵Mediā autem nocte Paulus et Silas adorantes laudabant Deum, et audiebant eos qui in custodiā erant. ²⁶Subito vero terraemotus factus est magnus, ita ut moverentur fundamenta carceris, et aperta sunt statim ostia omnia et universorum vincula soluta sunt. ²⁷Expergefactus autem custos carceris et videns apertas ianuas carceris evaginato gladio volebat se interficere, aestimans fugisse vinctos. ²⁸Clamavit autem Paulus magnā voce, dicens, "Nihil feceris tibi mali, universi enim hīc sumus."

Audiebant eos qui in custodiā erant: They must have been astonished by their prayers and perhaps even converted. This would explain their subsequent behavior. ***Ostia omnia . . . soluta sunt***: The entire jail complex was shaken open and the chains of all the prisoners were loosened, not just those of Paul and Silas. ***Mali***: complementary genitive after *nihil*. ***Universi enim hīc sumus***: That is, Paul and Silas, as well as everyone else in the jail complex.

29–34: The guard and his family are converted and baptized.

tollo, to rescue • **continuo**, immediately

²⁹Petitoque lumine introgressus est et tremefactus procidit Paulo et Silae, ³⁰et producens eos foras ait, "Domini, quid me oportet facere ut salvus fiam?" ³¹At illi dixerunt, "Crede in Domino Iesu et salvus eris, tu et domus tua." ³²Et locuti sunt ei verbum Domini cum omnibus qui erant in domo eius. ³³Et tollens eos in illā horā noctis lavit plagas eorum et baptizatus est ipse et omnes eius continuo. ³⁴Cumque perduxisset eos in domum suam adposuit eis mensam et laetatus est cum omni domo suā, credens Deo.

Cum omnibus qui erant in domo eius: Paul and Silas are taken by the jailor to his home, where his entire household is converted and baptized. Thereupon they share a meal. It's not in the text, but the jailor must have escorted them back to the prison.

35–40: They are released by the Roman authorities and continue their mission.

lictor, a Roman lictor • **indemnatus**, unconvicted • **occulte**, secretly

³⁵Et cum dies factus esset miserunt magistratūs lictores, dicentes, "Dimitte homines illos." ³⁶Nuntiavit autem custos carceris verba haec Paulo quia "Miserunt magistratūs lictores ut dimittamini. Nunc igitur exeuntes, ite in pace." ³⁷Paulus autem dixit eis, "Caesos nos publice indemnatos, homines Romanos, miserunt in carcerem, et nunc occulte nos eiciunt? Non ita! Sed veniant, ³⁸et ipsi nos eiciant." Nuntiaverunt autem magistratibus lictores verba haec timueruntque audito quod Romani essent. ³⁹Et venientes deprecati sunt eos et educentes rogabant ut egrederentur urbem. ⁴⁰Exeuntes autem de carcere introierunt ad Lydiam, et visis fratribus consolati sunt eos et profecti sunt.

Miserunt magistratūs lictores: The duumvirs send word to the jailor via the lictors that Paul and Silas were free to go. Paul and Silas respond that duumvirs have violated Roman law and must come release them personally. *Timuerunt*: As brutal as it could be, Roman rule was circumscribed by a strict adherence to law, and Luke makes a point of it. The one operating here is that no Roman citizen could be scourged under any circumstances. The magistrates were themselves guilty of a crime by having Paul beaten in public. Claiming that they didn't know Paul was Roman citizen would only make things worse, since it would underscore the fact that the punishment had been inflicted without a proper inquiry. An obvious question is why Paul didn't declare his citizenship before he was beaten. One possibility is that though it would have spared him, his companions, who were not Roman citizens, could nevertheless have been scoured in front of him as he watched. Perhaps Paul wanted to show solidarity with them and didn't try to escape the mistreatment they endured. *Audito quod*: *Audito* is a compressed ablative absolute followed by indirect statement: "[it] having been heard that . . . ," or "when they heard that . . . " *Venientes deprecati sunt*: Paul's condition amounted to getting an apology from the magistrates. *Visis fratribus*: This is a somewhat loosely engineered ablative absolute, since the pronoun *eos*, which refers to the *fratres*, is the accusative object of *consolati sunt*. A gradual relaxing the syntax of the ablative absolute is a feature of late Latin.

ACTS 17 AD 50-51

The mission arrives in Thessaloniki, where Paul preaches in a local synagogue, converting both Jews and Gentiles. Some conservative Jews agitate against him and arrange to have his host, Jason, and others brought before the local authorities on the charge of sedition against Roman rule. They are set free and go on to nearby Berea, where they find a more receptive audience. Troublemakers arrive from Thessaloniki. Sent on to Athens, Paul engages some philosophers in the marketplace and on the Areopagus Hill. He tells them that he is spreading the message about the creator of the universe, who can't be contained in an image and who doesn't live in a temple. They laugh at him when he mentions the promise of resurrection and eternal life. Some who heard him are converted, including Dionysius the Areopagite and his wife, Damaris.

1–4: Their preaching in Thessaloniki converts many Jews and Gentiles.

consuetudo, custom • **dissero**, to discuss • **adaperio**, to reveal • **insinuo**, to make known

Cum autem perambulassent Amphipolim et Apolloniam, venerunt Thessalonicam, ubi erat synagoga Iudaeorum. ²Secundum consuetudinem autem Paulus introivit ad eos, et per Sabbata tria disserebat eis de Scripturis, ³adaperiens et insinuans quia Christum oportuit pati et resurgere a mortuis, et quia "hĭc est Christus Iesus, quem ego adnuntio vobis." ⁴Et quidam ex eis crediderunt et adiuncti sunt Paulo et Silae, et de colentibus Gentilibusque multitudo magna et mulieres nobiles non paucae.

Oportuit pati et resurgere a mortuis: This is given special emphasis in the summary of Paul's address because while the predictions of the arrival of a heavenly king to restore and rule over Israel would have been known to most Jews, the claim that he was to was to suffer, die, and be resurrected would have seemed paradoxical at least, and blasphemous at worst. **Quidam ex eis**: "Some of them" contrasts with *multitudo magna* of "God fearing" Gentiles who believed. There is only a trickle of Jewish converts, but a flood of God-fearers. **Non paucae**: = *multae*.

5–9: Some Jews in the city agitate against them.

concito, to stir up • **adsisto**, to stand before • **accepto satis ab**, bail being posted by

⁵Zelantes autem Iudaei adsumentesque de vulgo viros quosdam malos et turbā factā concitaverunt civitatem. Et adsistentes domui Iasonis quaerebant eos producere in populum. ⁶Et cum non invenissent eos, trahebant Iasonem et quosdam fratres ad principes civitatis, clamantes quoniam, "Hi qui orbem concitant et huc venerunt, ⁷quos suscepit Iason, et hi omnes contra decreta Caesaris faciunt regem alium, dicentes esse Iesum." ⁸Concitaverunt autem plebem et principes civitatis, audientes haec. ⁹Et accepto satis ab Iasone et a ceteris dimiserunt eos.

Zelantes: not members of the Zealot faction who were to cause so much trouble back in Roman Judaea, but rather "very devout," or "strictly observant" Jews. By and large, most Jews in the synagogue were merely curious about Paul's message of the Christ and probably received him politely. Those who were more devout objected for any number of reasons, not the least of which would be that the appearance of a cult within Judaism proclaiming the arrival of a new king of the Jews would surely attract the unwelcomed attention of the Romans. The Romans had dismantled the unified kingdom of the Jews shortly after the death of Herod the Great in AD 4-6 and carved it up into three districts watched over by client "kings" of diminished power. If Paul was proclaiming a new king of the Jews, he would de facto be challenging the order of things in Roman Judaea and potentially wherever there was a concentration of Jews throughout the empire. ***Adsistentes domui Iasonis:*** "coming up to the house of Jason." This is Jason's only appearance in Acts. It's likely that he's the same man Paul calls his "countryman" in his letter to the Romans (16:21). We may rightly infer, however, that Jason was well-known to a great number of early believers for reasons that are now lost to us. ***Contra decreta***: among which is the prohibition against proselytizing new religions. It's one thing to cause a fuss within a recognized religion, and quite another to seek new converts. ***Concitaverunt . . . audientes haec***: Take *audientes* as accusative, agreeing with both *plebem* and *principes*. The translation still won't be smooth: "They stirred up the common people and the city leaders who were hearing these things." A paraphrase would be, "The people and the city leaders were stirred up when they heard these things." ***Accepto satis***: "with a fair amount having been received from Jason and others" = "when Jason and some others paid an appropriate bail (or fine)." This is a somewhat anticlimactic ending to what Luke sets up as a massive and dangerous insurrection in the city. The authorities essentially write Jason and his friends a ticket, which they pay, and they set them free. We might also suspect that the crowd wasn't as large and dangerous as Luke has been suggesting. It's difficult to believe that a mob would have been satisfied to see their targets walk off with only a fine to pay.

10–15: The same Jews who caused problems for them in Thessaloniki harass them in Berea; Paul is sent on to Athens.

nobilior, more decent • **aviditas**, eagerness • **scruto**, to search

¹⁰Fratres vero confestim per noctem dimiserunt Paulum et Silam in Beroeam. Qui cum advenissent, in synagogam Iudaeorum introierunt. ¹¹Hi autem erant nobiliores eorum qui sunt Thessalonicae, qui susceperunt verbum cum omni aviditate, cotidie scrutantes Scripturas si haec ita se haberent. ¹²Et multi quidem crediderunt ex eis et Gentilium mulierum honestarum et viri non pauci. ¹³Cum autem cognovissent in Thessalonicā Iudaei quia et Beroeae praedicatum est a Paulo verbum Dei, venerunt et illuc, commoventes et turbantes multitudinem. ¹⁴Statimque tunc Paulum dimiserunt fratres ut iret usque ad mare. Silas autem et Timotheus remanserunt ibi. ¹⁵Qui autem deducebant Paulum perduxerunt usque Athenas, et accepto mandato ab eo ad Silam et Timotheum ut quam celeriter venirent ad illum, profecti sunt.

Thessalonicae: locative case. ***Qui susceperunt***: The antecedent for this clause is the people in Berea. They are the ones who search Scripture, not the people in Thessalonicae. ***Scrutantes***: "checking over Scripture to see . . ." Various Christ communities, like the one here at Berea, would have engaged in a comprehensive search through Scripture to see if the Jesus story squared with the prophecies about the Messiah. The documents they produced were probably passed around to Christian groups and churches as a ready reference when and if their claims were questioned. When Matthew and Luke wrote their Gospel accounts, they had access to these "proof" documents and worked them into the narrative at key points. ***Gentilium mulierum honestarum***: The grammar is somewhat fractured here. We have a grammatical shift to the genitive of the whole for some reason after *multi*. This is followed up by the nominative *non pauci viri*, as a subject group for *crediderunt*, literally, "And indeed there believed many from them and of respectable Gentile women, and so did not a few men." = "And many of them believed, both respectable Gentile women and many men." ***Venerunt et illuc***: It's one thing for local Jews to protest this new preaching in their midst. It's another thing to shadow him on his travels. Who are these people and who is supporting them? Perhaps they are agents from Jerusalem dispatched to undo Paul's preaching, either the Jewish authorities or the original apostles. We've seen before that the compromise hammered out earlier (Chapter 15) about non-Jewish converts wasn't accepted by all the ethnic Jewish believers in Jerusalem. In addition, Paul's letter to the Galatians (2:11-14) reveals a great animosity between him and a faction of the Christ believers back in Jerusalem. At Philippians 3:3 he calls them "foul, busybody dogs," (*canes malos operarios*), and at 3:8 he says he's come to see that the Laws are *detrimentum* ("harmful"). ***Statimque . . . profecti sunt***: To keep him from harm in Berea, Paul's friends take him to the coast, presumably to get on a boat bound for Athens. Once in Athens, Paul sends for Timothy and Silas, who had stayed behind in Berea.

ACTS OF THE APOSTLES

16–21: Paul preaches to Jews and philosophers in Athens.

deditus, to devote • **vult** < **volo** • **seminiverbius**, word-seeder • **infers**, you are bringing • **velint** < **volo** • **vaco**, to make time for

¹⁶Paulus autem cum Athenis eos expectaret, incitabatur spiritus eius in ipso, videns idolatriae deditam civitatem. ¹⁷Disputabat igitur in synagogā cum Iudaeis et colentibus et in foro per omnes dies ad eos qui aderant. ¹⁸Quidam autem Epicurei et Stoici philosophi disserebant cum eo, et quidam dicebant, "Quid vult seminiverbius hĭc dicere." Alii vero: "Novorum daemoniorum videtur adnuntiator esset," quia 'Iesum' et 'Resurrectionem' adnuntiabat eis." ¹⁹Et adprehensum eum ad Ariopagum duxerunt, dicentes, "Possumus scire quae est haec nova quae a te dicitur doctrina? ²⁰Nova enim quaedam infers auribus nostris. Volumus ergo scire quidnam velint haec esse." ²¹Athenienses autem omnes et advenae hospites ad nihil aliud vacabant nisi aut dicere aut audire aliquid novi.

Athenis: locative, "at Athens." ***Idolatriae***: By this time, Athens had been reduced to a venerated but politically insignificant cultural center. Wealthy individuals and cities from around the Mediterranean sent gifts and in some cases even commissioned massive building projects as a way to leave their own personal mark in the revered city. Hence, Paul's Athens would have been a forest of statues and shrines to gods and heroes. It's no wonder that Paul saw it as a city completely dedicated to idol worship. ***In foro***: This probably isn't the ancient Greek *agora*, but the one more recently built in the first century AD by the Romans. ***Epicurei et Stoici philosophi***: Just about the only thing Stoics and Epicureans agreed on was that there was a no personal afterlife. ***Seminiverbius***: This made up word means "seed worder." Paul is accused of just cobbling together random philosophic terms from here and there and making a pretense of being a philosopher. ***Alii vero***: Some say Paul is talking gibberish, but others think he's proclaiming the new gods "Jesus" and another named "Resurrectio." Greek religious myth is replete with personified concepts, such as Victory, Fortune, Nemesis, Memory, and others. If Paul wants to deify "Resurrection," who's to stop him? ***Ad Ariopagum***: The Areopagus (Mars Hill) is a jagged outcropping of rock at the foot of the Acropolis, where trials used to be held. The philosophers probably took him there to get out of the noisy agora. The archaeology of the site is very ambiguous, but there is a report from the first century BC of a small building on it dating back to deep antiquity (Vitruvius, *De Architectura* 2:1.5). Paul's interview might have been conducted there. He could also have delivered his sermon in the open air in front of a gathering of no more than about thirty, seated on a bench, as was the ancient practice. ***Quidnam velint haec esse***: "what these [new things] want to be" = "what this means." ***Advenae hospites***: Though both are nouns, they must be taken together as "foreigner visitors."

CHAPTER 17

22–31: Paul gives a private address to a group of philosophers on the Areopagus Hill.

praetereo, to make one's way • **ara**, altar • **ignotus**, unknown • **indigeo**, to be in need • **adtracto**, to draw near • **quamvis**, however • **non longe** = near • **vivo**, to live • **argentum**, silver • **lapis**, stone • **tempora**, for a time • **despicio**, to disregard • **ubique**, everywhere • **aequitas**, fairness

---

²²Stans autem Paulus in medio Ariopagi, ait, "Viri Athenienses, per omnia quasi superstitiosiores vos video. ²³Praeteriens enim et videns simulacra vestra inveni et aram in quā scriptum erat, 'Ignoto Deo.' Quod ergo ignorantes colitis, hŏc ego adnuntio vobis. ²⁴Deus qui fecit mundum et omnia quae in eo sunt, hĭc caeli et terrae cum sit Dominus, non in manufactis templis inhabitat, ²⁵nec manibus humanis colitur indigens aliquo, cum ipse det omnibus vitam et inspirationem et omnia ²⁶fecitque ex uno omne genus hominum inhabitare super universam faciem terrae, definiens statuta tempora et terminos habitationis eorum ²⁷quaerere Deum, si forte adtractent eum aut inveniant, quamvis non longe sit ab unoquoque nostrum. ²⁸In ipso enim vivimus et movemur et

Stans autem Paulus in medio Ariopagi: This famous but short speech cannot be all that Paul had to say. It takes only about two minutes to declaim, and it's a mere string of assertions, which is hardly the philosophical account the Epicureans and Stoics were expecting. We should note, however, that Paul wasn't allowed to finish his address, as we'll see. *Quasi superstitiosiores*: Paul is paying the Athenians an ironic compliment. They are so "devout" that their city is packed with images of false gods. *Ignoto Deo*: There are numerous ancient references to an altar to the unknown gods in the agora, but none to just one unknown god. *Ergo*: This really isn't a rigorous logical inference from what came before. We can translate it as our "and so," which speakers often throw in to give the appearance of continuity. *Deus qui . . .*: Here begins a particularly complex series of thoughts that runs on to *nostrorum*, sixty-eight words in the Latin, all concatenated into one multi-part argument. We can summarize its essence like this: I'm announcing to you the God who created everything. Because he created everything and because all things are in him, he doesn't live in temples built by men. He's worshiped not because he's in need of anything made by human hands. He's the one who gave life and everything else to men. He made the entire human race and decided where men would live and how long. They are to seek to draw near to God and to find him, even though he is not far from anyone. *Cum sit Deus*: Now Paul is starting to weave his speech into one logical argument: "and since this [God] is the Lord of heaven and earth, he doesn't live in dwellings made by hands." If this is a part of the "stump speech" he's been delivering in the Jewish synagogues, it's little wonder that he caused such an uproar among practicing Jews. The Temple in Jerusalem was everywhere revered as God's one place on earth. *Cum ipse det*: "[he's not worshiped as if he needs anything] since he gives . . ." *Quaerere*: This is best taken as an infinitive of purpose,

sumus, sicut et quidam vestrum poetarum dixerunt, 'Ipsius enim et genus sumus.' ²⁹Genus ergo cum simus Dei, non debemus aestimare auro aut argento aut lapidi sculpturae artis et cogitationis hominis divinum esse simile. ³⁰Et tempora quidem huius ignorantiae despiciens Deus nunc adnuntiat hominibus ut omnes ubique paenitentiam agant. ³¹Eo quod statuit diem in quā iudicaturus est orbem in aequitate in viro, quem constituit, fidem praebens omnibus, suscitans eum a mortuis."

though it could be an indirect command. *Si forte*: another purpose clause following upon *Quaerere*: "to seek God, that they might perhaps draw near to him . . ." *Ex uno*: *ex uno viro*, i.e., Adam. It would make sense for him to omit this specific reference so as not distract his audience with a reference to texts they wouldn't be familiar with. ***Definiens statuta tempora***: This is a necessary explanation. Paul has just said that God made one race of humans over the entire world. If that's so, then why are there different races and nations? The reply is that it's part of God's plan to have things this way for a time. ***Quidam vestrum poetarum***: Paul cites only Aratus, though the verb *dixerunt* is plural. It was attracted to the plural of the final word in the subject group. *Vestrum* is a common syncopation for *vestrorum*. ***Genus ergo cum simus Dei***: Paul returns to his point about idolatry. ***Auro aut argento aut lapidi***: These are dative complements of the adjective simile: "we must not think the *divum esse simile* to . . ." ***Cogitationis hominis***: Are we to take this as a parallel to *sculpturae artis*? He might be referring to the human imagination that's needed to make sculpted images, as if to say, "God isn't like the material of the statues nor like what humans can imagine him to be." ***Omnes ubique paenitentiam agant***: This of course is the core of Paul's mission: God is now extending both the offer of salvation to the entire world and also requiring it to repent. Henceforth and until the end, God will not tolerate the ignorant practice of idolatry. ***Eo quod***: "wherefore." ***In viro, quem constituit***: The *viro*, of course, is Jesus. Jesus is the means of both judgment and salvation. ***Fidem praebens***: "offering proof." ***Suscitans eum a mortuis***: With this expression, Paul makes it clear he's not proclaiming two new gods, "Jesus" and "*Resurrectio*," as some of the philosophers had supposed. He means the literal raising of the dead. Once they understand that, the philosophers burst out into laughter and the sermon is effectively over.

CHAPTER 17

32-34: Some Athenians are converted, including Dionysus the Areopagite and his wife.

³²Cum audissent autem resurrectionem mortuorum, quidam quidem inridebant. Quidam vero dixerunt, "Audiemus te de hoc iterum." ³³Sic Paulus exivit de medio eorum. ³⁴Quidam vero viri adherentes ei crediderunt, in quibus et Dionisius Ariopagita et mulier, nomine Damaris, et alii cum eis.

Audiemus te de hoc iterum: This is almost certainly sarcastic, as in the English colloquialisms "later," or "some other time." ***Dionisius Ariopagita***: Nothing else is known about Dionysius the Areopagite, though he does have a lively mythic history in subsequent Christian traditions. Similarly his wife, Damaris, is mentioned only here in the New Testament. The epithet "Areopagite" indicates that he was a member of the Areopagite court, which was by this time reduced to superintending various traditional and religious matters in Athens.

Paul's Second Missionary Journey 49-53

Paul's second missionary journey is by far the longest and most extensive of his three, taking up all of Chapters 16 to 18.

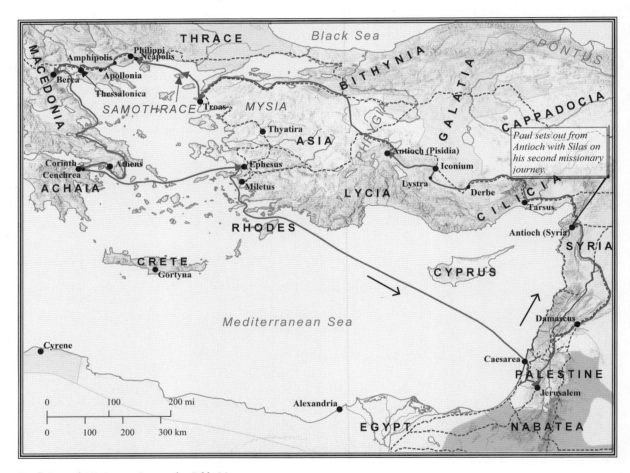

Paul's Second Missionary Journey by *Bible Mapper*.

ACTS 18  AD 52-53

Paul continues on to Corinth where he stays with two Christ believers, Aquila and his wife, Priscilla. He is soon joined by Silas and Timothy from Berea. Paul has little success with the local Jewish community, so he turns instead to preaching exclusively to Gentiles. Paul has a vision that the Lord will protect him during his stay, so he remains in Corinth for a year and a half. The local Jews, however, arraign Paul before the Roman governor at Corinth, who refuses to intervene in what he sees as a local religious matter of no interest to Rome. In their anger, they seize Sosthenes, a prominent member of the synagogue, and beat him. Taking Aquila and Priscilla with him, Paul travels to Ephesus. He leaves them there while he goes on to Caesarea, Jerusalem, and eventually to Antioch. In Ephesus, Aquila and Priscilla meet Apollos, a formidable disciple of John the Baptist from Alexandria. They explain Jesus to him and he is fully converted. Apollos is given a letter of introduction and sent to Corinth.

1–4: Paul stays with Aquila and his wife, Priscilla, in Corinth.

nuper, recently • **īdem**, the same • **scenofactoria**, tent making • **interpono**, to bring up

Post haec egressus ab Athenis venit Corinthum. ²Et inveniens quendam Iudaeum, nomine Aquilam, Ponticum genere, qui nuper venerat ab Italiā et Priscillam, uxorem eius (eo quod praecepisset Claudius discedere omnes Iudaeos a Romā) accessit ad eos. ³Et quia eiusdem erat artis, manebat apud eos et operabatur. Erat autem scenofactoriae artis.

Ponticum genere: Pontus is along the northern coast of modern-day Turkey on its border with the Black Sea. *Claudius*: At most Claudius tried to put a lid on the growth of the Jewish population in Rome. "With regard to the Jews, who were increasing in number again, it would have been hard to bar them from the city because of how many there were. He didn't drive them out, but he told them not to meet anymore, while allowing them to observe their ancestral ways" (*Cassio Dio* 60:6.6). *Eiusdem erat artis*: We learn for the first time that Paul was a tentmaker. He didn't have a steady source of support during his missions and often we hear that he had to settle in for a while and work to pay his expenses. *Apud eos*: Aquila and Priscilla become important Christ believers later on, but it may be that they weren't at this time. They may have taken Paul in simply as a coworker in their shop.

ACTS OF THE APOSTLES

5–11: He is opposed by many Jews but welcomed by others.

---

insto, to press on • **mundus**, innocent • **vado**, to go • **migro**, to move • **coniungo**, to join • **noceo**, to harm • **mensis**, month

---

⁵Cum venissent autem de Macedoniā Silas et Timotheus, instabat verbo Paulus, testificans Iudaeis esse Christum Iesum. ⁶Contradicentibus autem eis et blasphemantibus excutiens vestimenta dixit ad eos, "Sanguis vester super caput vestrum! Mundus ego! Ex hōc ad Gentes vadam!" ⁷Et migrans inde intravit in domum cuiusdam, nomine Titi Iusti, colentis Deum, cuius domus erat coniuncta synagogae. ⁸Crispus autem archisynagogus credidit Domino cum omni domo suā, et multi Corinthiorum audientes credebant et baptizabantur. ⁹Dixit autem Dominus nocte per visionem Paulo, "Noli timere, sed loquere et ne taceas. ¹⁰Propter quod ego sum tecum, et nemo adponetur tibi ut noceat te, quoniam populus est mihi multus in hāc civitate." ¹¹Sedit autem annum et sex menses, docens apud eos verbum Dei.

Cum venissent: Things become more contentious in Corinth when Silas and Timothy arrive and Paul increasingly preaches to Gentiles. *Migrans inde intravit*: He might actually have been asked to leave by Aquila and Priscilla. Whatever their personal convictions, they were running an important business in the city and didn't need to be caught up in any kind of disturbance. *Crispus autem archisynagogus*: His title doesn't necessarily mean that he was the spiritual leader of the Jewish community. The expression "leader of the synagogue" could mean only that the had some supervisory role in the maintenance of the synagogue. Still, the conversion of a highly visible Jew in the city would not have gone unnoticed. *Noceat te*: The dative follows the verb *noceo* in Classical Latin, and not, as here, the accusative.

CHAPTER 18

12–17: The Roman governor in Corinth refuses to intervene in the dispute between Paul and the Jewish leaderhsip in Corinth.

incipio, to begin • **facinus**, crime • **recte**, properly • **ino**, to threaten • **percutio**, to beat

¹²Gallione autem proconsule Achaiae, insurrexerunt uno animo Iudaei in Paulum, et adduxerunt eum ad tribunal, ¹³dicentes quia "contra Legem hïc persuadet hominibus colere Deum." ¹⁴Incipiente autem Paulo aperire os dixit Gallio ad Iudaeos, "Si quidem esset iniquum aliquid aut facinus pessimum, O viri Iudaei, recte vos sustinerem. ¹⁵Si vero quaestiones sunt de verbo et nominibus et Legis vestrae, vos ipsi videritis iudex. Ego horum nolo esse." ¹⁶Et minavit eos a tribunali. ¹⁷Adprehendentes autem omnes Sosthenen, principem synagogae, percutiebant ante tribunal, et nihil eorum Gallioni curae erat.

Gallione autem proconsule Achaiae: Corinth is the imperial capital of the province of Achaia. An inscription bearing Gallio's name found at Delphi dates his governorship of Achaia to 50-52. He was the brother of the philosopher Seneca, and like him was forced to commit suicide by the emperor Nero. ***Uno animo***: It was something less than a unanimous feeling among the Jews that something had to be done about Paul. There were at least some Jewish converts in Corinth, including Crispus and his entire household. ***Contra Legem***: The accusation is not false. The Romans had reached a kind of truce with Jews concerning their unusual religious practices. With only rare and temporary exceptions, they could worship as they saw fit within the empire but they were forbidden to seek new converts. ***Dixit Gallio ad Iudaeos***: Gallio would surely have heard of the rupture within the Jewish community in Corinth over Paul's teaching. He cuts off Paul before he can say a word in his defense. ***De verbo et nominibus***: To an outsider, the quarrels of the Jews would certainly seem to be about nothing more than words and ancient figures with unpronounceable names. ***Et Legis vestrae***: Grammatically, we'd expect *Lege vestrā* as the ablative object of *de*. ***Ego horum nolo esse***: "I want no part of these things." ***Sosthenen***: Why was an official of the synagogue beaten? Luke doesn't say he was a convert. It might be that Sosthenes didn't support the mob by speaking out and denouncing Paul in front of Gallio. Gallio, after all, did ask a question to the effect of, "Is this a serious matter? If it's just another one of your endless squabbles, count me out." That would have been Sosthenes's opportunity to speak up and denounce Paul, but he said nothing. ***Nihil eorum Gallioni curae erat***: "Nothing of these things were of a care to Gallio" = "Gallio didn't care about any of this." This is a parting shot at Gallio. If his concern is public order, one would imagine he'd intervene in a public beating of an innocent man right in front of him.

18–23: Paul, along with Aquila and Priscilla, leave Corinth for Ephesus. Leaving them in Ephesus, he travels on to Caesarea, Jerusalem, and finally to Antioch.

valefaciens, bidding farewell • **devenio**, to arrive at • **amplior**, more • **iterum**, again • **aliquantus**, some

¹⁸Paulus vero cum adhuc sustinuisset dies multos, fratribus valefaciens, navigavit Syriam, et cum eo Priscilla et Aquila, qui sibi totonderat in Cencris caput, habebat enim votum. ¹⁹Devēnitque Ephesum et illos ibi reliquit. Ipse vero ingressus synagogam disputavit cum Iudaeis. ²⁰Rogantibus autem eis ut ampliori tempore maneret non consensit, ²¹sed valefaciens et dicens, "Iterum revertar ad vos, Deo volente." Profectus est ab Epheso. ²²Et descendens Caesaream ascendit et salutavit ecclesiam et descendit Antiochiam. ²³Et facto ibi aliquanto tempore, profectus est perambulans ex ordine Galaticam regionem et Frygiam, confirmans omnes discipulos.

Habebat enim votum: This appears to be an example of the "Nazarite vow." As recorded by the contemporary historian Josephus (*Wars of the Jews* II, 15.1), those wishing to make an offering to the Temple in Jerusalem for a cure had to abstain from wine for thirty days prior and cut their hair. There is reason to believe that Paul has been suffering from some chronic ailment (see note at 27:1-6) that is beginning to overtake him. There is a noticeable lack of vigor in Paul's preaching from this point on in Acts. *Ascendit*: After a short stay in Ephesus, he "goes down" to Caesarea, from which he "goes up" to the *ecclesia* in Jerusalem. *Salutavit ecclesiam*: It's remarkable that this is all Luke has to report about the visit. Such a short visit suggests some coolness or even hostility toward him in Jerusalem. *Perambulans ex ordine Galaticam regionem*: Leaving from Antioch, Paul visits only Christ communities he'd already established. Other believers begin to do with work of winning new converts.

CHAPTER 18

24–26: Apollos, a follower of John the Baptist, receives instructions and is sent to Corinth to preach in Achaia.

eloquens, good at speaking • **ferveo**, to burn for • **revinco**, to defeat thoroughly

²⁴Iudaeus autem quidam, Apollo nomine, Alexandrinus natione, vir eloquens, devenit Ephesum potens in Scripturis. ²⁵Hĭc erat edoctus viam Domini et fervens spiritu, loquebatur et docebat diligenter ea quae sunt Iesu, sciens tantum baptisma Iohannis. ²⁶Hĭc ergo coepit fiducialiter agere in synagogā. Quem cum audissent Priscilla et Aquila, adsumpserunt eum et diligentius exposuerunt ei viam Dei. ²⁷Cum autem vellet ire Achaiam, exhortati fratres scripserunt discipulis ut susciperent eum. Qui cum venisset contulit multum his qui crediderant. ²⁸Vehementer enim Iudaeos revincebat, publice ostendens per Scripturas esse Christum Iesum.

Qui . . . crediderant: literally, "who when he came brought much to those who had believed." We might translate it, "when he arrived he was very helpful to (was an excellent resource for) . . ." Luke specifies that Apollos's thorough knowledge of Scripture gave ammunition to the local Christ believers in their confrontations with the local Jews. Despite this auspicious beginning, Apollos appears in 1 Corinthians 3: 11-15 to have been the instigator of a schism among the Christ believers in Corinth. This may be why Acts attributes his education to Priscilla and Aquila and not to Paul himself.

ACTS
 AD 53-55

Leaving from Antioch, Paul passes through "upper Asia" and arrives in Ephesus. There he rebaptizes some disciples of John the Baptist, who then receive the power of the Holy Spirit. In the face of opposition, he begins to teach only privately in a building owned by a local man named Tyrannus. Mimicking Paul, some Jewish exorcists try to cast out demons in Jesus' name, but to no effect. Many Ephesian sorcerers repent, become followers of Jesus, and burn their books of pagan magic. Paul decides to revisit Greece before returning to Jerusalem, his third and final mission. Paul sends his assistants Timothy and Erastus ahead of him to Macedonia. Before he can leave Ephesus, a local silversmith incites a riot against the Christ believers. The mob seizes two of them and takes them to a theater where it appears they will conduct some manner of trial. Paul's friends restrain him from going to help. An unnamed town clerk persuades the mob to disband.

1–10: Returning to Ephesus, Paul completes the baptism of some disciples of John, but then withdraws to teaching in private for two years.

fere, almost • **regnum**, kingdom • **induro**, to harden • **coram**, in front of • **biennium**, two years

Factum est autem cum Apollo esset Corinthi ut Paulus peragratis superioribus partibus veniret Ephesum et inveniret quosdam discipulos. ²Dixitque ad eos, "Si Spiritum Sanctum accepistis credentes?" At illi ad eum, "Sed neque si Spiritus Sanctus est audivimus." ³Ille vero ait, "In quo ergo baptizati estis?" Qui dixerunt, "In Iohannis baptismate." ⁴Dixit autem Paulus, "Iohannes baptizavit baptismā paenitentiae populum, dicens in eum qui venturus esset post ipsum ut crederent, hŏc est, in Iesum." ⁵His auditis baptizati sunt in nomine Domini Iesu. ⁶Et cum inposuisset

Corinthi: locative case. **Peragratis superioribus partibus**: ablative absolute, "when the upper districts had been traveled through." This means the inland districts of the Roman province of Asia. **Si**: See note at 7:1-5 for the use of *si* to introduce a question. **Quosdam discipulos**: It's generally assumed, and very likely, that they were followers of Apollos, who was a disciple of John the Baptist. All the Gospels pointedly say that John was preaching the arrival of one far greater (Matt 3:11; Mark 1:7; Luke 3:16; John 1:15), yet even after Jesus began his mission there were disciples of John who hadn't heard of Jesus, or didn't accept the emerging claim that he was the Messiah. Apollos was one of them. There were some people who believed that Jesus was in fact John, who'd been brought back from the dead after his execution by Herod Antipas (Matt 6:18; Mark 6:14, 8:28; Luke 9:7). John's disciples confront Jesus in the Gospel accounts, as at Matt 9:14, Mark 2:18, Luke 5:33. **In quo**: Add *baptismate*, "in what [baptism] were you [baptized]." *Baptismate* is ablative. It has a mixed declension, sometimes retaining its Greek ending and at other times behaving as if it were a first declension feminine noun. Later we'll see *baptismā* as the ablative. **In eum**: Dependent on *crederent*, "to believe in": literally, "saying that they should believe in the one who was coming after him; that is, in Jesus." **Baptizati sunt**: This is the

illis manum Paulus, vēnit Spiritus Sanctus super eos, et loquebantur linguis et prophetabant. ⁷Erant autem omnes viri fere duodecim. ⁸Introgressus autem synagogam, cum fiduciā loquebatur per tres menses, disputans et suadens de regno Dei. ⁹Cum autem quidam indurarentur et non crederent, maledicentes viam coram multitudine, discedens ab eis segregavit discipulos, cotidie disputans in scolā Tyranni. ¹⁰Hŏc autem factum est per biennium, ita ut omnes qui habitabant in Asiā audirent verbum Domini, Iudaei atque Gentiles.

first explicit reference to the conferral of the Holy Spirit by the laying on of hands. Luke apparently is making a point of it here to distinguish the complete conversion process from the partial one Apollos had above. **Duodecim**: These are the so-called "Ephesus Twelve." They had repented and were baptized, but without also believing that Jesus was the Messiah. **Maledicentes viam**: "speaking ill of the way." The word *via* comes to be shorthand for the life of a Christ Believer saved through Jesus and empowered by the Holy Spirit. The Greek word is *hodos*, which is visible in words like "Met<u>hod</u>ist", one who follows along (*met'*) the way (*hodos*). **Disputans in scolā Tyranni**: The Ephesus Twelve preach openly for three months, but there arises such hostility in the city that Paul begins to preach privately in a facility owned by a man named Tyrannus. This goes on for two years. A reason Luke includes the name of the owner of the building is that the structure might have been a well-known landmark in Ephesus, though there's no indisputable evidence of it today. **Omnes . . . audirent**: subjunctive in a relative clause of characteristic. *Omnes* is obviously a pious exaggeration, but if Paul's school was well established in Ephesus, the imperial capital of the province, its reputation could easily have filtered out along the established economic and social networks.

CHAPTER 19

11–16: Paul's great powers put local Jewish exorcists to shame, including seven sons of the priest Sceva.

quislibet, ordinary • **defero**, to bring • **semicintium**, work apron • **languor**, ailment • **nequam**, (*indeclinable*) worthless • **adiuro**, to entreat • **insilio**, to attack • **dominor** + *genitive*, to overpower • **invalesco**, to prevail

---

¹¹Virtutesque non quaslibet Deus faciebat per manūs Pauli, ¹²ita ut etiam super languidos deferrentur a corpore eius sudaria vel semicintia, et recedebant ab eis languores et spiritūs nequam egrediebantur. ¹³Temptaverunt autem quidam et de circumeuntibus Iudaeis exorcistis invocare super eos qui habebant spiritūs malos nomen Domini Iesu, dicentes, "Adiuro vos per Iesum, quem Paulus praedicat." ¹⁴Erant autem quidam Scevae Iudaei, principis sacerdotum, septem filii qui hŏc faciebant. ¹⁵Respondens autem spiritus nequam dixit eis, "Iesum novi, et Paulum scio, vos autem qui estis?" ¹⁶Et insiliens homo in eos, in quo erat daemonium pessimum, et dominatus amborum invaluit contra eos, ita ut nudi et vulnerati effugerent de domo illā.

Virtutesque non quaslibet: "not just any old miracles." *Recedebant . . . egrediebantur*: These two indicatives don't fit the syntax, which is fragmented enough as it is. The sense of it is that so great was his power that even his handkerchiefs and aprons could cure illnesses and run off demons. Literally it reads like this: "so that even handkerchiefs and aprons would be brought from his body over the sick, and their illnesses go away and evil spirits depart." **Nequam**: an indeclinable adjective agreeing with *spiritūs*. **Scevae . . . septem filii**: We don't know anything about a local priest named *Sceva* (*Skeva* in Greek) or his seven sons. It should be noted that there appears to be a curious network of word play underlying the original Hebrew/Aramaic. The Hebrew/Aramaic word for "seven" is *seba*, and both the verb "to perform an exorcism" (*nisha*) and the name of the priest (*Sce[b]a*) are related to it. If all of this is more than sheer coincidence, the story of the Jewish exorcists might have originally been a local fable or parable that got taken up into Acts. **Amborum**: Genitive complement of *dominatus* < *dominor, -ari, dominatus sum*, "to overpower." Why "both" when there were seven exorcists? There are two possibilities. Perhaps the Greek word *amphoterōn*, translated into Latin as *amborum*, can mean "all," and not strictly "both of two," hence "subdued them all." Other than this passage from Acts, however, there's little evidence for this sense. If "both of two" is the meaning, perhaps only two of the brothers were actually attempting the exorcism while the other five looked on.

149

17–20: The news of the failed exorcisms prompts widespread conversions and a book burning.

actus, deed • **curiosus**, mystical • **sector**, to follow eagerly • **confero**, to bing together • **conburo**, to burn up • **conputo**, to calculate • **denarius**, a Roman denarius • **quinquaginta**, fifty • **milia**, thousands

¹⁷Hŏc autem notum factum est omnibus Iudaeis atque Gentilibus qui habitabant Ephesi, et cecidit timor super omnes illos, et magnificabatur nomen Domini Iesu. ¹⁸Multique credentium veniebant confitentes et adnuntiantes actūs suos. ¹⁹Multi autem ex his qui fuerant curiosa sectati contulerunt libros et conbuserunt coram omnibus, et conputatis pretiis illorum invenerunt pecuniam denariorum quinquaginta milium. ²⁰Ita fortiter verbum Dei crescebat et confirmabatur.

Timor: a mixture of astonishment, reverence, and submission. *Actūs suos*: "their deeds," in this case, their misdeeds. *Qui fuerant curiosa sectati*: *Curiosa* is the neuter plural accusative object of the verb, "Those who had been chasing after mystical things" = "practicing magical arts." *Conputatis pretiis*: ablative absolute, "when their price had been added up." How Luke or anyone else could have calculated the value of these texts is hard to imagine, particularly if they'd proven to be worthless. *Denariorum quinquaginta milium*: The value of the denarius varied widely over time and even in different states in the same period. A rough estimate puts a denarius at one day's wages for an unskilled laborer. If we use the modern minimum wage as the basic rate, that would be $60 for one denarius. Hence the value of the cache materials would be in the neighborhood of $3,000,000.

21–22: Paul continues the plans for his mission.

²¹His autem expletis, posuit Paulus in spiritu, transitā Macedoniā et Achaiā, ire Hierosolymam, dicens quoniam "Postquam fuero ibi, oportet me et Romam videre." ²²Mittens autem in Macedoniam duos ex ministrantibus sibi, Timotheum et Erastum. Ipse remansit ad tempus in Asiā.

Transitā Macedoniā et Achaiā: ablative absolute, "after Macedonia and Achaia (= Corinth) had been traveled through." Judging by Paul's first letter to the Corinthians, perhaps written from Ephesus at this time, we're led to suspect that Luke has left out a considerable amount of detail. This is about the time that the Christ believers in Corinth were having great difficulties staying together. (See note at 18: 24-26.) In 1 Corinthians 4: 17 Paul first sent Timothy to Corinth to try to mediate. *Erastum*: Nothing else is known of Erastus, and he is not mentioned again in Acts. *Ad tempus*: "for a while." It couldn't have been for very long: weeks perhaps, and at most a couple of months.

23–27: A silversmith stirs up trouble for Paul in Ephesus.

argentarius, a silver worker • **aedes**, shrine • **argenteus**, of silver • **artifex**, craftsman • **opifex**, workman • **adquisitio**, profit • **periclito**, to be in danger • **redargutio**, refutation • **reputo**, to think of • **maiestas**, majesty

---

²³Facta est autem in illo tempore turbatio non minima de viā. ²⁴Demetrius enim quidam nomine, argentarius faciens aedes argenteas Dianae, praestabat artificibus non modicum quaestum, ²⁵quos convocans et eos qui eiusmodi erant opifices dixit, "Viri, scitis quia de hōc artificio adquisitio est nobis, ²⁶et videtis et auditis quia non solum Ephesi sed paene totius Asiae Paulus hĭc suadens avertit multam turbam, dicens quoniam non sunt dii qui manibus fiunt. ²⁷Non solum autem haec periclitabitur nobis pars in redargutionem venire, sed et magnae deae Dianae templum in nihilum reputabitur, sed et destrui incipiet maiestas eius quam tota Asia et orbis colit."

Aedes argenteas Dianae: "Silver shrines to Diana." Ephesus was the location of the Temple to Artemis, one of the seven ancient "Wonders of the World." Selling visitors souvenirs or votive offerings would have been a big business. ***Ephesi . . . totius Asiae***: both locatives. ***Avertit multam turbam***: "has led a lot of people astray." ***Haec . . . nobis pars***: literally, "the role to us," or "this our profession is in danger." ***Templum***: nominative, subject of *reputabitur*. Demetrius reveals in his complaint that he's agnostic about whether the goddess actually exits. His only concern is that people act as if she does and spend their money accordingly.

28–34: Shouting "Great Diana of the Ephesians," a mob drags two of the Christ believers to the central theater.

comes, companion • **reddo**, to offer up

---

²⁸His auditis repleti sunt irā et exclamaverunt, dicentes, "Magna Diana Ephesiorum!" ²⁹Et impleta est civitas confusione, et impetum fecerunt uno animo in theatrum, rapto Gaio et Aristarcho, Macedonibus, comitibus Pauli. ³⁰Paulo autem volente intrare in populum, non permiserunt discipuli. ³¹Quidam autem et de Asiae principibus qui erant amici eius miserunt ad eum, rogantes ne se daret in theatrum. ³²Alii autem aliud clamabant. Erat enim ecclesia confusa, et plures nesciebant quā ex causā convenissent. ³³De turbā autem detraxerunt Alexandrum, propellentibus eum Iudaeis. Alexander ergo manu silentio postulato volebat rationem reddere populo. ³⁴Quem ut cognoverunt Iudaeum esse, vox facta est una omnium quasi per horas duas clamantium, "Magna Diana Ephesiorum!"

Dicentes: The artisans and craftsmen are the ones stirring up the rest of the city. Simply shouting "Great Artemis of the Ephesians," even without specifying what the issue was with the goddess, would have been enough to get people out of their houses and into the streets, if for no other reason than to hear what all the yelling was about. ***Gaio et Aristarcho***: Aristarchus accompanies Paul on his travels after this and eventually to Rome. There is a Gaius mentioned in 20:4, but he is said to be a man from Derbe. ***Non permiserunt discipuli***: It's possible that this is a pious explanation for why Paul wasn't there. He'd been beaten by a mob before (in Antioch) so it would be perfectly understandable if he'd chosen to stay away from this scene. To answer the charge that he was a coward, verses 30-31 were added later. Nevertheless, the fact that Paul sat this out might have caused some lingering bad feeling toward him in Ephesus. On his final journey back to Jerusalem, he pointedly avoids the city (20:16), perhaps because he wasn't welcomed there. ***Ne se daret in theatrum***: indirect command: "that he not take present himself to the theater." ***De turbā autem detraxerunt Alexandrum, propellentibus eum Iudaeis***: During the tumult, Jews in the crowd find and push out Alexander. Luke doesn't tell us who this Alexander is, why he should be the one to speak, what he was expected to say, or why a Jew of any standing would be someone to address the crowd. It certainly couldn't have been to defend idolatry, for even Jews who weren't Christ believers wouldn't do that. We can only speculate that Alexander, as a Jew known to the Greeks for some reason, was to convince the crowd that not all Jews presented a threat to the business of the silversmiths. Whatever the intention, it didn't work, as we see in verse 34. ***Volebat rationem reddere populo***: He tried to reason with the crowd, but it's not clear he was successful. They recognized him as a Jew and shouted him down.

35–40: A town clerk calms the mob and saves the two men.

sedo, to calm • **proles**, child • **temere**, rashly • **quod si**, but if • **forensis**, legal • **accuso**, to pled a case • **arguo**, to charge with • **hodiernus**, today's • **obnoxius**, punishable

³⁵Et cum sedasset scriba turbas, dixit, "Viri Ephesii, quis enim est hominum qui nesciat Ephesiorum civitatem cultricem esse magnae Dianae Iovisque prolis? ³⁶Cum ergo his contradici non possit, oportet vos sedatos esse et nihil temere agere. ³⁷Adduxistis enim homines istos, neque sacrilegos neque blasphemantes deam vestram. ³⁸Quod si Demetrius et qui cum eo sunt artifices habent adversus aliquem causam, conventūs forenses aguntur, et pro consulibus sunt. Accusent invicem. ³⁹Si quid autem alterius rei quaeritis, in legitimā ecclesiā poterit absolvi. ⁴⁰Nam et periclitamur argui seditionis hodiernae, cum nullus obnoxius sit (de quo non possimus reddere rationem) concursūs istius." Et cum haec dixisset, dimisit ecclesiam.

Sedasset: seda[vi]sset. It might not have been hard to calm the crowd. If they'd been shouting the same thing for two hours, they'd be looking for a reason to stop. *Scriba*: The title *scriba* suggests that he was a recorder of deeds. A working knowledge of Roman law, both administrative and judicial, would have required years of study and a prodigious memory. When he does speak to the matter at hand, the scribe fittingly refers the crowd to the process Demetrius should be following. *Quis enim est hominum qui nesciat*: All the scribe knows is that a crowd has been shouting "Great Diana of the Ephesians" in the theater for nearly two hours. His first comment is along the lines of, "What are you shouting about? Everybody knows that Ephesus is the favored city of Artemis!" This might have embarrassed them because they must have known that they had no idea what the charges against these men were or what they were going to do about it. *Iovisque prolis*: Diana is the sister of Apollo, and both children of Zeus by Leto. *Oportet vos sedatos esse*: Among the other reasons for calming down is that a riot in the city is bad for business. No one wants the word to get around that there are weird enthusiasms breaking out over the cult of Diana. Visitors would be afraid to come and spend money. *Pro consulibus*: There is actually only one proconsul in control of the province of Asia at any one time. The scribe is probably speaking in general terms, saying that the system uses the proconsuls, whoever it may be at any particular year, to settle such suits. *Accusent*: jussive subjunctive, "Let them argue it out in turn." *Seditionis*: The charge is put into the genitive case. If the disquiet continues, the Romans may think they have an insurrection on their hands. *De quo non possimus reddere rationem*: a reminder that no one really knows what's going on.

Paul's Third Missionary Journey 53-57

After a short visit to Jerusalem (Chapter 18), Paul returns to Ephesus from Antioch, visiting the communities of Christ believers he had established in Pamphylia and Galatia. After more than two years in Ephesus, he travels to Greece, which merits only scant mention in Chapter 20, except for a healing in Troas on the return trip. On his way back to Jerusalem he meets with leaders from Ephesus in the nearby city of Miletus, where Paul bids them farewell.

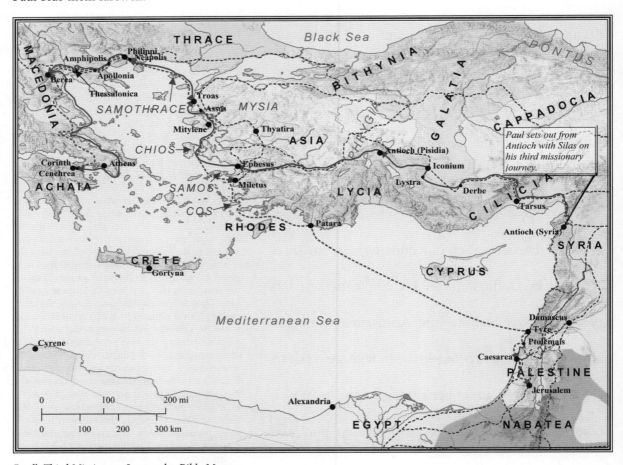

Paul's Third Missionary Journey by *Bible Mapper*.

ACTS **AD 56**

Paul leaves Ephesus, traveling north to make the passage to Macedonia, and then south into Greece. He stays in Corinth for some time. He changes his plans to sail back to Syria to avoid a plot against him and instead retraces his steps on land back to Macedonia. He meets up with others, and they travel on to Troas. There he restores a young man who'd fallen from the third floor of a house. Paul and his friends sail rapidly down the coast of Asia Minor, hoping to be in Jerusalem for the feast of the Pentecost. He stops at Miletus, where he summons the elders of the Christ believers from Ephesus to come for a final meeting. He reminds them of the sacrifices he made for the Gospel of Jesus and predicts that he will face trouble in Jerusalem. He warns them to be on their guard against members of their own community who will try to distort his teachings and replace them with their own. He shares one final, tearful prayer with them.

1–6: Paul and his companions travel to Greece and back, ending up in Troas.

---

comitor, to accompany • **praecedo**, to go on before • **sustineo**, to hold up and wait for • **demoror**, to stay

---

Postquam autem cessavit tumultus, vocatis Paulus discipulis et exhortatus eos, valedixit et profectus est ut iret in Macedoniam. ²Cum autem perambulasset partes illas et exhortatus eos fuisset multo sermone, vēnit ad Graeciam. ³Ubi cum fecisset menses tres, factae sunt illi insidiae a Iudaeis navigaturo in Syriam, habuitque consilium ut reverteretur per Macedoniam. ⁴Comitatus est autem eum Sopater Pyrri Beroensis, Thessalonicensium vero Aristarchus et Secundus et Gaius Derbeus et Timotheus, Asiani vero Tychicus et Trophimus. ⁵Hii cum praecessissent sustinebant nos

Vocatis Paulus discipulis et exhortatus eos: This clause combines an ablative absolute (*vocatis discipulis*) and a participial phrase (*Paulus exhortatus*): "with the disciples having been summoned and Paul encouraging them . . ." **Partes illas**: that is, where Paul had established communities of Christ believers: Philippi, Kavalla, Berea, and Thessaloniki. **Multo sermone**: "a long speech." **Ad Graeciam**: regions of Greece south of Macedonia. It's generally understood that he visited Corinth during this mission, even though it's not explicitly mentioned. **Navigaturo**: dative, agreeing with *Illi*: "against him as he was about to sail." **Comitatus est**: singular even though there are multiple subjects. We're not told why Paul undertook this mission, but judging from his letters (1 Cor. 16:1–4, 2 Cor.8:1–9:15, Rom. 15:31-32) at least part of its purpose was to collect funds for the Christ believers in Jerusalem. If that's so, then these other figures with Paul would be part of this mission, each bringing offerings from his home city. The plot against him could be nothing more than a plan to rob him at sea. Traveling by land, they must have thought, would be safer. **Cum praecessissent**: probably to make sure the embassy had lodgings. **Nos**: We're suddenly back in one of the "we" passages. The others are 16:10–17, 21:1–18, 27:1–37, and 28:1-16. This is most often assumed to mean that Luke joined Paul in Macedonia along with the others. **Post dies azymorum**: the seven days after Passover, when only unleavened bread was eaten.

Troade. ⁶Nos vero navigavimus post dies azymorum a Philippis et vēnimus ad eos Troadem in diebus quinque, ubi demorati sumus diebus septem.

7–12: Paul restores a young man thought to have died from a fall.

protraho, to draw out • **lampas**, a lamp • **fenestra**, window • **mergo**, *(in the passive)*, to sink • **tertius**, third • **sublatus** < **tollo**, to raise up • **incubo**, to lie on • **conplector**, to embrace • **nolite** < **nolo**, not to want • **turbo**, to trouble

⁷In unā autem Sabbati, cum convenissemus ad frangendum panem, Paulus disputabat eis, profecturus in crastinum protraxitque sermonem usque in mediam noctem. ⁸Erant autem lampades copiosae in cenaculo ubi eramus congregati. ⁹Sedens autem quidam adulescens, nomine Eutychus, super fenestram, cum mergeretur somno gravi (disputante diu Paulo), eductus somno cecidit de tertio cenaculo deorsum et sublatus est mortuus. ¹⁰Ad quem cum descendisset Paulus incubuit super eum et conplexus dixit, "Nolite turbari. Anima enim ipsius in eo est." ¹¹Ascendens autem frangensque panem et gustans satisque adlocutus usque in lucem, sic profectus est. ¹²Adduxerunt autem puerum viventem et consolati sunt non minime.

In unā autem Sabbati: "on [day] one of the Sabbath," = "the day after the Sabbath day" or "the first day of the week." Since a new day begins at sunset, this would mean to us the evening of the Sabbath day. *Disputante diu Paulo*: This could be a humorous comment. It's late at night, everyone has just had a big meal, the lighting in the room was dim, and, to make things worse for the young man, Paul is carrying on at length. It's little wonder he nodded off. *Sublatus est mortuus*: "He was picked up dead." A fall from a third-floor window could be fatal, but not necessarily. It's somewhat surprising that Luke, who is traditionally held to have been a physician and witnessed this accident, doesn't give us a more definitive diagnosis. It's not clear whether Eutychus was really dead or only appeared to be dead. *Incubuit super eum*: "he laid over the top of him," probably as a way of conferring as much healing power to him as possible.

13–16: Paul and others make their way toward Jerusalem.

adplico, to put in at • **transnavigo**, to sail by • **mora**, a delay • **festino**, to hurry

¹³Nos autem ascendentes navem enavigavimus in Asson, inde suscepturi Paulum, sic enim disposuerat ipse per terram iter facturus. ¹⁴Cum autem convenisset nos in Asson, adsumpto eo vēnimus Mytilenen. ¹⁵Et inde navigantes sequenti die vēnimus contra Chium, et alia adplicuimus Samum, et sequenti vēnimus Miletum. ¹⁶Proposuerat enim Paulus transnavigare Ephesum, ne qua mora illi fieret in Asiā. Festinabat enim, si possibile sibi esset, ut diem Pentecosten faceret Hierosolymis.

Disposuerat ipse per terram iter facturus: They may still be trying to elude robbers by going in separate groups. Luke and others sail around the peninsula to Assos, while Paul and others cut straight across it on land. *Vēnimus Mytilenen*: What follows is an accurate description of a sea voyage along the western coast of Asia Minor that anyone would have taken at this time. *Miletum*: Miletus is farther south on the coast than Ephesus. *Ne qua mora illi fieret*: "lest there be any delay for him." Luke offers a plausible explanation why Paul passed by it without stopping. Another consideration might be that he left Ephesus directly after a dangerous riot against him and other Christ believers. Perhaps he feared going back to Ephesus because his presence might reignite more troubles. *Diem Pentecosten*: Even though the Pentecost is now a strictly Christian holy day, Paul is referring to the Jewish celebration of the First Fruits that took place fifty days after the Passover. According to Acts, Jesus was with his disciples for forty days after his crucifixion. He was then taken up into heaven, and ten days later his followers received the gifts of the Holy Spirit. Hence they received the Holy Spirit on the same day as the Jewish festival of the First Fruits.

17–24: In Miletus, Paul tells church elders from Ephesus of his past struggles preaching the word and of his plans to travel on to Jerusalem.

mitto, to send a message to • **maiores natu**, ancestors • **qualiter**, in what manner • **lacrima**, a tear • **subtraho**, to withhold • **utilis**, useful • **quominus**, that . . . not • **protestor**, to declare publicly • **maneo**, to await • **vereor**, to fear • **pretiosus**, valuable • **dummodo**, while • **consummo**, to fulfill

---

[17]A Mileto autem mittens Ephesum vocavit maiores natu ecclesiae, [18]qui cum venissent ad eum et simul essent, dixit eis, "Vos scitis a primā die quā ingressus sum in Asiam qualiter vobiscum per omne tempus fuerim, [19]serviens Domino cum omni humilitate et lacrimis et temptationibus quae mihi acciderunt ex insidiis Iudaeorum, [20]quomodo nihil subtraxerim utilium quominus adnuntiarem vobis et docerem vos publice et per domos, [21]testificans Iudaeis atque Gentilibus in Deum paenitentiam et fidem in Dominum nostrum, Iesum Christum. [22]Et nunc ecce: alligatus ego Spiritu vado in Hierusalem, quae in eā eventura sint mihi ignorans, [23]nisi quod Spiritus Sanctus per omnes civitates protestatur mihi, dicens quoniam vincula et tribulationes me manent. [24]Sed nihil horum vereor, nec facio animam pretiosiorem quam me, dummodo consummem cursum meum et ministerium quod accepi a Domino Iesu testificari evangelium gratiae Dei."

Maiores natu: literally, "the greater in birth." The Greek is *presbyteroi*, from which our word "priest" is derived. It won't be long until the first communities begin to develop a specialized clergy to oversee their ritual practices, but not yet. These "elders" are leaders who have acquired some informal leadership role among their peers because of their personal stature, or just their willingness to take on the role. *Fuerim*: perfect subjunctive in indirect question: "you know how I was [how I conducted myself]." Is this a rhetorical argument or is there some specific accusation that has been made against him? His time in Ephesus couldn't be called entirely successful: the opposition was so fierce that he stopped preaching openly and taught in a closed building, and he caused a citywide disruption—which he did nothing to quell—and left shortly thereafter. Perhaps there is some lingering hostility toward him in Ephesus. *Ex insidiis Iudaeorum*: These would be the Jews who actively opposed him, not just those who weren't convinced. Who were they? Were they local Jewish authorities in the cities Paul visited, or where they paid persecutors from Jerusalem? Paul had enemies from many different sides: Jews, who saw him as the representative of a heretical sect; Romans, who saw him as a potential revolutionary against their rule; Christ believers who didn't support his radical approach to Gentile converts; and even, potentially, his own followers, who found his autocratic dogmatism at odds with the notion of a community of believers. *Quominus adnuntiarem vobis et docerem vos*: *Quominus* is somewhat challenging to translate. Literally it means "whereby . . . the less," which isn't especially helpful. It nearly always follows a verb of hindering or preventing, so it can be thought of as kind of negative indirect command. One approach is to translate *quominus* as "from" and to turn its clause into a gerund. In English we might say something like, "What's keeping you from getting your work done?" or "I'm going to stop you from doing anything silly." Hence we could translate this expression as "[you know] how I withheld nothing useful from announcing to you and teaching you . . ." To move another step away from the literal translation, we could render it, "I did everything I could to announce to you and teach you . . ." *Quae in eā eventura sint*: indirect question after *ignorans*. The antecedent of *eā* is Jerusalem.

25–38: He encourages them to watch over their brethren carefully and to be on guard against frauds rising up among them.

quapropter, for which reason • **adtendo**, to tend to • **episcopus**, an overseer • **adquiro**, to acquire • **discessio**, departure • **lupus**, wolf • **parceo** + *dative,* to spare • **vigilo**, to keep watch • **triennium**, three years • **hereditas**, inheritance • **mimini** + *genitive,* to remember • **fletus**, weeping

---

²⁵"Et nunc ecce ego scio quia amplius non videbitis faciem meam vos omnes, per quos transivi praedicans regnum Dei. ²⁶Quapropter contestor vos hodiernā die quia mundus sum a sanguine omnium, ²⁷non enim subterfugi quominus adnuntiarem omne consilium Dei vobis. ²⁸Adtendite vobis et universo gregi in quo vos Spiritus Sanctus posuit episcopos regere ecclesiam Dei, quam adquisivit sanguine suo. ²⁹Ego scio quoniam intrabunt post discessionem meam lupi graves in vos, non parcentes gregi. ³⁰Et ex vobis ipsis exsurgent viri loquentes perversa ut abducant discipulos post se. ³¹Propter quod vigilate, memoriā retinentes quoniam per triennium nocte et die non cessavi cum lacrimis monens unumquemque vestrum. ³²Et nunc commendo vos Deo et verbo gratiae ipsius, qui potens

Mundus sum a sanguine omnium: "I am clean of the blood of all." This rather striking expression appears to mean no more than "I'm not responsible for what happens next." ***Episcopos***: This is a mere transliteration of the Greek word, which means "overseer." Eventually, this designation will come to acquire the technical ecclesiastic sense of "bishop," which is indeed derived from it. At this stage in Christian history, it's very unlikely that the clergy and lay people have grown to be distinct classes of believers. ***Ex vobis ipsis***: "from your own numbers." Paul makes it clear that there will be adversaries arising both from the outside and from the inside. The orthodox Jews want to see the entire movement stamped out, and heretics from within may pervert Paul's clear teachings. Indeed Paul's letters frequently warn of false apostles teaching doctrines that are different from his. ***Argentum aut aurum aut vestem nullius concupivi***: This line and the rest of his speech appear out of place. Paul has just rounded of his speech with a soaring and impassioned farewell, but then it resumes with a rather petty self-defense against charges that he'd been lining his pockets and envying the clothing of others during his missions. For this and other reasons verses 33-35 have long been considered to be later additions, or misplaced. ***Beatius est magis dare quam accipere***: Although a noble and famous sentiment, Jesus is never reported to have said this. Of course, this doesn't mean that Jesus didn't say it, only that we don't have any other attestations that he did. What makes it more striking is that Paul hardly ever quotes or paraphrases anything Jesus actually said (1 Cor. 7:10-11; 11:23-6; and 2 Cor. 12:9). The one time he does in Acts is a saying that's not attested anywhere else in the New Testament. ***Positis genibus suis***: literally, "with his knees having been placed" = "he got down on his knees." ***Non essent visuri***: The subjunctive is used to represent what they were thinking, "since [as they thought] they would not see his face again."

est aedificare et dare hereditatem in sanctificatis omnibus. [33]Argentum aut aurum aut vestem nullius concupivi. [34]Ipsi scitis quoniam ad ea quae mihi opus erant et his qui mecum sunt ministraverunt manūs istae. [35]Omnia ostendi vobis, quoniam sic laborantes oportet suscipere infirmos ac meminisse verbi Domini Iesu, quoniam ipse dixit, 'Beatius est magis dare quam accipere.'"

[36]Et cum haec dixisset, positis genibus suis, cum omnibus illis oravit. [37]Magnus autem fletus factus est omnium, et procumbentes super collum Pauli osculabantur eum, [38]dolentes maxime in verbo quo dixerat, quoniam amplius faciem eius non essent visuri. Et deducebant eum ad navem.

ACTS

 AD 56-57

Paul travels on to Jerusalem, making several stops along the way. In Caesarea, he stays at the house of Philip, one of the seven assistants appointed by the apostles early on. A prophet predicts that Paul is going to be abused in Jerusalem. In Jerusalem, James and the rest of the apostles question him about reports they have heard that he has been telling even Jewish converts that they need no longer observe Mosaic laws. They instruct Paul to purify himself by joining others who are about to undergo a ritual of spiritual cleansing. Toward the end of the seven-day process, some Jews from Asia accuse him of taking a Gentile into a restricted area of the Temple. A mob drags him out of the Temple, and he is rescued by the Roman centurion of the guard. Paul is allowed to speak.

1–7: Paul and his companions work their way down the western coast of Asia Minor on their way to Jerusalem.

---

abstraho, to separate from • **transfreto**, to transport • **pareo**, to arrive at • **sinister**, on the left • **expono**, to deliver • **onus**, freight • **litus**, shore • **in suā**, *sc.* **domo**

Cum autem factum esset ut navigaremus abstracti ab eis, recto cursu vēnimus, et sequenti die Rhodum et inde Patara. ²Et cum invenissemus navem transfretantem in Foenicen, ascendentes navigavimus. ³Cum paruissemus autem Cypro et relinquentes eam, ad sinistram navigabamus in Syriam et vēnimus Tyrum. Ibi enim navis erat expositura onus. ⁴Inventis autem discipulis mansimus ibi diebus septem, qui Paulo dicebant per Spiritum ne ascenderet Hierosolymam. ⁵Et explicitis diebus, profecti ibamus. Deducentibus

Ut navigaremus: The narrative becomes more detailed and almost novelistic from this point on. This isn't surprising, since Luke is now one of Paul's constant companions and a first-hand witness of these events. Conversely, as the story becomes more entertaining, it becomes less of a source for the history of the early church. It's the story of Paul's adventures and perils. For example, the first seven verses of this chapter contribute little new information, aside from confirming the already well-known sailing routes from Asia Minor to the area of modern-day Syria. ***Diebus septem***: This would be the accusative of duration of time in Classical Latin: "for seven days." ***Per Spiritum***: It can't be that the Holy Spirit is trying to dissuade Paul from going to Jerusalem. His trial there sets in motion the series of events that will bring him to Rome, something that must happen. Having been informed by the Holy Spirit that Paul would be persecuted there, his friends naturally want him to take steps to avoid it. They don't understand how his persecution is part of a larger plan. ***Ne . . .***: negative indirect command, best translated here as an infinitive clause, "not to . . ." ***Nos***: is the object of the participle *deducentibus*. ***Usque foras civitatem***: In post-Classical Latin, the adverb *foras* can be used as a preposition governing the accusative case: "up to outside the city," = "to outside of the city."

nos omnibus cum uxoribus et filiis usque foras civitatem, et positis genibus in litore oravimus. ⁶Et cum valefecissemus invicem, ascendimus in navem, illi autem redierunt in suā. ⁷Nos vero navigatione explicitā a Tyro descendimus Ptolomaida, et salutatis fratribus mansimus die unā apud illos.

8–16: In Caesarea there are warnings that Paul will be harshly treated in Jerusalem.

zona, belt • **fleo**, to cry

⁸Aliā autem die profecti vēnimus Caesaream. Et intrantes in domum Philippi, evangelistae, qui erat [unus] de septem, mansimus apud eum. ⁹Huic autem erant filiae, quattuor virgines, prophetantes. ¹⁰Et cum moraremur per dies aliquot, supervenit quidam a Iudaeā propheta, nomine Agabus. ¹¹Is cum venisset ad nos, tulit zonam Pauli et alligans sibi pedes et manūs dixit, "Haec dicit Spiritus Sanctus, 'Virum cuius est zona haec sic alligabunt in Hierusalem Iudaei et

Evangelistae: The epithet distinguishes him from Philip the Apostle. *[Unus] de septem*: one of the seven deacons appointed at 6:1-6. *Prophetantes*: I.e., the girls were actively proclaiming the Gospel of Jesus, not making predictions about the future. *Nomine Agabus*: almost certainly the same Agabus who predicted a famine "in the whole world" at 11:27-28. *Sibi*: dative of possession, referring to Agabus. Agabus dramatizes the treatment Paul will receive by taking Paul's belt and tying up his own feet and hands with it. *Virum . . . Gentium*: The word order of the Holy Spirit's dictum is highly inflected, thus giving it the feel of an oracular pronouncement. In more natural word order it might be: *Sic Iudaei in Hierusalem alligabunt virum cuius zona est haec et tradent [eum] in manūs Gentium.* ***Tradent in manūs Gentium***: This indeed does come about, but only because Paul will request that he be tried in Rome by a Roman magistrate and not in Jerusalem by the Sanhedrin. *Quod*: a resumptive relative: "Which when we had heard," = "When we had heard this." *Ne ascenderet Hierosolymam*: indirect command after *rogabamus*. *Adducentes apud quem hospitaremur*: We need to read a lot in *apud quem* to translate this phrase:

tradent in manūs Gentium.'" ¹²Quod cum audissemus, rogabamus nos et qui loci illius erant ne ascenderet Hierosolymam. ¹³Tunc respondit Paulus et dixit, "Quid facitis flentes et adfligentes cor meum? Ego enim non solum alligari sed et mori in Hierusalem paratus sum propter nomen Domini Iesu." ¹⁴Et cum ei suadere non possemus, quievimus, dicentes, "Domini voluntas fiat." ¹⁵Post dies autem istos praeparati ascendebamus Hierusalem. ¹⁶ Venerunt autem et ex discipulis a Caesareā nobiscum adducentes apud quem hospitaremur, Mnasonem quendam, Cyprium, antiquum discipulum.

"bringing [us] to the home of the man with whom we were to stay." This is followed by the name of the man in apposition to *quem*. **Mnasonem**: The fact that Luke mentions him by name suggests he had some particular significance that's lost to us. Luke says he's Cypriot, so it's possible that he was converted during Paul and Barnabas's mission there in Chapter 13. He might also have been a source of information for the earliest years of the Jesus movement that Luke was not present for—before he joined Paul midway through the second missionary journey (16:10). His name, perhaps not insignificantly, means "remembering" in Greek.

ACTS OF THE APOSTLES

17–22: In Jerusalem, the disciples are pleased to hear of Paul's successful missions, but they are concerned about allegations that he's been propagating false teachings about the Law.

libenter, with pleasure • **per singula**, in detail • **aemulator**, one who is zealous for

¹⁷Et cum venissemus Hierosolymam, libenter exceperunt nos fratres. ¹⁸Sequenti autem die introibat Paulus nobiscum ad Iacobum, omnesque collecti sunt seniores. ¹⁹Quos cum salutasset, narrabat per singula quae fecisset Deus in Gentibus per ministerium ipsius. ²⁰At illi cum audissent, magnificabant Deum dixeruntque ei, "Vides, frater, quot milia sint in Iudaeis qui crediderunt et omnes aemulatores sunt Legis. ²¹Audierunt autem de te quia discessionem doceas a Mose eorum qui per Gentes sunt Iudaeorum, dicens non debere circumcidere eos filios suos neque secundum consuetudinem ingredi. ²²Quid ergo est? Utique oportet convenire multitudinem, audient enim te supervenisse."

Ad Iacobum: I.e., James, the brother of Jesus, not the James the son Zebedee, one of the original disciples. Sometimes the brother of Jesus is called "James the Lesser" to distinguish him from the son of Zebedee, who can be called "James the Greater." Remember that "James" is by tradition and convention the translation for the name "Jacob" in New Testament Scripture (1:12-14). James the Greater was executed by Agrippa II at 12:1-2. This James has become the nominal leader of the Jerusalem brethren. We don't have much information about what has been going on in Jerusalem during the time of Paul's missions, but it's safe to assume that the Christ believers found some way to accommodate themselves to the larger community of orthodox Jews. This would mean defusing to some degree the tension that existed between them about the Law. Paul's teachings about these matters is going to be a problem for them, particularly as he's present in the heart of Judaism. The brethren would have known that the Jewish authorities would be watching him and them closely. ***Per singula***: "one-by-one," or "in detail." As can be inferred from his letters, Paul would also be bringing back a substantial amount of money he'd collected for the welfare of the poor in Jerusalem (1 Cor. 16:1-4; 2 Cor. 8:1-9:15; Rom. 15:14-32). The fact that this isn't mentioned in Acts is a curious omission. ***Qui crediderunt***: That is, those who believe in Jesus. The elders in Jerusalem get right to the heart of the matter. They tell Paul that he can see in Jerusalem how Jewish converts to the Jesus movement are faithful to the Law. Their point is that it's possible to be both a Christ believer and an observant Jew. ***Eorum qui per Gentes sunt Iudaeorum***: The elders say that converts to Jesus become Jews, and as such have certain obligations to the traditions of the Laws. ***Dicens***: agrees with the implied subject of *doceas*. ***Eos filios suos***: The earlier agreement worked out between Paul and the elders in Jerusalem was that new Gentile converts need not be circumcised, but that expectation didn't necessarily apply to their newborn sons. ***Secundum consuetudinem***: It appears that the elders are saying they saw the exceptions for new non-Jewish converts as temporary measures only for the first generation of converts. After that their family was to be raised as fully Jewish and fully observant of the Laws. ***Quid ergo est***: "So, what are we going to do?" It's potentially divisive even to have Paul in the city, given what people know about his teachings. ***Multitudinem***: the entire body of believers in Jerusalem. This will have to be an open discussion, since Paul's presence in Jerusalem can't be kept secret.

23–26: They require him to purify himself.

sanctifico, purify • **inpendo**, to pay • **rado**, to shave • **oblatio**, an offering

²³"Hŏc ergo fac quod tibi dicimus. Sunt nobis viri quattuor votum habentes super se. ²⁴His adsumptis sanctifica te cum illis, et inpende in illis ut radant capita, et scient omnes quia quae de te audierunt falsa sunt sed ambulas et ipse custodiens Legem. ²⁵De his autem qui crediderunt ex Gentibus nos scripsimus, iudicantes ut abstineant se ab idolis immolato et sanguine et suffocato et fornicatione." ²⁶Tunc Paulus adsumptis viris posterā die purificatus cum illis, intravit in Templum, adnuntians expletionem dierum purificationis donec offerretur pro unoquoque eorum oblatio.

Votum: The ritual of a *votum* is a very public act. The elders want the *multitudo* to see Paul in the city, hair shorn off and wearing the garments of a penitent, so they will know that his teachings about the Law have been thoroughly repudiated. ***De . . . fornicatione***: This rehearsal of the original ordinance seems forced at this point. It could be a later marginal note that was incorporated into the text as a way of reminding readers what the understanding about Gentile converts was. ***In Templum***: That is, Paul and the others are required to go into the Temple and make a public announcement that they are going to be purified for their transgressions.

ACTS OF THE APOSTLES

27–30: Some Jews from Asia stir up more trouble for Paul in Jerusalem.

concursio, a gathering

²⁷Dum autem septem dies consummarentur, hi qui de Asiā erant Iudaei cum vidissent eum in Templo, concitaverunt omnem populum, et iniecerunt ei manūs, clamantes, ²⁸"Viri Israhelitae, adiuvate! Hĭc est homo qui adversus populum et Legem et locum hunc, omnes ubique docens insuper et Gentiles induxit in Templum et violavit sanctum locum istum." ²⁹Viderant enim Trophimum Ephesium in civitate cum ipso, quem aestimaverunt quoniam in Templum induxisset Paulus. ³⁰Commotaque est civitas tota, et facta est concursio populi, et adprehendentes Paulum trahebant eum extra Templum, et statim clausae sunt

De Asiā: This probably means they were from Ephesus, as they recognize an Ephesian walking with Paul in the city. Paul had mixed success at best in Ephesus, and the controversy he stirred up there has followed him. ***Trophimum Ephesium***: In 20:4, Trophimus is one of the eight Greeks who were accompanying Paul back to Jerusalem. There he is said to be "of Asia." ***Aestimaverunt quoniam***: The syntax is somewhat fractured after *quem*. Literally, it reads, "whom they figured that Paul had taken into the Temple." We can smooth it over either by understanding *et eum* for *quem*—"and they supposed Paul had taken him into the Temple"—or by deleting the *quoniam* and taking *aestimaverunt* as parenthetical—"whom, they supposed, Paul had taken into the Temple." ***Templum***: Luke must mean to an area of the Temple compound where only Jews are allowed. (See the image of the Temple on page 24.) Luke appears to deny the charge, saying that this is something these Asiatic Jews only supposed Paul had done. But the question behind the question is why it would have made a difference. Trophimus is certainly a Gentile convert to the Jesus movement, and the instigators of the uproar must have known that. The fact that they protest reveals that some Jews at least didn't accept the notion that a Gentile convert to the Jesus movement was fully Jewish. ***Ianuae***: These would be the gates that marked off the area Gentiles could not enter.

ianuae.

31–36: Paul is rescued from the violence of a mob by the Roman commander of the guard, who takes him into protective custody.

---

confundo, to put into an uproar • **gradus**, stairway • **contigit**, it came about

---

³¹Quaerentibus autem eum occīdere, nuntiatum est tribuno cohortis quia tota confunditur Hierusalem. ³²Qui statim adsumptis militibus et centurionibus decucurrit ad illos. Qui cum vidissent tribunum et milites, cessaverunt percutere Paulum. ³³Tunc accedens tribunus adprehendit eum et iussit alligari catenis duabus et interrogabat quis esset et quid fecisset. ³⁴Alii autem aliud clamabant in turbā, et cum non posset certum cognoscere prae tumultu, iussit duci eum in castra. ³⁵Et cum venisset ad gradus, contigit ut portaretur a militibus propter vim populi. ³⁶Sequebatur enim multitudo populi, clamans, "Tolle eum!"

Quaerentibus autem eum occidere: The participle is a compressed ablative absolute. Supply *eis*. The infinitive *occidere* is complementary: "While they were seeking to kill him." **Tribuno**: dative after *nuntiatum est*. The tribune will be named later as Claudius Lysias (23:26). His rank was roughly equivalent to a modern-day colonel, in charge of a detachment of six hundred to one thousand soldiers. **Decucurrit**: The Roman garrison was housed in the Tower of Antonia, so "ran down" is accurate. **Qui**: a resumptive relative, whose antecedent is *illos*: "who, when they saw the tribune and the soldiers" = "And when they saw the tribune and the soldiers." **Ad gradus**: to the steps leading up into the Tower of Antonia. There Paul is picked up by the soldiers and passed over the crowd.

37–40: The commander allows Paul to address the crowd.

nosti, < **novisti** • **nonne**, expects the answer "yes" to a question • **concitasti**, < **concitavisti** • **sicarius**, assassin • **municeps**, resident

³⁷Et cum coepisset induci in castra, Paulus dicit tribuno, "Si licet mihi loqui aliquid ad te?" Qui dixit, "Graece nosti? ³⁸Nonne tu es Aegyptius, qui ante hos dies tumultum concitasti et eduxisti in desertum quattuor milia virorum sicariorum?" ³⁹Et dixit ad eum Paulus, "Ego homo sum quidem Iudaeus a Tarso Ciliciae, non ignotae civitatis municeps. Rogo autem te, permitte mihi loqui ad populum." ⁴⁰Et cum ille permisisset, Paulus stans in gradibus annuit manu ad plebem et magno silentio facto adlocutus est, Hebraeā linguā dicens:

Graece novisti: supply *loqui* or *dicere* after *novisiti*: "you know how to speak Greek?" **Nonne tu es Aegyptius**: There was in fact at the time a foreign born insurgent/messianic leader from Egypt who had been stirring up trouble in Jerusalem (Josephus *Jewish War*, 2.259-263; *Jewish Antiquities*, 20.169-171). He was still at large at this time. When Paul spoke Greek, Lysias realized that Paul was no uneducated trouble-maker from Egypt as he had assumed. **Hebraeā linguā**: Not Hebrew, but Aramaic. This isn't an error on Luke's part, as "Hebrew" is often used for "Aramaic."

ACTS

AD 57

Paul tells his story in Aramaic. "I was born a Jew and lived in strict observation of the Law. I was even officially authorized to persecute the belivers and assented to the stoning of Steven. I was converted by Jesus himself on my way to Damascus and helped by a local man. Jesus told me to be purified in Jerusalem. In Jerusalem, Jesus appeared to me and told me to leave the city because of their stubbornness and preach to the Gentiles." The mob is enraged and the tribune rescues him again, but intends to flog and interrogate him. Paul protests to a nearby centurion that because he is a Roman citizen he cannot be flogged. The centurion presents him again to the Roman tribune. The tribune orders the Jewish authorities to assemble for an inquiry into the matter.

1–5: "I was born and raised an observant Jew in Tarsus, later even becoming a prosecutor of the Way."

---

praesto, to maintain • **nutritus**, raised • **secus** + *accusative*, near • **eruditus**, educated • **aemulator**, keeper • **natus**, birth • **pergo**, to travel through • **punio**, to punish

---

"Viri, fratres et patres, audite quam ad vos nunc reddo rationem." ²(Cum audissent autem quia Hebraeā linguā loquitur ad illos, magis praestiterunt silentium.) ³Et dixit, "Ego sum vir Iudaeus, natus Tarso Ciliciae, nutritus autem in istā civitate secus pedes Gamalihel eruditus iuxta veritatem paternae Legis, aemulator Legis, sicut et vos omnes estis hodie. ⁴Qui hanc viam persecutus sum usque ad mortem, alligans et tradens in custodias viros ac mulieres, ⁵sicut princeps sacerdotum testimonium mihi reddit et omnes maiores natu, a quibus et epistulas accipiens ad fratres, Damascum pergebam ut adducerem inde vinctos in Hierusalem uti punirentur."

Gamalihel: This is the same Gamaliel who urged patience with the Jesus movement at 5:34. ***Usque ad mortem***: The only execution Paul is known to have been involved in Acts is Stephen's (7: 59). See note at 26: 9-11. ***Epistulas accipiens ad fratres***: Take *ad* in the hostile sense of "against." Paul received a writ, a kind of legal document from the authorities condemning the first followers of Jesus.

ACTS OF THE APOSTLES

6–11: "While on my way to Damascus in search of the Christ believers there, Jesus appeared and spoke to me."

adpropinquo, to approach • **copiosus**, abundant • **claritas**, brillance

⁶"Factum est autem eunte me et adpropinquante Damasco mediā die subito de caelo circumfulsit me lux copiosa, ⁷et decidens in terram audivi vocem dicentem mihi, 'Saule, Saule! Quid me persequĕris?' ⁸"Ego autem respondi, 'Quis es, Domine?' "Dixitque ad me, 'Ego sum Iesus Nazarenus quem tu persequĕris.' ⁹Et qui mecum erant lumen quidem viderunt, vocem autem non audierunt eius qui loquebatur mecum. ¹⁰"Et dixi, 'Quid faciam, Domine?' "Dominus autem dixit ad me, 'Surgens, vade Damascum, et ibi tibi dicetur de omnibus quae te oporteat facere.' ¹¹Et cum non viderem prae claritate luminis illius, ad manum deductus a comitibus veni Damascum."

Factum est: This is the second of the three accounts in Acts of Paul's conversion (9:3-20; 22: 3-20; 26: 12-18). See Appendix A, "Three Accounts of Paul's Conversion," for a brief discussion and side-by-side comparison. ***Damasco***: dative after the participle *adpropinquante*. ***Circumfulsit***: Classical Latin would introduce this clause after *factum est* with an *ut* and use the imperfect subjunctive to follow the sequence of tenses. Switching to the present tense indicative, however, makes the narrative more vivid. ***Persequĕris***: present tense; *persequēris* would be the future.

12–16: "Ananias in Damascus cured my blindness, told me God's plan, and instructed me to confess and be baptized."

abluo, to wash away

¹²"Ananias autem quidam, vir secundum Legem testimonium habens ab omnibus habitantibus Iudaeis, ¹³veniens ad me et adstans dixit mihi, 'Saule, frater, respice.' Et ego eādem horā respexi in eum. ¹⁴"At ille dixit, 'Deus patrum nostrorum praeordinavit te ut cognosceres voluntatem eius, et videres iustum et audires vocem ex ore eiusn ¹⁵quia eris testis illius ad omnes homines eorum quae vidisti et audisti. ¹⁶Et nunc quid moraris? Exsurge, baptizare et ablue peccata tua, invocato nomine ipsius.'"

Secundum Legem testimonium habens: It's fitting that in this version of his conversion he would emphasize Ananias's well-known faithfulness to the Law, whether he's a convert or not, since Paul is standing before a mob of angry, orthodox Jews. ***Baptizare***: not an infinitive, but a passive imperative, "be baptized."

17–21: "Jesus appeared to me in Jerusalem to tell me he was sending me to the Gentiles."

concludo, to close up • **festino**, to make haste • **asto**, to stand near • **consentio**, to assent • **vestimentum**, clothing

¹⁷"Factum est autem revertenti mihi in Hierusalem et oranti in Templo fieri me in stupore mentis ¹⁸et videre illum dicentem mihi, 'Festina et exi velociter ex Hierusalem, quoniam non recipient testimonium tuum de me.' ¹⁹Et ego dixi, 'Domine, ipsi sciunt quia ego eram concludens in carcerem et caedens per synagogas eos qui credebant in te. ²⁰Et cum funderetur sanguis Stephani testis tui, ego astabam et consentiebam et custodiebam vestimenta interficientium illum.' ²¹Et dixit ad me, 'Vade, quoniam ego in nationes longe mittam te.'"

Revertenti . . . oranti: Paul is visited again by Jesus in a vision, this time in Jerusalem. Strictly speaking, it's not a variation of the conversion accounts because by this time, Paul has already been baptized. It's difficult to square, however, with 9: 26-31, where it's the disciples who send him away and not for the reasons Paul cites here. Paul does allude to other transcendent experiences of the divine he had at 2 Cor. 12: 1-7, and perhaps this is one of them.

22–25: The tribune rescues Paul from the infuriated mob but intends to imprison him and have him whipped.

iusmodi, of this sort • **vocifero**, to raise a shout • **aer**, air • **flagellum**, a whip • **torqueo**, to torture

²²Audiebant autem eum usque ad hŏc verbum, et levaverunt vocem suam, dicentes, "Tolle de terrā eiusmodi, non enim fas est eum vivere." ²³Vociferantibus autem eis et proicientibus vestimenta sua et pulverem iactantibus in aerem, ²⁴iussit tribunus induci eum in castra et flagellis caedi et torqueri eum, ut sciret propter quam causam sic acclamarent ei.

Usque ad hŏc verbum: What sets them off is his comment that God sent him to convert Gentiles, the aspect of his mission that was so controversial. Paul had been grafting large numbers of Gentiles on to the Jewish nation, but at the same time he was granting them lenient conditions for membership. Traditional, orthodox Jewish believers never actively sought converts to Judaism. Quite the contrary, Judaism's extensive body of Law and traditions were an impediment to conversion, as Judaism always held that it was a nation that was apart from the world. Diluting the Jewish experience and Jewish identity, Paul was worse than a heretic. He was a revolutionary. ***Tolle de terrā eiusmodi***: = "Away with [a man] of this sort." ***Iussit tribunus induci eum in castra***: The mob is demanding that Paul be executed, a punishment that could be inflicted legally only by the Romans. Hence the tribune's involvement at this point. He could have looked the other way if the mob had stoned him themselves, as was Stephen's fate earlier, but letting a mob do what it wants only invites more trouble later on. ***Torqueri eum***: The extra *eum* isn't strictly necessary. This isn't Paul's punishment. This is the prelude to an inquiry. The tribune wants to know what Paul has done, so he has to torture him, before the inquest could begin. It was common practice to torture a slave or non-Roman for information even if he was willing to talk. The assumption is that a person will say anything to avoid torture, so he's not a reliable source until after he's been tortured!

ACTS OF THE APOSTLES

26–28: Paul declares he is a Roman citizen and reminds the centurion that as such he can't be whipped. The centurion reports the matter to the Roman tribune.

adstringo, to tie up • **lorum**, rope • **indemnatus**, uncondemned • **flagello**, to whip • **summa**, sum • **civitas**, legal status (of citizenship)

²⁵Et cum adstrinxissent eum loris, dixit adstanti sibi centurioni Paulus, "Si hominem Romanum et indemnatum licet vobis flagellare?" ²⁶Quo audito centurio accessit ad tribunum et nuntiavit, dicens, "Quid acturus es? Hĭc enim homo civis Romanus est!" ²⁷Accedens autem tribunus dixit illi, "Dic mihi, tu Romanus es?" At ille dixit, "Etiam." ²⁸Et respondit tribunus, "Ego multā summā civitatem hanc consecutus sum." Et Paulus ait, "Ego autem et natus sum."

Indemnatum: *"uncondemned."* Of course, it wasn't permitted to punish a Roman citizen until after he'd been tried and convicted, a fact Paul knows well. In any case, no Roman citizen could be whipped, convicted or not. ***Ego multā summā civitatem hanc consecutus sum***: literally, "I too achieved this status for a very great sum" = "I paid a pretty penny to become a Roman citizen." Those who were not born Roman citizens could acquire it either by special dispensation after performing a notable service to Rome, such as serving in the army, or by buying it outright. ***Ego autem et natus sum***: Paul's father was a Roman citizen, so this status was passed on to his children. We're not told how Paul verified this claim, though it seems the tribune didn't just accept Paul's word for it. He looked into the matter *diligentius* and finally came to know for sure *rescivit* that Paul was in fact a Roman citizen. As before in Philippi (16:35-40), Paul may have presented some documentation.

29–30: The Roman tribune summons the Sanhedrin to meet and explain their case against Paul.

protinus, immediately • **rescio**, to know for sure • **diligentius**, very carefully

---

²⁹Protinus ergo discesserunt ab illo qui eum torturi erant. Tribunus quoque timuit postquam rescivit quia civis Romanus esset et quia alligasset eum. ³⁰Posterā autem die volens scire diligentius quā ex causā accusaretur a Iudaeis solvit eum, et iussit sacerdotes convenire et omne concilium, et producens Paulum statuit inter illos.

Qui eum torturi erant: "those who were going to torture him." *Quā ex causā accusaretur*: The tribune so far has performed his legal duty admirably. He can't hold a Roman citizen without charge, let alone torture him, but he can't look the other way if a citizen has committed a crime in his jurisdiction. He lets Paul go for the time being, but tells the Sanhedrin to make their case against him the next day.

ACTS

 AD 57

Paul addresses the Sanhedrin. As he begins, he is struck on the mouth by the orders of the high priest. Paul in turn insults the high priest. He gets the two major parties on the Sanhedrin to quarrel among themselves by mentioning the afterlife, angels, and spirits, matters about which they are fiercely opposed. This causes a ruckus, and the tribune has to rescue Paul from being lynched. A conspiracy of forty men develops to kill Paul. When he learns of their plot from Paul's nephew, the tribune arranges to have Paul escorted to Caesarea under heavy guard. The tribune sends a letter to the governor there, requesting that he continue the investigation into the charges.

1–5: Paul insults the high priest.

---

paries, wall • **dealbatus**, white-washed • **iudico**, to pass judgment • **maledico**, to curse

---

Intendens autem concilium Paulus ait, "Viri, fratres, ego omni conscientiā bonā conversatus sum ante Deum usque in hodiernum diem." ²Princeps autem sacerdotum Ananias praecepit adstantibus sibi percutere os eius. ³Tunc Paulus ad eum dixit, "Percutiet te Deus, paries dealbate! Et tu sedens iudicas me secundum Legem, et contra Legem iubes me percuti!" ⁴Et qui adstabant dixerunt, "Summum sacerdotem Dei maledicis?" ⁵Dixit autem Paulus, "Nesciebam, fratres, quia princeps est sacerdotum. Scriptum est enim: 'Principem populi tui non maledices.'"

Adstantibus sibi: The participle is the dative complement of the verb *praecepit*; *sibi* is dative complement of the participle *Adstantibus*: literally, "he gave an order to those standing near himself," (not those standing near Paul). *Percutere os eius*: We can't know why Ananias ordered Paul to be struck. It may be because of what Paul said, or simply because of some violation of some court procedure. Similarly, Paul's rebuke of the high priest may be based on a number of things. He may be indicating that Ananias doesn't understand that the Law allows a defendant to speak, or that he has inflicted punishment before the defendant had been properly tried and convicted. *Nesciebam*: Why Paul didn't recognize Ananias is an enduring question. Perhaps Ananias became the high priest while Paul was away on his missions, and thus he didn't know who he was. Another possibility is Paul's oft-mentioned affliction (2 Cor. 12:7, for example) that affected his eyes, resulted in near-sightedness, so perhaps he literally couldn't see who issued the order (see note at 27: 1-6). Then again, maybe Paul is being sarcastic by saying that no real high priest would have ordered that he be struck in violation of the Law. *Scriptum est enim*: Exodus 22:28. It's only by later tradition that this office was equated with the more general phrase "leader of the people." With this reference, Paul establishes himself as one who is well acquainted with Jewish Scripture. It may also be yet another dig at the office of high priest. Paul could be saying subtly that he doesn't accept the fact that the high priest was the *princeps populi*.

6–8: He claims his only "offense" is that he has been preaching the resurrection of the dead.

uterque, both

⁶Sciens autem Paulus quia una pars esset Sadducaeorum et altera Pharisaeorum, exclamavit in concilio, "Viri, fratres, ego Pharisaeus sum, filius Pharisaeorum. De spe et resurrectione mortuorum ego iudicor." ⁷Et cum haec dixisset, facta est dissensio inter Pharisaeos et Sadducaeos, et soluta est multitudo. ⁸Sadducaei enim dicunt non esse resurrectionem, neque angelum neque spiritum, Pharisaei autem utrumque confitentur.

Ego Pharisaeus sum: Paul knows that there were both Pharisees and Sadducees in the Sanhedrin. He leverages their mutual antipathy by identifying himself as a Pharisee to his advantage. ***Ego iudicor***: Of course, it's not true that Paul is being put on trial because of his belief in the afterlife. Nowhere in Acts has Paul been challenged on this, except in Athens, where the pagan philosophers merely laughed at him. On the contrary, he's been repeatedly challenged on the questions surrounding his new non-Jewish converts and their relationship to the Law. But if he had tried to argue those questions, he would have found no sympathy on the court from either side. Essentially, Paul has reframed the trial from what he is doing to an entirely unrelated issue. He says, in effect, "We all know what this is really about. It's just the Sadducees trying to stamp out a growing number of Jews who believe in the afterlife." ***Facta est dissensio***: It's almost impossible to believe that Paul's tactic worked. Surely at least one of these educated men would have seen through Paul's diversion. One explanation for how this provocation broke up the trial is that the animosity between Pharisees and Sadducees was so deep that it blinded them all to how they were being manipulated. ***Sadducaei enim dicunt***: Luke's editorial comment illustrates that his intended audience wouldn't have known this about the Pharisees and Sadducees. That would mean he's writing not for Jews, even diasporic Jews, who surely would have known this. Perhaps this indicates that Theophilus, the named audience for Acts (1:1), is not Jewish, but a pagan convert.

9–11: Chaos erupts in the Sanhedrin, and Paul is whisked away by the tribune.

dissensio quarrel • **discerpo**, to tear apart • **esto**, second person singular imperative of *sum*

⁹Factus est autem clamor magnus. Et surgentes quidam Pharisaeorum pugnabant, dicentes, "Nihil mali invēnimus in homine isto. Quod si spiritus locutus est ei aut angelus?" ¹⁰Et cum magna dissensio facta esset, timens tribunus ne discerperetur Paulus ab ipsis, iussit milites descendere et rapere eum de medio eorum ac deducere eum in castra. ¹¹Sequenti autem nocte adsistens ei Dominus ait, "Constans esto, sicut enim testificatus es de me Hierusalem, sic te oportet et Romae testificari."

Nihil mali invēnimus: The Pharisees close ranks around Paul, whom they see as one of their own, apparently forgetting what the original charge was. *Quod si . . . angelus*: "What if an angel or a spirit spoke to him.? That is, suppose he got this news about the afterlife from an angel? Since the Sadducees didn't believe in angels or spirits either, this would have provoked them all the more. *Timens tribunus*: The tribune isn't acting entirely out of concern for Paul's well-being. Allowing a mob of Jews to murder a Roman citizen right before his eyes would hardly have helped his career as a soldier. *Hierusalem*: locative: "at Jerusalem."

12–15: A conspiracy to kill Paul develops in Jerusalem.

colligo, to gather together • **devovo**, to swear • **donec**, until • **coniuratio**, conspiracy • **devotio**, oath • **gusto**, to eat • **tamquam**, as if • **aliquid certius** = information/intelligence • **adpropio**, to arrive

¹²Factā autem die collegerunt se quidam ex Iudaeis et devoverunt se, dicentes neque manducaturos neque bibituros donec occīderent Paulum. ¹³Erant autem plus quam quadraginta qui hanc coniurationem fecerant. ¹⁴Qui accesserunt ad principes sacerdotum et seniores et dixerunt, "Devotione devovimus nos nihil gustaturos donec occīdamus Paulum. ¹⁵Nunc ergo vos notum facite tribuno cum concilio ut producat illum ad vos, tamquam aliquid certius cognituri de eo, nos vero priusquam adpropiet parati sumus interficere illum."

Manducaturos neque bibituros: Swearing to undergo physical hardships until an oath has been fulfilled was common. It also set an effective "do-by" date. ***Ut producat illum ad vos***: This is indirect command that's implied in the adjective *notum*, "make it known . . . that he [the tribune Lysias] should present [Paul] to you, as if you are going to reveal something about him . . ." ***Certius***: literally, this means "more certain." The absolute comparative is used in expressions like "make known," "reveal," "inform," "report," etc. ***Priusquam adpropiet***: "before he appears [before the Sanhedrin]. I.e., they will kill him while he's in transit, presumably when a small Roman guard is leading him through the crowded Temple compound.

16–21: The plot is revealed to Paul and then to the tribune.

indico, to reveal • **vinctus**, prisoner • **secedo**, to go apart • **seorsum**, privately • **convēnit**, it came in mind • **inquiro**, to request • **insidior**, to plot against • **promissus**, an order

¹⁶Quod cum audisset filius sororis Pauli insidias, vēnit et intravit in castra, nuntiavitque Paulo. ¹⁷Vocans autem Paulus ad se unum ex centurionibus ait, "Adulescentem hunc perduc ad tribunum, habet enim aliquid indicare illi." ¹⁸Et ille quidem adsumens eum duxit ad tribunum, et ait, "Vinctus Paulus, vocans rogavit me hunc adulescentem perducere ad te habentem aliquid loqui tibi." ¹⁹Adprehendens autem tribunus manum illius secessit cum eo seorsum, et interrogavit illum, "Quid est quod habes indicare mihi?" ²⁰Ille autem dixit, "Iudaeis convēnit rogare te ut crastinā die Paulum producas in concilium, quasi aliquid certius inquisituri sint de illo. ²¹Tu vero ne credideris illis. Insidiantur enim ei ex eis viri amplius quadraginta, qui se devoverunt non manducare neque bibere donec interficiant eum, et nunc parati sunt expectantes promissum tuum."

Filius sororis Pauli: This agonizingly brief reference to Paul's family is all we know about it. There is no mention anywhere else and in the New Testament, not even in Paul's letters, of any of his family members. (At 22:28, Paul says he was born a Roman citizen, from which we can deduce that his father was a Roman citizen. But Paul doesn't name his father or even use the word "father.") Deepening the mystery is how Paul's nephew learned about the plot. Was he familiar with the group of men who took part? All we can say is that Paul had a sister, and her son was present in Jerusalem at this time. This boy also cared enough about his uncle to take steps to prevent his assassination. *Intravit in castra*: There's no reason to speculate how Paul's nephew got past the guards and into the *castra*. The tribune, knowing that he was holding a Roman citizen, would likely have treated him well and would have allowed visitors. *Vinctus Paulus*: "the prisoner Paul." *Adprehendens autem tribunus manum illius*: This touching gesture indicates that Paul's nephew was probably a child. It also humanizes the Roman tribune in particular and the Roman authorities in general. Assuming, as we are, that Luke isn't adding details on his own, this scene could only have come from the nephew himself. *Seorsum*: so that no one would overhear what Paul's nephew had to say. This is to protect him from any possible retribution from the conspirators for informing on them.

22–25: The tribune orders Paul to be sent to Caesarea under armed guard.

ne cui = *ne alicui* • **iumentum**, draught animal • **praeses**, governor

²²Tribunus igitur dimisit adulescentem, praecipiens ne cui loqueretur quoniam haec nota sibi fecisset. ²³Et vocatis duobus centurionibus dixit illis, "Parate milites ducentos ut eant usque Caesaream et equites septuaginta et lancearios ducentos a tertiā horā noctis, ²⁴et iumenta praeparate ut inponentes Paulum salvum perducerent ad Felicem praesidem."²⁵

Ne cui: = *ne [ali]cui*, dative after *loqueretur*, "that he not say to anyone." ***Sibi***: The antecedent is the tribune, not Paul's nephew. ***Ducentos . . . septuaginta . . . ducentos***: It seems excessive to dispatch a force of 470 men in arms to sneak one man out of the city under cover of night (*a tertiā horā noctis*), especially when the number of the conspirators was known to be about forty. This figure is usually dismissed as a pious exaggeration, or perhaps Paul is merely being added to a movement of forces that had already been scheduled. ***Ad Felicem praesidem***: Lacking the authority to put a Roman on trial against the accusations of the local population, he did the right thing shipping him off to the governor of the province for processing there.

26–30: The tribune sends a letter to the Roman governor to explain the situation.

supervenio, to intervene • **crimen**, crime • **denuntio**, to order

²⁶ Scribens epistulam continentem haec: "Claudius Lysias optimo praesidi, Felici, salutem. ²⁷Virum hunc, conprehensum a Iudaeis et incipientem interfici ab eis, superveniens cum exercitu eripui, cognito quia Romanus est. ²⁸Volensque scire causam quam

Haec: It's not impossible that Luke is quoting the actual letter itself. The feel of the letter, with its short, declarative style and simple syntax, does square with what we'd expect from a tribune. It is a model of concision and completeness. ***Claudius Lysias***: The tribune is finally named. ***Incipientem***: "was going to be" or "was about to be." ***Cognito***: a compressed ablative absolute, "it being learned that." Of course, this isn't an entirely truthful account of what happened. He didn't intervene to rescue Paul because he knew he was a Roman citizen. He didn't know that until after he had him arrested and taken to prison to be tortured. But we

obiciebant illi deduxi eum in concilium eorum. ²⁹Quem inveni accusari de quaestionibus Legis ipsorum, nihil vero dignum morte aut vinculis habentem crimen. ³⁰Et cum mihi perlatum esset de insidiis quas paraverunt ei, misi ad te, denuntians et accusatoribus ut dicant apud te. Vale."

can sympathize with Lysias's wish to gloss over the precise chronology. **Quem**: A *resumptive* relative = *Et cum eum* . . . **Dignum**: Agrees with *crimen*, not *quem*. Paul had not committed a crime worthy of death or chains (= imprisonment). **Perlatum esset**: This is the impersonal use of the verb, "When it was reported to me about . . ." *Ei* = dative of indirect object after *paraverunt*.

31–35: Paul is delivered to the governor in Caesarea.

---

praetorium, governor's custody

---

³¹Milites ergo secundum praeceptum sibi adsumentes Paulum duxerunt per noctem in Antipatridem. ³²Et posterā die dimissis equitibus ut irent cum eo reversi sunt ad castra. ³³Qui cum venissent Caesaream et tradidissent epistulam praesidi, statuerunt ante illum et Paulum. ³⁴Cum legisset autem et interrogasset de quā provinciā esset et cognoscens quia de Ciliciā, ³⁵"Audiam te," inquit, "cum et accusatores tui venerint." Iussitque in praetorio Herodis custodiri eum.

Sibi: dative after *praeceptum*, "according to what had been ordered to them," = "as they had been ordered." **Per noctem in Antipatridem**: Antipatris is midway between Jerusalem and Caesarea, so it would have been on the road, but it's still about thirty-five to forty miles away. If the convoy left at 3 a.m. (as per verse 23), they could not have reached the town before dawn. **Et posterā die**: The meaning of this verse is clear but the grammar isn't easy: "On the next day, the cavalry being split off [*dimissis*] to go with him [Paul], they [the soldiers] returned to the *castra* [in Jerusalem]." **Cognoscens quia de Ciliciā**: This little detail supports the notion that Luke was an eye-witness to these events or received an accurate and complete report from someone who was there. **In praetorio Herodis**: Herod the Great built an elaborate palace compound in Caesarea, where the Roman governor resided. It even included a small number of jail cells. Paul was to be kept in one of them as much for his own protection as for any other reason.

ACTS AD 57-59

The high priest and other authorities arrive in Caesarea from Jerusalem. A lawyer for the Jewish leaders lays out their complaints against Paul, among which is that he was inappropriately removed from their jurisdiction by Roman tribune in Jerusalem. Paul replies that they have no evidence he violated their laws. He says the real reason he was arraigned is that he teaches the doctrine of the resurrection. If there were any reason for the Jews to suspect him of sedition, he continues, the ones to indict him would be from Asia, where he has been spending most of his time preaching. The Roman governor in Caesarea dismisses the court but keeps Paul in custody for two years, hoping to get a bribe to release him. During that time, his wife and he visit Paul frequently and talk with him about his teachings. Felix, the Roman governor at the time, is succeeded by Porcius Festus, who keeps Paul in jail.

1–9: Felix hears charges against Paul.

clementia, indulgence • **pestiferus**, destructive

Post quinque autem dies descendit princeps sacerdotum, Ananias, cum senioribus quibusdam et Tertullo quodam oratore, qui adierunt praesidem adversus Paulum. ²Et citato Paulo coepit accusare Tertullus, dicens, "Cum in multā pace agamus per te et multa corrigantur per tuam providentiam, ³semper et ubique suscipimus, optime Felix, cum omni gratiarum actione. ⁴Ne diutius autem te protraham, oro breviter audias nos pro tuā clementiā. ⁵Invēnimus hunc hominem pestiferum et concitantem seditiones omnibus Iudaeis in universo orbe et auctorem

Tertullo quodam oratore: The term orator (*rhētor* in the Greek) combines "speaker," "lawyer," and "politician," as they were virtually indistinguishable in Greek and Roman practice. Tertullus might have been fluent in Greek and thus able to make the case for the Sanhedrin, whose Greek might not have been up to the task. ***Cum in multā pace***: It was standard practice first to flatter the sitting judge in ancient trials and to thank him for taking the time to hear the case, but this is a shameless exaggeration. The rule of Antonius Felix from about 52-58 was notorious for corruption and violent oppression. At the end of his term, he barely escaped being convicted of misrule himself. The charges against him, incidentally, were brought by the Jewish leaders themselves, some of whom might have been in this embassy. ***Cum omni gratiarum actione***: "with every gesture of thanks," or "with all conceivable gratitude." ***Pro tuā clementiā***: We might say, "with your indulgence," or "by your leave." The doting proemium of Tertullus' sspeech takes up more than half of Luke's summary. Why would Luke devote so much of his available space to the introduction and give only the sparsest account of the actual charges? Perhaps Luke was so shocked by its insincerity that he wanted it preserved. ***Audias***: Supply *ut*. ***Seditiones***: This is the word that would get Felix's attention. The Romans cared little for the local religious enthusiasms of the peoples in its empire, so long

seditionis sectae Nazarenorum, ⁶qui etiam Templum violare conatus est, quem et adprehendimus, [et voluimus secundum Legem nostrum iudicare. ⁷Superveniens autem tribunus, Lysias, cum vi magnā eripuit eum de manibus nostris,] ⁸a quo poteris ipse iudicans de omnibus istis cognoscere de quibus nos accusamus eum." ⁹Adiecerunt autem et Iudaei, dicentes haec ita se habere.

as it didn't disrupt their rule. Tertullus needs to make the case that this is no small squabble in Jerusalem, but part of an international cult that has the potential of spawning widespread revolution. **Sectae Nazarenorum**: The adjective *Christianus* was coined, probably as a slur, in Antioch (11:26), and was not in wide circulation. Even Tertullus might not have been familiar with it. The word he does use has the effect of isolating the movement geographically away from Jerusalem and outside of the mainstream of Jewish thought. **Et voluimus … de manibus nostris**: Even though the Latin manuscripts contain these words, as do some of the Greek manuscripts, the majority opinion is that they are a clumsy, later interpolation. It's hard to believe a skilled speaker would charge Lysias with interfering in their affairs before another Roman official, especially when it's only to bring up an insignificant detail. Further, if the words are deleted, the text folds back together seamlessly: "and we apprehended him, from whom you will be able to learn about the things . . ." **Ita se habere**: *Se* is the direct object of *habere*, "that these things held themselves thus" = "that this was so."

10–21: Paul defends himself.

offendiculum, a trifling offense • **praesto**, (*indeclinable adjective*) at hand • **stem** < sto

¹⁰Respondit autem Paulus (annuente sibi praeside dicere): "Ex multis annis esse te iudicem genti huic sciens bono animo pro me satisfaciam. ¹¹Potes enim cognoscere quia non plus sunt dies mihi quam duodecim ex quo ascendi adorare in Hierusalem, ¹²et neque in Templo invenerunt me cum aliquo, disputantem aut concursum facientem turbae, neque in synagogis neque in civitate. ¹³Neque probare possunt tibi de quibus nunc accusant me. ¹⁴Confiteor autem hŏc tibi quod secundum sectam, quam dicunt heresim, sic deservio patrio Deo meo, credens omnibus quae in Lege et prophetis scripta sunt, ¹⁵spem habens in Deum, quam et hi ipsi expectant: resurrectionem futuram iustorum et iniquorum. ¹⁶In hōc et ipse studeo sine offendiculo conscientiam habere ad Deum et ad homines semper. ¹⁷Post annos

Annuente sibi praeside dicere: an ablative absolute expression, with *sibi* as the indirect object of the participle and the subject of the infinitive. ***Ex multis annis***: Though this is a bit of an exaggeration—Felix served as governor from just 52-58—Paul's opening remarks aren't nearly so flattering as Tertullus's. All he says is, "I know you're the governor and this is what I have to do." He admits only that he recognizes Felix as the properly installed Roman governor. Whether Felix was pleased by this faint praise or not is something we can only guess at. ***Pro me satisfaciam***: "I will make satisfaction [give an account] on my own behalf." This distinguishes him from the paid advocate of the Sanhedrin, who spoke for them. He also might be boasting a little that he speaks Greek fluently, thus positioning himself as a citizen of the larger Roman world. The members of the Sanhedrin, he's insinuating, are just locals hicks. ***Potes enim cognoscere***: Paul is leading up to why he was in the Temple. ***Quia non plus sunt dies . . . in Hierusalem***: In other words, how could he have been the cause of so much turmoil in Jerusalem? He'd been there only twelve days. ***Quod secundum sectam . . . patrio Deo meo***: I.e., this isn't some new religion that should concern Rome. It's in fact the proper way to observe the old Jewish religion. ***Heresim***: This is merely a transliteration of the Greek word in the accusative singular. The distinction Paul is making between a *secta* and a *heresis* is key. The first is a legitimate variation of Jewish practice and theology, which nevertheless is within the bounds of Judaism. In Roman imperial policy, Judaism was a recognized religion and acceptable because of its antiquity. A *heresis*, by contrast, is a reinterpretation of Judaism that is so radical that its adherents can no longer be considered to be Jewish. The Romans tolerated different religions, but it didn't allow new ones to spring up. ***Resurrectionem . . . iniquorum***: Add *esse* to *futuram* to complete the indirect statement implied after *spem*. The demonstrative *hi* might demonstrate that the Sadducees were not represented at the hearing. They were a dying sect at this time, and the majority of Jews were aligned with the Pharisees. Under the circumstances, Paul would feel free to avoid complicating his defense

autem plures elemosynas facturus in gentem meam veni et oblationes et vota, [18]in quibus invenerunt me purificatum in Templo, non cum turbā neque cum tumultu. [19]Quidam autem ex Asiā Iudaei quos oportebat apud te praesto esse et accusare si quid haberent adversum me, [20]aut hi ipsi dicant si quid invenerunt in me iniquitatis cum stem in concilio, [21]nisi de unā hāc solummodo voce quā clamavi inter eos stans, quoniam 'De resurrectione mortuorum ego iudicor hodie a vobis.'"

by bringing up all the different minority opinions within Judaism. *Ipse studeo*: This is a dodge. His intention is not at issue. His actions and his teachings are. **Facturus**: future active participle showing purpose. This is the first time any reason is given for his return in Acts, and it squares with what he says in his letters. He has been collecting offerings from the community of believers he had established to bring back funds to Jerusalem. Whether he donated what he had collected to the Temple's general welfare fund or only to the Christ believers in Jerusalem is something we don't know. **Me purificatum**: Paul leaves out a critical detail. He underwent the purification ritual as penance for allegedly teaching heresy about the Law. **Quidam autem ex Asiā Iudaei**: The sentence doesn't have a complete main clause. Literally, "Some Jews from Asia, whom it is fitting to be present before you and to make the charge if they have anything against me . . ." We might smooth this over as, "There are Jews in Asia who should come . . ." or "It's fitting that Jews from Asia be present…" Paul is asking, "Where are my accusers, the ones who say I violated the Temple?" We know from other sources that the Romans were running out of patience with anonymous informants who didn't appear in court to be questioned. **Praesto**: an indeclinable adjective in the accusative case. (Remember, "case" is the grammatical role a word plays in a sentence, not an word ending. Hence though "case" is nearly always expressed in Latin as an ending, it isn't always.) **Hii ipsi dicant**: Now he's referring to the mob that followed the high priest and other officials to the trial. Stem: first person singular active subjunctive in a *cum* clause from the verb *sto, stare*. **Ego iudicor**: Paul returns to his original defense, which is no defense at all, since this isn't what he's being charged with.

CHAPTER 24

22–27: Paul is returned to prison and held for two years, during which time Felix and his wife, Drusilla, visit him often.

---

distulit < **differo**, to dimiss • **de suis [amicis]** • **castitas**, chastity • **Quod nunc adtinet** = "that's enough for now" • **bienium**, period of two years

---

²²Distulit autem illos Felix, certissime sciens de viā, dicens, "Cum tribunus Lysias descenderit, audiam vos." ²³Iussitque centurioni custodiri eum et habere requiem nec quemquam prohibere de suis ministrare ei. ²⁴Post aliquot autem dies veniens Felix cum Drusillā uxore suā, quae erat Iudaea, vocavit Paulum et audivit ab eo fidem quae est in Iesum Christum. ²⁵Disputante autem illo de iustitiā et castitate et de iudicio futuro, timefactus Felix respondit, "Quod nunc adtinet! Vade. Tempore autem oportuno accersiam te." ²⁶Simul et sperans quia pecunia daretur a Paulo, propter quod et frequenter accersiens eum loquebatur cum eo. ²⁷Biennio autem expleto, accepit successorem Felix Porcium Festum. Volens autem gratiam praestare Iudaeis, Felix reliquit Paulum vinctum.

De viā: that is, the Jesus movement. As it turns out, this fact about Felix has no bearing on his conduct or his decisions. ***Audiam vos***: Felix doesn't render a verdict; he announces a continuance. ***Ministrare ei***: Was Paul ill? See note at 27: 1-6 at *curam sui*. ***Cum Drusillā uxore suā, quae erat Iudaea***: Felix's relationship to Drusilla was a fresh, high-profile scandal at the time of Paul's incarceration. She was a daughter of Herod Agrippa I, the client king for the Romans in Judaea. Her father first married her off to a pagan priest-king, who agreed to be circumcised and converted to Judaism. Shortly thereafter, Felix was so enamored by her beauty that he arranged to have her leave her first husband, some say by employing a sorcerer. We don't know whether the first marriage was actually dissolved or whether she just left, but we certainly know that Felix didn't convert to Judaism, not even just for show. ***Timefactus***: Inasmuch as Paul talks with him about *iustitia*, *castitas*, and a future judgment, Felix would have good reason to be *timefactus*. ***Quod nunc adtinet***: = "That will do for now." ***Quia pecunia daretur a Paulo***: Though it was officially frowned on, expecting and even demanding bribes was commonplace for Roman governors. ***Accepit successorem***: The transfer of power probably occurred in AD 59. ***Felix reliquit Paulum vinctum***: Luke's point seems to be that Felix could have released Paul so as not to leave any lingering unfinished business behind for Festus to deal with, similar to the way one office manager might tidy up affairs before a new manager is set to take over. But so as not to inflame the Jews, he left Paul where he was.

ACTS 25 AD 59

Festus, the new Roman governor, arrives in Jerusalem, where he is confronted by the Jewish authorities, who still want Paul to be executed. He tells them that he is on his way to Caesarea, where Paul is being held. If they want to make a formal charge against him, he says, they can do it there. At the hearing in Caesarea, Paul says he has committed no crimes against the Temple or Rome. He turns down Festus's offer to be tried in Jerusalem before the Sanhedrin, and appeals to Caesar himself. Before Paul can be sent to Rome, the new Jewish ruler of the Judaean Jews, Herod Agrippa II, and his wife, Bernice, arrive in Caesarea with a grand entourage to pay their respects to the new Roman governor. Festus tells them about Paul, who'd been leftover from the previous governor. Festus is uncertain about the charges the Jews are bringing against Paul and hopes that Agrippa II and others can explain them to him. He will use the information they provide in a brief for the imperial court in Rome.

1–6: Festus, the new Roman governor, tells the Jews in Jerusalem that they should come to Caesarea if they want to present their case against Paul.

triduum, three days • **tendo**, to intend • **maturius**, shortly • **profecturum** < **proficiscor**

Festus ergo cum venisset in provinciam, post triduum ascendit Hierosolymam a Caesareā. ²Adieruntque eum principes sacerdotum et primi Iudaeorum adversus Paulum, et rogabant eum, ³postulantes gratiam adversum eum, ut iuberet perduci eum Hierusalem, insidias tendentes ut eum interficerent in viā. ⁴Festus autem respondit servari Paulum in Caesareā, se autem maturius profecturum. ⁵"Qui ergo in vobis," ait, "potentes sunt descendentes simul, si quod est in viro crimen, accusent eum." ⁶Demoratus autem inter eos dies non amplius quam octo aut decem, descendit Caesaream, et alterā die sedit pro tribunali et iussit Paulum adduci.

Festus: This is Porcius Festus, who replaced Antonius Felix when the latter was recalled to Rome to face charges of misrule in the province of Judaea. There is no sure evidence for the date of Festus's tenure, but the period of 59-62 is the most widely accepted. Only a few years after his rule the final revolt against Roman rule would begin in 66, leading ultimately to the destruction of Jerusalem in 70. ***Post triduum***: If his province was in turmoil, a new governor would want to meet with the leaders of the Jewish community almost immediately after his arrival. ***Ut eum interficerent in viā***: The Jewish authorities tried this ruse before (23:15), when Paul was to be escorted from Jerusalem to Caesarea. Then the Roman tribune learned of the plot and took steps to frustrate it. In this instance, Festus makes the reasonable observation, without necessarily suspecting a plot, that it would be more convenient if they were to present their case in Caesarea. ***Non amplius quam octo aut decem***: This seemly superfluous detail does indicate, as before, that he is relying on eyewitness accounts, perhaps his own. ***Alterā die***: that is, on the day after he arrived in Caesarea. This signals that Paul's trial was a priority both for him and for the Jewish authorities, as it occurred as soon as possible after their meeting in Jerusalem.

ACTS OF THE APOSTLES

7–12: In Caesarea, Paul appeals to Caesar himself.

probo, to prove • **praesto**, to present to • **noceo**, to harm • **melius**, better • **nosti** < **nosco** • **recuso**, to refuse • **vero**, but • **appellasti** < **appello**

---

⁷Qui cum perductus esset, circumsteterunt eum qui ab Hierosolymā descenderant Iudaei, multas et graves causas obicientes quas non poterant probare. ⁸Paulo autem rationem reddente quoniam "Neque in Legem Iudaeorum neque in Templum neque in Caesarem quicquam peccavi." ⁹Festus autem volens Iudaeis gratiam praestare, respondens Paulo dixit, "Vis Hierosolymam ascendere et ibi de his iudicari apud me?" ¹⁰Dixit autem Paulus, "Ad tribunal Caesaris sto, ubi me oportet iudicari. Iudaeis non nocui, sicut tu melius nosti. ¹¹Si enim nocui aut dignum morte aliquid feci, non recuso mori. Si vero nihil est eorum quae hi accusant me, nemo potest me illis donare. Caesarem appello!" ¹²Tunc Festus cum consilio locutus respondit, "Caesarem appellasti. Ad Caesarem ibis."

Qui ab Hierosolyma descenderant Iudaei: We can safely assume this is another embassy from the Sanhedrin. The high priest himself is not reported to have attended this hearing, and in any case it wouldn't have been Ananias who was present at the hearing before Felix (24:1). He had been deposed in 57 by King Agrippa II. ***Paulo autem rationem reddente***: He essentially pleads "*Nolo contendere.*" We can infer from Paul's response that the authorities leveled the old charges again: committing crimes against Jewish Law, profaning the Temple, and fomenting trouble for the Romans. ***Iudaeis gratiam praestare***: As the incoming governor of a troubled province, Festus tried to win over the local authorities with a little favor. What's not so understandable is what Festus means by *ibi de his iudicari apud me*. If this means, as it appears, that he's offering only to move the venue of the trial to Jerusalem, without suggesting that Paul will actually be tried by the Sanhedrin, then Festus's offer seems like a compromise. Paul will still be tried by a Roman. It's also remarkable that Paul is given the choice. One idea is that Festus is suggesting a trial in Jerusalem that would combine all the charges. The Sanhedrin would rule on the crimes against the Law and the Temple, but Festus would rule on the charges the Romans would be concerned with. This interpretation is supported by Paul's answer. ***Ad tribunal Caesaris sto***: Paul's answer is that the charge that he has violated the Laws and the Temple is baseless. Hence there's no reason to transfer the trial to Jerusalem before the Sanhedrin. The only charge left is that of stirring up trouble for the Romans, which should be adjudicated by a Roman tribunal at the imperial capital of the province. ***Dignum morte aliquid feci***: Paul's argument is subtle: "The only capital crime in their brief against me is sedition against Roman rule, and that has to be tried in a Roman court. So there's no reason for me to be sent to Jerusalem to be tried there, even if you are going to superintend the trial. We are in the proper venue in Caesarea right now." ***Nemo potest me illis donare***: Paul says that Festus knows no such crimes have been committed against the Jews, but does he? He has arrived in the province only recently, and even experienced governors could make little sense of Jewish religious practices. ***Caesarem appello***: Festus was probably relieved to hear Paul's appeal

because it extricated him from a politically sensitive position. He didn't want his tenure as governor of Judaea to begin with an affront to the very people he needed to work with to maintain order, but then again he couldn't just hand over a Roman citizen to a local, non-Roman court for trial and punishment (as he will say at verse 16 below).

13–21: Festus tells Agrippa and Bernice about his dealings with Paul and the Jews from Jerusalem.

transigo, to go through • **saluto**, to greet • **derelictus** < **derelinquo** • **dilatio**, a delay • **suspicor**, to suspect • **defungor**, to be dead • **cognitio**, trial

¹³Et cum dies aliquot transacti essent, Agrippa Rex et Bernice descenderunt Caesaream ad salutandum Festum. ¹⁴Et cum dies plures ibi demorarentur, Festus regi indicavit de Paulo, dicens, "Vir quidam est derelictus a Felice vinctus, ¹⁵de quo, cum essem Hierosolymis, adierunt me principes sacerdotum et seniores Iudaeorum, postulantes adversus illum damnationem. ¹⁶Ad quos respondi quia 'Non est consuetudo Romanis donare aliquem hominem priusquam is qui accusatur praesentes habeat accusatores locumque defendendi accipiat ad abluenda crimina.' ¹⁷Cum ergo huc convenissent, sine ullā dilatione sequenti die sedens pro

Agrippa Rex et Bernice: Herod Agrippa II would be the last client king ruling on behalf of the Romans. He was expelled by his countrymen in 66 when the great rebellion against Rome that he desperately tried to prevent got underway. It would take an extended commentary to untangle the complex web of family relations in the Herodian dynasty that brought Agrippa and Bernice together, but two points are relevant here. One is that Agrippa and Bernice were brother and sister, and rumors swirled that their relationship was incestuous. Hence their forthcoming interview with Paul is a parallel to the earlier meeting Paul had with Felix. There Paul lectured the governor about morality, knowing that Felix was wrongfully living with Drusilla. It also is an echo of John the Baptist's imprisonment and eventual execution at the hands of Herod Antipas, who was also in an unsanctioned relationship with his consort. Bernice would have been instantly recognizable as a famous beauty like Cleopatra. She would eventually carry on an affair with Titus, the Roman general and future emperor of Rome, who commanded the Roman forces against the final Jewish Revolt (66-70). Thus what appears to moderns to be a simple courtesy call by Herod Agrippa II and his consort would have been alive with all kinds of lurid overtones to the first readers of Acts. ***Quaestiones vero . . . Paulus vivere***: It's surprising to see this claim about Jesus come up so late in the process, but it does form a necessary piece of the charge the Jewish authori-

tribunali iussi adduci virum. ¹⁸De quo cum stetissent accusatores nullam causam deferebant de quibus ego suspicabar malum, ¹⁹quaestiones vero quasdam de suā superstitione habebant adversus eum et de quodam Iesu defuncto, quem adfirmabat Paulus vivere. ²⁰Haesitans autem ego de huiusmodi quaestione dicebam si vellet ire Hierosolymam et ibi iudicari de istis. ²¹Paulo autem appellante ut servaretur ad Augusti cognitionem, iussi servari eum donec mittam eum ad Caesarem."

ties are making. The Romans would be concerned only if a religious superstition presented a political threat. Paul's sect is in fact claiming a new king of the Jews, but this king had been executed. It's critical to add, therefore, that Paul asserts this king has been resurrected and still lives. **Paulo autem appellante**: ablative absolute, "with Paul appealing," or "since/when Paul appealed," followed by the indirect command *ut servaretur*. **Donec mittam**: anticipatory subjunctive, "Until I [should] send him."

22–23: Paul is presented to King Agrippa, Bernice, and other leaders.

ambitio, entourage

²² Agrippa autem ad Festum, "Volebam et ipse hominem audire." "Cras," inquit, "audies eum." ²³ Alterā autem die, cum venisset Agrippa et Bernice cum multā ambitione et introissent in auditorium cum tribunis et viris principalibus civitatis, et iubente Festo adductus est Paulus.

Cum venisset: singular because Luke sees the two of them as one couple. ***Cum multā ambitione***: This isn't a small, informal event. The royal couple enters with a grand entourage of officials and other worthies.

24–27: Festus repeats that he needs help understanding the case against Paul so that he can prepare a brief for the imperial court in Rome.

interpello, to confront • **amplius**, anymore • **dominus** = Caesar • **maxime**, especially • **sine ratione** = inappropriate

²⁴Et dixit Festus, "Agrippa rex et omnes qui simul adestis nobiscum viri, videtis hunc, de quo omnis multitudo Iudaeorum interpellavit me Hierosolymis petens, et hīc clamantes non oportere eum vivere amplius. ²⁵Ego vero conperi nihil dignum eum morte admisisse. Ipso autem hōc appellante Augustum, iudicavi mittere, ²⁶de quo quid certum scribam domino non habeo. Propter quod produxi eum ad vos et maxime ad te, rex Agrippa, ut interrogatione factā habeam quid scribam. ²⁷Sine ratione enim mihi videtur mittere vinctum et causas eius non significare."

De quo . . . non habeo: This somewhat awkwardly hangs at the end of the sentence. Grammatically, *Augustum* should be the antecedent of the relative pronoun *quo*, but clearly that's not what's meant. *Domino* appears as a doublet for *Augustum*, perhaps to straighten out the ambiguity of the antecedent. The fact that Festus is writing a letter is brought out at the end of verse 26: *quid habeam scribere*, "that I may have something to write." *Significare*: "to specify" or "to indicate." Festus is duty bound to prepare a brief for the superior court in Rome and not just to pass the entire mess up without any explanation.

ACTS OF THE APOSTLES

St. Paul Speaking Before King Agrippa

Saint Paul Speaking Before King Agrippa by Giorgio Vasari 1573 (The Met)

ACTS 26

AD 59

Paul explains himself to King Agrippa II, hoping that another Jew will understand the doctrinal disputes which underlie the charges against him. He begins by saying that everyone knows he was a strict Pharisee and even an officially sanctioned persecutor of the new Jesus sect in Jerusalem and elsewhere. He repeats his conversion experience on the road to Damascus. He reasserts his conviction that far from being a departure from Judaism, the Gospel of Jesus and his call for repentance is firmly rooted in Jewish laws and its prophetic traditions. And why, he adds, should it be difficult to believe that God can raise the dead? Festus thinks Paul has lost his mind, and Agrippa II jokes that if Paul should continue, he may be converted himself. After the guests file out of the room, there is still no clear idea of what the charge against Paul is. Agrippa says that Paul could have been released already if he hadn't appealed to Caesar.

1–3: Paul begins his explanation by complimenting King Agrippa's "well-known" expertise in Jewish affairs.

temet, = **te** + the intensive, indeclinable suffix *met* • **beatus**, blessed • **consuetudo**, custom

Agrippa vero ad Paulum ait, "Permittitur tibi loqui pro temetipso." Tunc Paulus extentā manu coepit rationem reddere: ²"De omnibus quibus accusor a Iudaeis, rex Agrippa, aestimo me beatum, apud te cum sim defensurus me hodie, ³maxime te sciente omnia quae apud Iudaeos sunt, consuetudines et quaestiones. Propter quod obsecro patienter me audias."

Agrippa vero ad Paulum ait: There's no reason Festus can't allow Agrippa to take the lead as this is only an extra-legal meeting and not a trial. *Cum sim defensurus*: Paul means this in a non-legal sense. The issue is not whether Paul will be tried in Rome, but what kind of background information Festus is going to provide the court. *Te sciente*: The compression of the ablative absolute gives Paul's exordium a sense of formality.

ACTS OF THE APOSTLES

4–8: He continues: "Everyone knows I was raised in the most strictly observant sect of the Jews."

iuventus, childhood • **praescio**, to know already • **velint** < **volo** • **tribus**, tribe • **devenio**, to arrive

⁴"Et quidem vitam meam a iuventute, quae ab initio fuit in gente meā in Hierosolymis, noverunt omnes Iudaei, ⁵praescientes me ab initio (si velint testimonium perhibere) quoniam secundum certissimam sectam nostrae religionis vixi Pharisaeus. ⁶Et nunc in spe quae ad patres nostros repromissionis facta est a Deo sto iudicio subiectus, ⁷in quam duodecim tribūs nostrae, nocte ac die deservientes, sperant devenire, de quā spe accusor a Iudaeis, rex. ⁸Quid incredibile iudicatur apud vos si Deus mortuos suscitat?"

Et quidem vitam meam a iuventute: Readers of Acts are already well acquainted with Paul's life, but this will all be new to Festus and Agrippa. ***Certissimam sectam***: Inasmuch as the Pharisees imposed extensive and detailed restrictions on behavior and ritual practices, they could be called the most exacting. The Sadducees, naturally, would differ, as they held that the body of derived law hadn't the same authority as the original Mosaic codes. It's also a fact that many of the Pharisees became followers of Jesus (cf. 15:5), though they split with Paul over the question of Gentile converts. ***In spe quae***: To what expectation or hope is Paul referring? From what follows, it appears to be the resurrection of the dead (verse 28), and not the arrival of the Messiah. Paul has pointed out before that the real reason for the trial is not so much his evangelizing for Jesus as it is his belief in a personal afterlife. He may or not be accurately representing the charges against him, but that's what Luke says he said. It's also no accident that Paul never says in his defense that Jesus is the one true king of the Jews, probably so as not to concern Festus. The Romans had done away with that title after Herod the Great and preferred to rule over a fractured province with three client kings serving at their pleasure.

9–11: "I was even an active prosecutor of the followers of Jesus both in Judea and abroad."

detuli < **defero** • **insanio**, to rage

⁹"Et ego quidem existimaveram me adversus nomen Iesu Nazareni debere multa contraria agere, ¹⁰quod et feci Hierosolymis, et multos sanctorum ego in carceribus inclusi, a principibus sacerdotum potestate acceptā, et cum occīderentur detuli sententiam. ¹¹Et per omnes synagogas frequenter puniens eos conpellebam blasphemare, et amplius insaniens in eos persequebar usque in exteras civitates."

Cum occiderentur: Is this an exaggeration, or were many of Jesus' first followers executed on the orders of the Sanhedrin? We read of harassment, floggings, and threats (5:39-42; 8:1-3; 9:1-2; 21), but only Stephen (7:56-59) is actually murdered. Even then, it doesn't seem to have been the result of official policy. Stephen was stoned by an enraged mob. At 22:4, Paul says that his persecution included execution (*usque ad mortem*), but he could be referring just to Stephen's. It's possible that the persecution of the first Christ believers included executions; we just don't have any evidence for it. **Detuli sententiam**: "I kept back my opinion," = "I held my tongue." It's true that James the Elder was executed by Agrippa I in about AD 44, but Paul was not in Jerusalem then.

ACTS OF THE APOSTLES

12–14: "But Jesus spoke to me while I was on the road to Damascus in pursuit of Jesus' followers."

supra, beyond

¹²"In quibus dum irem Damascum cum potestate et permissu principum sacerdotum, ¹³die mediā in viā vidi, rex, de caelo supra splendorem solis circumfulsisse me lumen et eos qui mecum simul erant. ¹⁴Omnesque nos cum decidissemus in terram, audivi vocem loquentem mihi hebraicā linguā: 'Saule, Saule, quid me persequĕris? Durum est tibi contra stimulum calcitrare.'"

Cum potestate et permissu principum sacerdotum: Paul repeats the source of his authority (verse 10 above). It underscores the fact that his Jewish accusers are well aware of his background and of his service to them. ***In quibus dum irem Damascum . . .***: This is the third and final account of Paul's conversion on the road to Damascus. The first was told in the third person by Luke at 9:3-20, and the second by Paul before an angry mob in Jerusalem at 22:6-21. The three versions are listed side-by-side in a table in Appendix A "Three Accounts of Paul's Conversion" for comparison.

15–18: "He told me that I was to bring the word to the Gentiles."

¹⁵"Ego autem dixi, 'Quis es, Domine?' Dominus autem dixit, 'Ego sum Iesus, quem tu persequĕris.¹⁶Sed exsurge, et sta super pedes tuos. Ad hoc enim apparui tibi, ut constituam te ministrum et testem eorum quae vidisti et eorum quibus apparebo tibi, ¹⁷eripiens te de populo et Gentibus, in quas nunc ego mitto te ¹⁸aperire oculos eorum ut convertantur a tenebris ad lucem et de potestate Satanae ad Deum, ut accipiant remissionem peccatorum et sortem inter sanctos per fidem quae est in me.'"

De potestate Satanae: The only other mention of the power of Satan in Acts is at 5:3. In that scene, Satan tempted Ananias and his wife, Saffira, to hold back some money from the apostles. The comment and the verses that follow are exclusive to this account of his conversion. Paul had been evangelizing for nearly thirty years at this point. It would be surprising if he weren't gaining clarity and new insights about his mission.

19–23: "I obeyed the vision and preached the Gospel of Jesus from the time of my conversion with God's protection. This is the reason the Jews want to kill me."

adiuvo, to help • **minori atque maiori** = to unimportant and important people

¹⁹"Unde, rex Agrippa, non fui incredulus caelestis visionis, ²⁰sed his qui sunt Damasci primum et Hierosolymis et in omnem regionem Iudaeae et Gentibus adnuntiabam ut paenitentiam agerent et converterentur ad Deum, digna paenitentiae opera facientes. ²¹ex causā me Iudaei, cum essem in Templo, conprehensum temptabant interficere. ²²Auxilio autem adiutus Dei usque in hodiernum diem sto, testificans minori atque maiori, nihil extra dicens quam ea quae prophetae sunt locuti futura esse et Moses: ²³si passibilis Christus, si primus ex resurrectione mortuorum lumen adnuntiaturus est populo et Gentibus."

Caelestis visionis: complementary genitives after the adjective *incredulus*, "I was not faithless of [about] the heavenly vision." Inasmuch as his belief led him to act, this could also be translated, "I was not disobedient to the heavenly vision." ***His qui sunt Damasci primum***: This is an accurate, if incomplete geographical summary of his mission as recorded in Acts. He preaches first in Damascus (9:20-22), and next in Jerusalem (9:26-28). This may be what Paul means by *in omnem regionem Iudaeae*, though there's no record of a wide-ranging missionary trip in Judea proper. At 9:30, however, the disciples in Jerusalem send him away to his home in Tarsus. He appears next some years later at 11:25-26, when Barnabas summons him from Tarsus to help him preach in Antioch. Thus begins his evangelizing to the Gentiles. ***Hāc ex causā***: Paul again misrepresents the case against him. His life and work before his conversion are not in question. The charges against him are that since his conversion he has been preaching new doctrines. He is accused of saying that obedience to the law is optional, even for Jewish converts, and of profaning the Temple by bringing a Gentile into areas where they are forbidden. These are accusations that even his brethren in Jerusalem might support. ***Testificans minori atque maiori***: "testifying to the low and the high." ***Si passibilis Christus, si primus…***: These two propositions are what Paul says are affirmed in the prophets: that the Christ suffers, and that as the first one to be resurrected he confers to the world the light of this promise.

24–27: "I'm not insane, Festus, as you think. Agrippa knows what I'm saying was clearly stated by the prophets."

litterae, literature • **lateo**, to be hidden • **angulus**, a [street] corner • **gestum est** < **gero**, to carry on

²⁴ Haec loquente eo et rationem reddente, Festus magnā voce dixit, "Insanis Paule! Multae te litterae ad insaniam convertunt!" ²⁵At Paulus, "Non insanio," inquit, "optime Feste, sed veritatis et sobrietatis verba eloquor. ²⁶Scit enim de his rex, ad quem et constanter loquor. Latere enim eum nihil horum arbitror. Neque enim in angulo quicquam horum gestum est. ²⁷Credis, Rex Agrippa, prophetis? Scio quia credis."

Multae te litterae ad insaniam convertunt: The Jews were constantly poring over their Scripture, interpreting and re-interpreting them with exceptionally close readings of every sentence, phrase and word. *Latere eum nihil eorum*: "none of these things escape [lie hidden from] him." Paul's reply to the critique that his defense is nothing but literary obscurantism is that the events that prove his understanding of Scripture occurred in broad daylight. *Credis, Rex Agrippa, prophetis*: This is a contentious argument. It's possible to believe in the prophets without committing to any particular interpretation of their proclamations.

28–29: Agrippa jokes that Paul might convert him into a Christian.

in modico [tempore] • **suadeo**, to persuade • **non tantum . . . sed et**, not only . . . but also • **tales qualis**, such as

²⁸Agrippa autem ad Paulum, "In modico suades me Christianum fieri!" ²⁹Et Paulus [ait], "Opto apud Deum et in modico et in magno non tantum te sed et omnes hos qui audiunt hodie fieri tales qualis et ego sum, exceptis vinculis his."

Me Christianum fieri: This is the second of two uses of the word *Christianus* in Acts. Again it is meant as a slur. See note at 11: 19-26. In this verse, Agrippa is sneering at the idea that he could ever become a silly "Christian" like Paul. *Exceptis vinculis his*: This is a rare moment of wit in Acts. Paul said he wishes everyone would become a Christian like him, "Well," he adds, holding up his manacled hands, "except for these chains."

30–32: Neither Festus nor Agrippa find Paul guilty of anything that merits imprisonment.

praeses, governor

³⁰Et exsurrexit rex et praeses et Bernice et qui assidebant eis. ³¹Et cum secessissent, loquebantur ad invicem, dicentes quia "Nihil morte aut vinculorum dignum quid facit homo iste." ³²Agrippa autem Festo dixit, "Dimitti poterat homo hĭc, si non appellasset Caesarem."

Quid: = *aliquid*. **Si non appellasset Caesarem**: It's not easy to know how to take this. Festus could end this affair by dropping the charges. If the charges are dropped at the local level, then the appeal for a change of venue would be moot. It's likely that both Festus and Agrippa are using the appeal as a cover. They can't drop the charges without enraging the Sanhedrin, so they pretend their hands are tied. Perhaps they're hoping that faced with the expense and inconvenience of sending a delegation to Rome to present their case the locals will lose interest and forget the whole matter.

Saint Paul

Saint Paul by Michel Aubert 1726 (The Met)

ACTS

 AD 59

Paul now begins his voyage to Rome under Roman guard. Starting from Caesarea, he and his companions make their way up the coast to Sidon, and then pass along the eastern coast of Cyprus on to a major port, Myra, in southern, modern-day Turkey. They are taken by another vessel toward the south of Crete, where they'd hoped to spend the winter. They are driven away from the southern coast of Crete by a storm and into the open sea. Paul's judgment becomes increasingly valued on the journey until he becomes the de facto captain of the boat. The sailors are reassured in their darkest hour when Paul tells them an angel told him everyone will survive. Paul prevents a mutiny by the crew, who consider abandoning the ship to save themselves. Finally, they run their battered ship onto a beach on the island of Malta.

1–6: Paul and his companions are taken from Caesarea to Lystra in southern, modern-day Turkey, where they are put on a ship bound for Italy.

---

reliquus, the other • **custodia**, prisoner • **persevero**, to persevere • **humane**, kindly • **tracto**, to treat • **subnavigo**, to sail on the leeward side • **propterea quod**, because • **pelagus**, sea

---

Ut autem iudicatum est eum navigare in Italiam et tradi Paulum cum reliquis custodiis centurioni, nomine Iulio, cohortis Augustae. ²Ascendentes autem navem Hadrumetinam, incipientem navigare circa Asiae loca, sustulimus, perseverante nobiscum Aristarcho Macedone Thessalonicense. ³Sequenti autem die devēnimus Sidonem. Humane autem tractans Iulius Paulum permisit ad amicos ire et curam sui agere. ⁴Et inde cum sustulissemus subnavigavimus Cypro, propterea quod essent venti contrarii. ⁵Et pelagus

Ut autem iudicatum est eum navigare in Italiam: Working back from other datable evidence in Chapter 18, we can fix their departure to late August. *Cohortis Augustae*: Julius might have been an officer in one of the five cohorts that were stationed in Roman Judaea, and the Augustus cohort might have been one of them. *Hadrumetinam*: "a ship from Hadrumetina," a harbor near Carthage in North Africa. This is assumed to be a transcription error in the Latin. In the Greek, the ship is said to be from Hadrumythia, a port in the city of Troas. *Incipientem*: "as it was beginning its run to the Asian ports." Julius didn't have a dedicated military transport for his prisoners. He booked passage on transport ships. *Sustulimus*: Thus begins the last of the "we-passages," implying that Luke is with Paul at this point on. The inclusion of precise details affirms a first-hand witness of the events. *Aristarcho*: This is no doubt the same Aristarchus mentioned as one of Paul's companions at 19: 29 and 20: 4. He plays no role in the sea voyage narrative and isn't mentioned again. *Ad amicos*: The centurion actually allowed Paul shore leave and let him go to his friends, certainly other Christ believers in or near the city. *Curam sui*: sui is objective genitive of the reflexive pronoun: "undergo care of himself." Was Paul ill? In Galatians 4: 13-15, Paul talks about

Ciliciae et Pamphiliae navigantes vēnimus Lystram, quae est Lyciae, ⁶et ibi inveniens centurio navem Alexandrinam navigantem in Italiam transposuit nos in eam.

a weakness of his flesh (*infirmitas carnis*), and in 2 Corinthians 12: 7-9, he says he has a "thorn in his flesh" (*stimulus carnis*) inflicted on him by Satan. At Acts 24: 23, we read that Lysias allowed Paul's friends to come to take care of him (*ministrare ei*) in prison. Explanations of these passages cover the whole range of possibilities, but if Paul means a literal physical illness, and not just a spiritual weakness, it's likely that it was in his eyes. In his letter to the Galatians at 4: 15, he says they loved him so, that if it had been possible they would have torn out their eyes and given them to him. Also in Galatians 6: 11, he says that he had to write in large letters (*videte qualibus litteris scripsi vobis mea manu*), perhaps so that he could see what he'd written. **Subnavigavimus**: This is the technical sailing term for passing "under the lee," that is, using the island as protection from the wind coming from the open sea. It would have been shorter to pass on the western coast of Cyprus, but passing by the eastern coast was safer. **Lystram**: The Greek has Myra, which was a major port for grain ships sailing from Alexandria to Rome. **Alexandrinam**: This would have been one of the large grain transports. As we learn later in the

7–8: Slowed by contrary winds, they sail to Crete, where they finally reach a small port city of Fair Havens (*Boni Portŭs*).

tarde, late • **vix**, with difficulty • **adnavigo**, to sail to the leeward side • **iuxta**, close to (the coast)

⁷Et cum multis diebus tarde navigaremus et vix devenissemus contra Cnidum. Prohibente nos vento, adnavigavimus Cretae secundum Salmonem, ⁸et vix iuxta navigantes vēnimus in locum quendam qui vocatur Boni Portūs, cui iuxta erat civitas Thalassa.

Prohibente nos vento: As we see here, the winds in the eastern Mediterranean were already picking up. It was extremely rare that a ship would dare sailing during the "closed season," that started from the first weeks of November and lasted until the beginning of spring. ***Vix devenissemus contra Cnidum***: The ship is hugging the coast because of the wind, using the island of Rhodes for protection. ***Secundum Salmonem***: The ship covers a short expanse of open sea, though somewhat protected by a string of small islands, until it touches the northeastern-most port of Crete, Salmone. Thence it will go south along the eastern coast of Crete and follow the island's southern coast. ***Boni Portūs... Thalassa***: There's no material evidence for Fair Haven, though traditionally it is identified with Kaloi Limenes in Crete, a little to the east of the modern resort town of Matala. The Latin name of the city, furthermore, is a corruption of the Greek Lasaia or Alassa. It has never been firmly identified either.

ACTS OF THE APOSTLES

9–11: The centurion ignores Paul's warning of dangerous times ahead if they should leave Fair Haven.

iam, by now • **consolor**, to give advice • **ieiunium**, hunger • **damnum**, loss • **gubernator**, helmsman • **nauclerius**, ship's owner

⁹Multo autem tempore peracto, et cum iam non esset tuta navigatio, eo quod et ieiunium iam praeterisset, consolabatur Paulus, ¹⁰dicens eis, "Viri, video quoniam cum iniuriā et multo damno non solum oneris et navis sed etiam animarum nostrarum incipit esse navigatio." ¹¹Centurio autem gubernatori et nauclerio magis credebat quam his quae a Paulo dicebantur.

Eo quod et ieiunium iam praeterisset: The fast must be the celebration of Yom Kippur or the Day of Atonement, which fell between the end of September and the beginning of October. *Consolabatur Paulus*: Knowing that the officers of the ship have decided to try to move to a larger port on Crete and winter there, Paul issues his warning. *Centurio autem gubernatori et nauclerio*: As this was a ship in the imperial maritime fleet, the decision to sail or not to sail rested with the centurion. It's natural that he would listen to the helmsman and owner of the ship, and not to one of his prisoners, who had no experience in sailing.

12–15: They are blown out into the open sea when trying to reach Phoenix, another port on Crete they deemed more suitable for spending the winter.

---

aptus, suited for • **hiemo**, to spend the winter • **plurimi**, the majority • **respicio**, to face • **auster**, (gentle) south wind • **propositum**, objective • **subfero**, to lift up (anchors), **lego**, to sail near the coast of • **arripio**, to snatch up • **conor**, to hold course • **flatus**, a blast of air

---

¹²Et cum aptus portus non esset ad hiemandum, plurimi statuerunt consilium navigare inde, si quo modo possent devenientes Phoenice hiemare, portum Cretae respicientem ad Africum et ad Chorum. ¹³Adspirante autem austro, aestimantes propositum se tenere, cum sustulissent, de Asso legebant Cretam. ¹⁴Non post multum autem misit se contra ipsam ventus typhonicus qui vocatur Euroaquilo, ¹⁵cumque arrepta esset navis et non posset conari in ventum, datā nave flatibus ferebamur.

Phoenice hiemare: "to winter in Phoenix." The town has not been excavated, but its location is known. Luke's description is that it is a two-sided bay, with one that faces *ad Africam* (southwest) and another that faces *ad Choram* (northeast). This is consistent with the two-sided inlet found about fifty miles farther to the west of Fair Haven on the southern coast of Crete, today known as Chora Skafio. As it happens, it is the southern terminus of a popular hiking trail through the Samaria Gorge. **Adspirante austro**: This would indeed be propitious because a gentle south wind would allow them to stay close to the shore line. **Propositum se tenere**: "that they were obtaining their objective." With Phoenix only fifty miles away and there being a favorable wind, it appears they were about to reach their destination. **De Asso legebant Cretam**: There is no city of Asson. *De Asson* is a misinterpretation of the Greek adverb *anchi*, meaning "close by." The expression therefore is literally "they picked (their way) close by Crete." *Ipsam*: sc. *navem*. **Euroaquilo**: This is a composite of a Greek word *euro*, meaning "east-southeast wind," and a Latin term *aquilo*, meaning "north-east wind." The topography of the area would funnel wind down off the mountains of Crete. This is what suddenly blows the ship away from the coast and out into the open sea. **Datā nave flatibus ferebamur**: They had no choice but to pull the sails down and let the storm drive the ship along.

16–20: They are driven out to the open sea to the west of Crete and toward north Africa.

decurro, to pass to the leeward side of • **scapha**, small boat • **adiutor**, rope • **utor** + *ablative case*, to use • **accingo**, to bind up • **Syrtim**, the sand bars of Syrtim • **vas**, baggage • **valide**, powerfully • **iactum**, a thowing out (of things on the ship) • **armamenta**, (*plural*), equipment • **sidus**, star • **exiguus**, small • **inmineo**, to threaten

---

¹⁶Insulam autem quandam decurrentes quae vocatur Caudam, potuimus vix obtinere scapham, ¹⁷quā sublatā, adiutoriis utebantur, accingentes navem. Timentes ne in Syrtim inciderent, submisso vase, sic ferebantur. ¹⁸Valide autem nobis tempestate iactatis, sequenti die iactum fecerunt. ¹⁹Et tertiā die suis manibus armamenta navis proiecerunt. ²⁰Neque sole autem neque sideribus apparentibus per plures dies et tempestate non exiguā inminente, iam ablata erat spes omnis salutis nostrae.

Decurrentes . . . Caudam: "running under an island which was called Cauda." Cauda is only a little southwest of Fair Haven. Running "underneath" it, that is on the south side, afforded them enough time to haul in the small boat (*scapha*), used for transporting passengers to the shore. Assuming they would soon reach Phoenix, they didn't think it necessary to pull it up out of the water and lash it to the ship. But now in the storm it would be very dangerous to have it trailing behind, tethered by a rope. It could break loose, or worse, be driven against the ship itself. *Adiutoriis utebantur accingentes navem*: "They used supports, binding up the ship." It appears that they wrapped their mooring ropes (the *adiutoriis*) around the ship's hull to prevent it from breaking apart if they ran aground on the sand bars. *In Syrtim*: Now called the Gulf of Sidra, the Syrtis is a notoriously dangerous shallow area of the Mediterranean Sea to the north of modern-day Libya. The fact that they feared running aground on the Syrtis, which is nearly two hundred miles from their actual location, indicates just how lost they were. *Submisso vase*: "with their personal baggage having been thrown overboard." *Iactum fecerunt*: "They made a throwing" or "They threw some of the cargo overboard." This was to lessen the draft of the hull in anticipation of a possible encounter with the sandbars. *Armamenta*: The crew now turns to the ship's rigging and other equipment.

21–26: Paul tells everyone an angel assured him they would all survive.

ieiunatio, time without eating • **tollo**, in sailing, to set sail • **lucrum**, goods • **iactura**, a discarding • **amissio**, loss • **praeterquam**, other than • **adsto**, to stand before • **adsisto** = **adsto** • **estote** < **sum**, **quemadmodum**, just as

---

²¹Et cum multa ieiunatio fuisset tunc stans Paulus in medio eorum dixit, "Oportebat quidem, O viri, audito me non tollere a Cretā lucrique facere iniuriam hanc et iacturam. ²²Et nunc suadeo vobis bono animo esse, amissio enim nullius animae erit ex vobis, praeterquam navis. ²³Adstitit enim mihi hāc nocte angelus Dei cuius sum ego et cui deservio, ²⁴dicens, 'Ne timeas, Paule. Caesari te oportet adsistere, et ecce: donavit tibi Deus omnes qui navigant tecum.' ²⁵Propter quod bono animo estote, viri, credo enim Deo quia sic erit quemadmodum dictum est mihi. ²⁶In insulam autem quandam oportet nos devenire."

Multa ieiunatio: The crew hadn't the time, or perhaps the interest, to prepare a meal, so desperate was their situation. *Audito me*: as he warned them at verse 10. We could translate this ablative absolute as the protasis of a condition, "if you had listened to me." *Praeterquam navis*: Add *amissionem*: "except for the loss of the ship." *Cuius sum ego*: "of whom I am," or "whom I belong to." *Estote*: second person plural imperative of *sum*. *In insulam autem quandam*: This is the island of Malta.

27–32: After they anchor the ship, Paul informs the centurion that the sailors are considering abandoning ship.

submitto, to lower a sounding line • **passus**, distance of approximately five feet • **viginti**, twenty • **pusillum**, a little • **separo**, to go away • **asper**, perilous • **puppis**, the stern • **opto**, to pray for • **obtentus**, pretense • **prora**, the front of a ship • **funis**, rope • **excīdo**, to fall down

---

²⁷Sed posteaquam quartadecima nox supervenit, navigantibus nobis in Hadriā circa mediam noctem, suspicabantur nautae apparere sibi aliquam regionem. ²⁸Qui submittentes invenerunt passūs viginti, et pusillum inde separati invenerunt passūs quindecim. ²⁹Timentes autem ne in aspera loca incideremus, de puppi mittentes anchoras quattuor optabant diem fieri. ³⁰Nautis vero quaerentibus fugere de navi, cum misissent scapham in mare sub obtentu quasi a prora inciperent anchoras extendere, ³¹dixit Paulus centurioni et militibus, "Nisi hi in navi manserint, vos salvi fieri non potestis." ³²Tunc absciderunt milites funes scaphae et passi sunt eam excīdere.

In Hadriā: The modern-day Adriatic Sea is the expanse of the Mediterranean between eastern Italy and the western coast of the Balkans, which would make no sense here. In antiquity, however, it was thought to encompass the area south of that, from Sicily to Greece and Crete. *Suspicabantur*: It may be that they came to this suspicion because of the soundings they took. *Passūs viginti*: literally, "twenty paces" = approximately one hundred feet. A *passus* was two strides taken by an adult male at a normal walking pace, or about five feet. *Passūs quindecim*: "fifteen paces," or "sixty-five feet." After progressing only a little (*pusillum inde separati*), they found the water was thirty-five feet more shallow, a good indication they were approaching land somewhere. *Incideremus*: "run aground." To prevent this from happening, the sailors dropped (*mittentes*) four anchors from the stern (the rear) of the ship to wait for daylight. *Nautis quaerentibus*: A group of sailors decide to abandon ship and make their way to whatever land is out there on the *scapham*. Their pretext (*sub obtentu quasi*) is that they are going out to set more anchors, this time from the front of the ship (*a prora*). *Inciperent*: The subjunctive indicates the counter-factual nature of their pretext: "under the guise that they were going to . . . " *Centurioni et militibus*: that is, to the military authorities and not the owner of the ship. The ship was under imperial authority, hence the centurion outranked the civilian crew. Just as importantly, the soldiers were the ones with the means to head off the mutiny. *Excīdere*: "to fall off" the ship. The *scapha* had been hoisted up out of the water by the *funae*, which the soldiers cut to prevent the mutiny.

33–38: Paul convinces everyone to take time to eat and restore their spirits.

capillus, a thread of hair • **animaequior**, of better spirits • **ducenti**, two hundred • **septuaginta**, seventy • **adlevio**, to lighten • **triticum**, grain

³³Et cum lux inciperet fieri rogabat Paulus omnes sumere cibum, dicens, "Quartadecimā hodie die expectantes ieiuni permanetis, nihil accipientes. ³⁴Propter quod rogo vos accipere cibum pro salute vestrā quia nullius vestrum capillus de capite peribit." ³⁵Et cum haec dixisset, sumens panem gratias egit Deo in conspectu omnium, et cum fregisset coepit manducare. ³⁶Animaequiores autem facti omnes, et ipsi adsumpserunt cibum. ³⁷Eramus vero universae animae in navi ducentae septuaginta sex. ³⁸Et satiati cibo adleviabant navem, iactantes triticum in mare.

Vestrum: genitive plural of the pronoun, indicating a genitive of the whole: "a hair of none (*nullius*) of you (*vestrum*)." **Gratias egit Deo in conspectu omnium**: This could conceivably be a reenactment of the Eucharist, but since there were only three Christ believers aboard, it seems more likely it's just an ordinary meal. Paul's words *pro salute vestrā* don't suggest a sacred ritual. **Iactantes triticum in mare**: This is the first mention of the cargo. Dumping the wheat would have been a laborious task, but a necessary one if the ship was to be driven on to a shore.

ACTS OF THE APOSTLES

39–41: The next day they see a bay and decide to make for whatever habor it may provide.

agnosco, to recognize • **sinum**, a bay • **litus**, shore • **laxo**, to untie • **iunctura**, binding • **gubernaculum**, rudder • **artemon**, main-sail • **bithalassus**, seagirt • **inpingo**, to run a ground • **solvo** to break apart

³⁹Cum autem dies factus esset, terram non agnoscebant, sinum vero quendam considerabant habentem litus, in quem cogitabant, si possent, eicere navem. ⁴⁰Et cum anchoras abstulissent, committebant se mari, simul laxantes iuncturas gubernaculorum, et levato artemone secundum flatum aurae, tendebant ad litus. ⁴¹Et cum incidissemus in locum bithalassum, inpegerunt navem et prora quidem fixa manebat, inmobilis puppis vero solvebatur a vi maris.

Terram non agnoscebant: That is, none of the sailors recognized the island. The narrative is full of more technical sailing terms that make for slow reading. We can summarize the events as follows. The sailors see a bay (*sinum*) and its shoreline (*litus*). They decide to enter the bay and drive the ship onto the shore (*in quem . . . eicere navem*). They cut free the anchors (*abstulissent*), put to sea (*commitebant se mari*), and untie the rudders (*laxantes iuncturas gubernaculorum*). They hoist up the mainsail (*levato artemone*), let it fill up with the wind (*secundum flatum aurae*), and head for the shore (*tendebant ad litus*). Things don't work out as they'd hoped. Instead of reaching the shore, the ship becomes stuck (*inpegerunt navem*), caught fast (*prora quidem fixa manebat*) in the shallows in the middle of the bay (*in locum bithalassum*), where it is being torn apart by the power of the sea (*solvebatur a vi maris*).

42–44: The centurion overrules the idea of killing the prisoners to keep them from swimming away and escaping.

custodia, prisoner • **enato**, to swim away • **tabula**, plank

⁴²Militum autem consilium fuit ut custodias occīderent, ne quis cum enatasset effugeret. ⁴³Centurio autem volens servare Paulum prohibuit fieri, iussitque eos qui possent natare mittere se primos et evadere et ad terram exire. ⁴⁴Et ceteros alios in tabulis ferebant quosdam super ea quae de navi essent. Et sic factum est ut omnes animae evaderent ad terram.

Militum: genitive plural: "this was the soldiers' plan." *Effugeret*: Even the ordeal they had been through would not excuse the soldiers from letting any of the prisoners escape. If they killed them and disposed of their bodies, they could claim that they were lost at sea. *Servare*: This doesn't necessarily imply any affection for Paul. The centurion has his orders, and he's determined to carry them out. *Primos*: In this way, those who could swim would be on the shore to help the others who'd used planks stripped off the ship for floats.

Paul's Journey to Rome

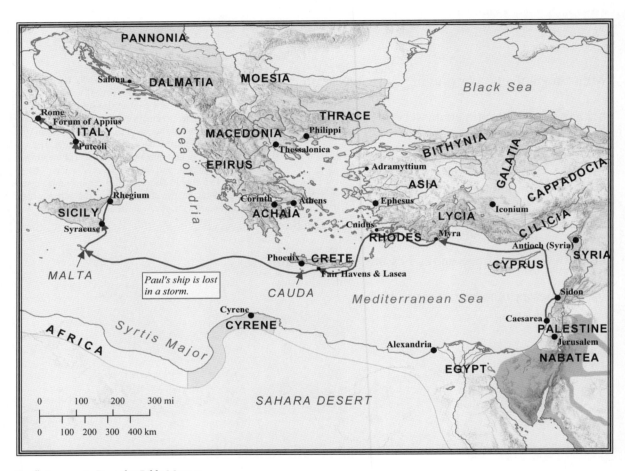

Paul's Journey to Rome by *Bible Mapper.*

ACTS 28  AD 60-63

The local people on Malta help the shipwrecked passengers and crew. They are amazed when Paul is unharmed by a snake. Paul performs many miraculous cures. Three months later they board a ship for Rome. They are welcomed there by other Christ believers. Though he is under house arrest Paul is not restricted from meeting with his friends and others. He explains to several Jewish leaders in Rome how he was interrogated in Jerusalem and why he invoked his right to appeal to the emperor. He spends an entire day trying to persuade them that Jesus is the Messiah predicted in Scripture. Some are convinced; others are not. Since the Jews have rejected God's salvation, it's now being offered to Gentiles, and they will accept it. For two more years he is free to teach the Gospel of Jesus in Rome.

1–6: Now safe on the island of Malta, Paul survives the bite of a poisonous snake to the astonishment of the local people.

---

pyra, camp fire • **imber**, rain • **frigus**, cold • **sarmentorum**, a twig • **aliquantus**, some • **vipera**, snake • **calor**, heat • **bestia**, animal • **utique**, most assuredly • **homicida**, a murderer • **tumor**, a swelling • **ultio**, any longer • **sino**, to permit

---

Et cum evasissemus tunc cognovimus quia Militene insula vocatur. Barbari vero praestabant non modicam humanitatem nobis. ²Accensā enim pyrā reficiebant nos omnes propter imbrem qui inminebat et frigus. ³Cum congregasset autem Paulus sarmentorum aliquantam multitudinem et inposuisset super ignem, vipera a calore cum processisset invasit manum eius. ⁴Ut vero viderunt barbari pendentem bestiam de manu eius, ad invicem dicebant, "Utique homicida est homo hĭc, qui cum evaserit de mari, ultio non sinit

Militene: There's no serious disagreement that this is the island of Malta. **Barbari**: people whose native tongue was not Greek or Latin. Malta was an outpost of Carthage, and the people spoke a Punic dialect, akin to Hebrew and Aramaic. Paul, who spoke both, as well as Greek, was probably able to make himself understood. **Modicam humanitatem**: The local people took in 276 survivors, which would have been a considerable strain on their resources. They may have been motivated by a combination of natural generosity and the presence of imperial soldiers among the survivors. **A calore**: This is a necessary editorial remark, for snakes would have been inactive at this time of the year. The fire stirred them up. **Ultio non sinit vivere**: The fact that Paul survived more than two weeks at sea in a blinding storm, only to be bitten by a poisonous snake at the moment of his rescue would seem to a superstitious people to have been divine punishment. **Sperantibus**: "expecting," not "hoping."

vivere." ⁵Et ille quidem excutiens bestiam in ignem nihil mali passus est. ⁶At illi existimabant eum in tumorem convertendum et subito casurum et mori. Diu autem illis sperantibus et videntibus nihil mali in eo fieri, convertentes se dicebant eum esse deum.

7–10: Paul performs many miraculous cures.

praedium, estate • **febris**, fever • **iaceo**, to be lying down

⁷In locis autem illis erant praedia principis insulae, nomine Publii, qui nos suscipiens triduo benigne exhibuit. ⁸Contigit autem patrem Publii febribus et dysenteriā vexatum iacere, ad quem Paulus intravit. Et cum orasset et inposuisset ei manūs, salvavit eum. ⁹Quo facto et omnes qui in insulā habebant infirmitates accedebant et curabantur, ¹⁰qui etiam multis honoribus nos honoraverunt, et navigantibus inposuerunt quae necessaria erant.

In locis autem illis: "in this area." The ancient capital of the island was only a few miles from where Paul was shipwrecked. ***Principis insulae***: Malta was included in the imperial province of Sicily. The designation "leader of the island" probably doesn't signify that Publius held any official position, but only that as a wealthy islander he was a notable contact for the Romans. ***Febribus et dysenteriā***: Luke's description of the disease is not inconsistent with what came to be known as the Maltese Fever (brucellosis), which was endemic to the island until the early twentieth century. It is a pathogen present in unpasteurized milk and cheese from infected animals or their undercooked meat.

CHAPTER 28

11–16: The passengers eventually sail from Malta; Paul is greeted at Rome.

insigne, insignia • **secundus**, favorable • **fiducia**, trustworthiness • **sibimet** = sibi

¹¹Post menses autem tres navigavimus in nave Alexandrinā quae in insulā hiemaverat, cui erat insigne Castorum. ¹²Et cum venissemus Syracusam, mansimus ibi triduo. ¹³Inde circumlegentes devēnimus Regium et post unum diem flante austro secundā die vēnimus Puteolos, ¹⁴ubi inventis fratribus rogati sumus manere apud eos dies septem, et sic vēnimus Romam. ¹⁵Et inde cum audissent fratres occurrerunt nobis usque ad Appii Forum et Tribus Tabernis, quos cum vidisset Paulus gratias agens Deo accepit fiduciam. ¹⁶Cum venissemus autem Romam, permissum est Paulo manere sibimet cum custodiente se milite.

Post menses autem tres: Following the chronology of the narrative, this would mean February of 60 AD, since they arrived on Malta sometime in November of 59. It's still too early in the season for sailing in the open sea, but given the short distances to be covered on individual legs of the journey and the fact that they could stay close to land all along the way it's not unthinkable that the crew of the grain ship would set out before the official beginning of the season. The southernmost coast of Sicily is only about sixty-five miles from Malta; thence the ship would work its way up the eastern coast of the island, which would protect it from a winter storm from the northwest, until it passed through the straights between Sicily and the tip of Italy. From there it would move up the western coast of Italy, staying always within sight of land until it reached its final destination of Puteoli (modern-day Naples). ***Castorum***: of the twin brothers Castor and Pollux, who were protectors of sailors. Many ships would have images of them fixed on their prow. ***Inventis fratribus***: Paul could hardly have been expected by Christ believers among the Jews in Puteoli after his voyage. They had to be found. ***Dies septem***: We need to remember that Paul is still accompanied by a small Roman guard. They must have been very accommodating to have allowed Paul to linger with his friends there for a full week. ***Et sic vēnimus Romam***: Luke appears to conclude the travel narrative at this point. In the next verse, however, Paul is back outside of Rome proper. The Three Taverns is known to be about thirty miles south of Rome. The Forum of the Appius is a few miles south of that. Several explanations are possible. One is that the verb *vēnimus* (*ēlthamen* in Greek) has to be taken not as "we arrived at Rome," but "we set out for Rome." This has the difficulty of redefining the verb to fit the context. Another is that Luke uses *Roma* to mean the greater Roman area, in the same way we might say New York, when actually we mean Brooklyn or the Bronx. In verse 16, however, Luke uses *Roma* to mean the city proper, and not the greater Roman area. Another solution is to take verse 15 as a later interpolation inserted very early on in the tradition. If it is excised, verses 14 and 16 fit together seamlessly. ***Sibimet***: "to remain to himself" or "to be at liberty."

221

17–22: Meeting with Jewish leaders in Rome, Paul explains why he didn't want to be tried by Jews in Jerusalem and appealed to Caesar.

¹⁷Post tertium autem diem convocavit primos Iudaeorum. Cumque convenissent dicebat eis, "Ego, viri, fratres, nihil adversus plebem faciens aut morem paternum vinctus ab Hierosolymis traditus sum in manūs Romanorum, ¹⁸qui cum interrogationem de me habuissent, voluerunt me dimittere, eo quod nulla causa esset mortis in me. ¹⁹Contradicentibus autem Iudaeis coactus sum appellare Caesarem, non quasi gentem meam habens aliquid accusare. ²⁰Propter hanc igitur causam rogavi vos videre et adloqui. Propter spem enim Israhel catenā hāc circumdatus sum." ²¹At illi dixerunt ad eum, "nos neque litteras accepimus de te a Iudaeā, neque adveniens aliquis fratrum nuntiavit aut locutus est quid de te malum. ²²Rogamus autem a te audire quae sentis, nam de sectā hāc notum est nobis quia ubique ei contradicitur."

Convocavit primos Iudaeorum: Knowing nothing about Paul, the leaders of the Jewish community would be interested in learning who he is and why he has been brought under guard from Jerusalem. He was not, it should be pointed out, invited to speak at the synagogue on the Sabbath, as had been his practice before. ***Non quasi***: The Jewish leaders would have correctly suspected that Paul was trying to avoid a just prosecution by the Jews in Jerusalem by appealing to the emperor. ***Vos***: object, not subject, of *videre* and *adloqui*. Paul called for meeting to assure them he's not just an ordinary criminal. ***Propter spem enim Israhel***: This might have been enough to signal to the Jewish leaders that Paul was a member of the Jesus cult they'd heard about. ***Litteras***: It is not surprising the Jews in Rome would have received no information about Paul from Jerusalem. His voyage began at the very end of the sailing season. If it hadn't been for the storm that blew them from Crete to Malta, they wouldn't have reached Rome for several more weeks. There is no chance that a letter from Jerusalem could have arrived any earlier than Paul did.

23–28: Paul explains the Gospel of Jesus to a large gathering, convincing some but not others.

mane, dawn • **vespera**, evening • **incrasso**, to thinken • **sano**, to heal • **salutare**, salvation

²³Cum constituissent autem illi diem, venerunt ad eum in hospitium plures quibus exponebat, testificans regnum Dei suadensque eos de Iesu ex Lege Mosi et prophetis a mane usque ad vesperam. ²⁴Et quidam credebant his quae dicebantur, quidam vero non credebant. ²⁵Cumque invicem non essent consentientes discedebant, dicente Paulo unum verbum, quia "Bene Spiritus Sanctus locutus est per Esaiam prophetam ad patres nostros, ²⁶dicens, 'Vade ad populum istum, et dic, 'Aure audietis et non intellegetis, et videntes videbitis et non perspicietis. ²⁷Incrassatum est enim cor populi huius, et auribus graviter audierunt, et oculos suos conpresserunt, ne forte videant oculis et auribus audiant et corde intellegant et convertantur et sanem illos.' ²⁸Notum ergo sit vobis quoniam Gentibus missum est hŏc salutare Dei, ipsi et audient."

Eos de Iesu ex Lege Mosi: The Jews would not need to hear the scriptural evidence for the Messiah rehearsed in detail. The specific issue is whether Jesus is the Messiah and had fulfilled the appropriate prophecies. ***Invicem***: "with one another." ***Per Esaiam prophetam ad patres nostros***: This is the most extensive Old Testament passage in Acts. Isaiah 29:10 will be attributed directly to Jesus in the first three Gospels—yet to be written—to explain the purpose and effect of his parables (Mk. 4:12; Mtt. 13:14-15; and Lk. 8:10). ***Ne forte***: The negative purpose clause has made this one of the most difficult of Jesus' sayings, one that has been hotly debated since antiquity. ***Salutare***: Despite its appearance, this isn't the infinitive of *saluto*.

29–31: For the next two years Paul spreads the Gospel of Jesus in Rome.

conductum, lodgings • **suscipio**, to receive

[²⁹Et cum haec dixisset, exierunt ab eo Iudaei, multam habentes inter se quaestionem.] ³⁰Mansit autem biennio toto in suo conducto et suscipiebat omnes qui ingrediebantur ad eum, ³¹praedicans regnum Dei et docens quae sunt de Domino Iesu Christo cum omni fiduciā sine prohibitione.

Et cum haec dixisset: The Latin includes this verse, though it is omitted in the best Greek manuscripts. It only repeats what has been said in verse 25. ***Biennio toto***: probably until AD 63. The abrupt ending has spawned a wide-ranging search for an explanation. Maybe Luke had envisioned a third volume, which he never got around to or which has been lost. Maybe Paul was killed during Nero's persecution in Rome in 64 and Luke lost his sources of information. Maybe Luke knew Paul was executed by the Romans and wanted to spare his readers the pain of reading about it for one reason or another. These all assume that Acts doesn't end as Luke had originally intended. If Acts ends precisely as Luke had intended, then another explanation is possible. Theophilus can be thought to have asked Luke two questions: (1) what is Christianity, and (2) how did it expand out of the exclusive religion of the Jews, winning non-Jewish converts on its way to Rome itself. Luke answers the first question with his Gospel. The second is answered with Acts. When Paul is preaching the Gospel of Christ to Gentiles in Rome, the promise to Theophilus has been fulfilled.

GLOSSARY OF LATIN TO ENGLISH WORDS

The glossary seeks to provide translations that are immediately applicable to the text of Acts. Not all shades of meaning are explored. For a more comprehensive study of these words, students should consult a classical Latin language dictionary, such as the online Lewis and Short at the Perseus site (www.perseus.tufts.edu), and note in particular the information for late-classical usage.

Proper nouns and place names are not included. As they are often non-Latinate words, many of them have only one form for all cases. When they do inflect, even the ancient authors can differ on how to decline them. The name Abraham, for instance, is indeclinable as **Abraham** in some texts and in others it inflects in the genitive as **Abrahae**. At other times, a non-Latin word fits easily into a Latin declension, such as **Antiochia**, which inflects as **Antiochiae**, **Antiochiae**, and so on. The rare examples of endings or forms that may be wholly unfamiliar to the intermediate student are treated in the notes.

I will list highly inflected forms of verbs or pronouns that may be challenging for the students at this level to analyze. For example, **abstulissent** will be presented with a reference to its root form, **abfero**. Similarly, "**casurum**, see **cado**," "**cuius**, see **qui**"; "**vobiscum**, see **cum**." My decision when to include a little extra help was based only on experience and not a set rule. Similarly, entries for verb stems are abbreviated more or less depending on how likely they are, in my judgment, to baffle new readers. The verb "to sink," for example, is listed as **mergo (3), mersi** [not simply as **-si**]**, mersum** [not simply as **-sum**], but the verb "to offer forth" is listed as **perhibeo (2), -ui** [not **-hibui**]**, -itum** [not **-hibitum**].

I have included long marks over vowels when they are important for determining the stem of a verb. The stem vowel of the third principal part of **venio**, for example, will be marked long when needed, since the unmarked form **venit**, for example, could be both present or perfect. Thus, the perfect will be written as **vēni**. This corresponds to my policy of indicating long vowels in the text where they make a difference in the inflection or conjugation of a word. In this way, for example, **hōc** (masculine/neuter ablative singular) is distinguished from **hoc** (neuter nominative or accusative), and **ancillā** (ablative singular) is distinguished from **ancilla** (nominative singular).

Finally, the text I chose to use comes from the **Perseus** website. It doesn't assimilate consonants with prepositional prefixes. It may be puzzling at first for students trained in classical Latin to see forms like **adfero** in place of **affero**, **adpono** for **appono**, **adsumo** but not **assumo**. These forms and others like them will become familiar with experience.

GLOSSARY

a(b)(s) + ablative, from, away from; by
abduco (3), -duxi, -ductum, to lead away; remove
abeo (4), -ii or -ivi, -itum, to depart; leave
ablata, see **abfero**
abluo (3), -ui, -utum, to wash away
abnego (1), to refuse; deny
abominatio, -onis, f., abomination
abominor, -ari, abominatus sum, to detest; abominate
abscindo (3), -scidi, -scissum, to cut away; cut out
absconditum, -i, n., cellar
abscondo (3), -scidi or -scididi, -sciditum, to hide; conceal
absolvo (3), -solvi, -solutum, to absolve; settle
abstineo (2), -tinui, -tentum, to keep away from
abstraho (3), -traxi, -tractum, to separate from
abstulissent, see **abfero**
absum, -esse, -fui, -futurum, to be away from; be distant from
abundo (1), to overflow; be abundant
ac, and
accedo (3), -cessi, -cessum, to go; draw near to
accendo (3), -di, accensum, to kindle; set on fire
acceptor, -oris, m., an acceptor + **personarum,** one who plays favorites
accersio (4), -ii or -ivi, -itum, to call for; summon
accido (3), -cidi, to happen; fall upon
accingo (3), -cinxi, -cinctum, to bind up
accio (3), -civi, -citum, to summon
accipio (3), -cepi, -ceptum, to get; acquire; take up
accola, -ae, m., resident of a nearby country
accuso (1), to reproach; plead a case
accusor, -oris, m., plaintiff
actio, -onis, f., action; gesture
actus, -us, m., deed
ad + accusative, to, toward; **with gerunds/gerundives to show purpose**
ad invicem, back and forth; in turn; one after another; to one another
adaperio (4), -aperui, -apertum, to open; reveal
adclamo (1), to proclaim
adcurro (3), -curri, -cursum, to run to; approach; come to
adduco (3), -duxi, -ductum, to lead to
adeo (4), -ii or -ivi, -itum, to come to
adfero, -ferre, -tuli, -latum, to bring to; present
adficio (3), -feci, -fectum, to visit upon; treat
adfigo (3), -fixi, -fixum, to put a sign on; brand
adfirmo (1), to confirm; insist
adflictio, -onis, f., pain; suffering
adfligo (3), -flixi, -flictum, to strike; cause trouble for
adhaereo (2), -haesi, -haesum, to adhere to; cling to
adhuc, still
adicio (3), -ieci, -iectum, to throw to; put near
adimpleo (2), -imlpevi, -impletum, to complete
adiungo (3), -iunxi, -iunctum, to join
adiuro (1), to swear to; swear; entreat
adiutor, -is, m., supports; stays; ropes
adiutorium, -ii, n., help; support
adiuvo (1), -iuvi, -iutum, to help
adlevio (1), to lighten
adlevo (1), to raise up
adloquor, -i, adlocutus sum, to speak to; address
administro (1), to serve; carry out
admiror, -ari, admiratus sum, to admire; be amazed
admitto (3), -misi, -missum, to allow; permit; let in

227

adnavigo (1), to sail (to the leeward side)
adnumero (1) to number; add to
adnuntiator, -oris, m., a proclaimer; an advocate of
adnuntio (1), to announce; proclaim
adoro (1), to pray to; curse
adplico (1), to steer toward; put in at
adplico (3), -plicui, -plicitum, to join with; arrive at
adpono (3), -posui, -positum, to set next to; add to
adprehendo (3), -di, -prehensum, to take hold of
adprobo (1), to approve
adpropinquo (1), to approach; arrive at + **dative**
adpropio (1), to draw near; arrive
adquiro (3), -quisivi, -questum, to acquire
adquisitio, -onis, f., profit; livelihood
adsideo (2), -sedi, -sessum, to sit near
adsigno (1), to mark out; point out
adsisto (3), -stiti, to stand before
adspiro (1), to blow on
adsto, -āre, -steti, -stitum, to stand near; stand before; keep watch
adstringo (3), -strinxi, -strictum, to tie up
adsum, -esse, -fui, -futurum, to be pr-essent; nearby
adsumo (3), -sumpsi, -sumptum, to take up
adtendo (3), -di, -tentum, pay attention to; tend to
adtineo (2), -ui, -tentum, to hold fast; **idiomatically, quod nunc adtinet,** that's enough for now
adtracto (1), to draw near to oneself
adtulit, see **adfero**
adulescens, -entis, m., a young man
adulterium, -ii, n., adultery
adultero (1), to commit adultery
adulterus, -a, -um, debauched; adulterous
advena, -ae, m., visitor; migrant
advenio (4), -vēni, -ventum, to come to; arrive
adventus, -us, m., approach; arrival

adversum + accusative, against; in the presence of
adversus + **accusative,** to; against
advesperascit, -ere, -vesperavit, impersonal, to become dark; become evening
advoco (1), to summon
advolvo (3), -volvi, -volutum, to roll upon
aedes, -is, f., dwelling place; shrine
aedificatio, -onis, f., construction
aedifico (1), to build
aeger, -gra, -grum, sick
aegrotus, -a, -um, sick
aemulator, -oris, m., one who is zealous for
aemulor, -ari, aemulatus sum, to revile with; be envious of
aequitas, -tatis, f., fairness; equality
aequus, -a, -um, fair; equal; just
aer, -is, m., air
aestimo (1), to think
aeternus, -a, -um, everlasting
ager, agri, m., field; farm
agnosco (3), -novi, -nitum, to recognize
agnus, -i, m., lamb
ago (3), egi, actum, to make; perform; do
ait, aiunt, he says/they say
albus, -a, -um, white
Alexandrinus, -a, -um, of the city Alex-andria
alibi, elsewhere
alienigena, -ae, m., foreigner
alienus, -a, -um, foreign
alligo (1), to tie up
aliquantus, -a, -um, of a certain amount; some
aliquis, aliquid, someone; something
aliquot, several; some
alius, -a, -ud, other; another; **alius . . . alius,** the one . . . the other
alo (3), alui, alitus/altum, to feed; nourish
alterus, -a, -um, the other of two
alteruter, alterautera or alterutera, alterumuterum or alterutorum, one another
amaritudo, -inis, f., bitterness
ambigo (3), to go around; debate about

ambitio, -onis, f., entourage; pomp
ambo, -ae, -o, both
ambulo (1), to walk
amicus, -i, m., friend; friendly to
amissio, -onis, f., loss
amoveo (2), -movi, -motum, to take away; pass on; die
amplior, comparative of amplus
amplius, anymore; more; further
amplus, -a, -um, of a large extent; great
an, in an indirect alternative question, or
anchora, -ae, f., anchor
ancilla, -ae, f., female servant; slave
angelus, -i, m., messenger
angulus, -i, m., angle; corner
anima, -ae, dative and ablative animabus, f., soul
animaequior, comparative of animaequus
animaequus, -a, -um, of good spirits; of calm mind
animus, -i, m., soul; mind
annum, -i, n., year
annuntio (1), to announce
annuo (3), -nui, -nutum, to nod approval
ante + accusative, in front of; before; **as an adverb,** previous; before
antequam, before
antiquus, -a, -um, old; ancient
aperio (4), -ui, apertum, to uncover; open
apostolatus, -us, m., the role of Apostle
apostolus, -i, m., apostle; one who is sent out
appareo (2), -parui, -paritum, to appear
appello (1), to call upon
Appius, -ii, m., the Appian Way
aptus, -a, -um, suited for + **ad**
apud + accusative, nearby; in the house of
aqua, -ae, f., water
aquila, -ae, f., eagle
ara, -ae, f., altar
arbitror, -i, arbitratus sum, to think
archisynagogus, -i, m., a leader of a synagogue
argentarius, -ii, m., a sliver worker

argenteus, -a, -um, of silver
argentum, -i, n., silver
argumentum, -i, n., discussion topic
arguo (3), argui, argutum, to charge with + **genitive**
armamenta, -orum, n., equipment
arripio (3), -ripui, -reptum, to lay hold of; to snatch up
ars, artis, m., skill; craft
artemon, -is, m., main-sail
artifex, -icis, m., craftsman
artificium, -ii, n., trade; means of employment
ascendo (3), -di, -censum, to rise up
asper, -a, -um, harsh; perilous
aspicio (3), -spexi, -spectum, to look at; behold
at, but; and
atque, also
auctor, -oris, m., author; creator
audenter, courageously; boldly
audeo (2), ausus sum, to dare
audio (4), -ii or **-ivi, -itum,** to hear
auditorium, -ii, n., hall; lecture room
augeo (2), agui, auctum, to increase
Augustus, -a, -um, of Augustus; imperial
Augustus, -i, m., the emperor
aura, -ae, f., wind
auris, -is, m., ear
aurum, -i, n., gold
ausculto (1), to listen to attentively
auster, -tris, m., the south wind
aut, or; **aut . . . aut,** either . . . or
autem, however, moreover
auxilium, -ii, n., help
averto (3), -verti, -versum, to turn away; remove
aviditas, -tatis, f., eagerness
azyma, -orum, n., Feast of the Unleavened Bread

B

baiulo (1), to carry
baptisma, -atis, ablative, -mate, n., washing; baptism

baptismum, -i, n., baptism
baptizo (1), to baptize
barbarus, -a, -um, barbarian
basis, -is, f., base, foot
beatus, -a, -um, blessed; happy
bene, well
benedico (3), -dixi, -dictum, to bless
benefacio (3), -feci, -factum, to do a good deed
benigne, kindly
bestia, -ae, f., (wild) animal
bibo (3), bibi, bitum, to drink
biduum, -i, n., two days
biennium, -ii, n., two years
bithalassus, -a, -um, bounded on both sides by the sea; seagirt
blasphemia, -ae, f., blaspheme
blasphemo (1), to blaspheme
bonus, -a, -um, good
brachium, -ii, n., arm
brevis, -e, short; brief
breviter, briefly

C

cado (3), cecĭdi, casum, to fall; die
caecus, -a, -um, blind
caedes, -is, f., destruction; slaughter
cado (3), cecĭdi, casum, to fall down
caedo (3), cecīdi, caesum, to beat
caelestis, -e, heavenly
caelum, -i, n., sky; heaven
Caesar, -is, m., generic title for a Roman emperor
caesus, -a, -um, see **caedo**
calceo (1), to put on shoes; wear shoes
calciamentum, -i, n., shoe
calcium, -ii, n., sandal
calcitro (1), to kick; trample on
caligo, -inis, f., fog
calor, -oris, m., heat
candidus, -a, -um, bright
capillus, -i, m., a thread of hair
caput, -itis, n., head
carcer, -eris, m., prison

carus, -a, -um, dear; beloved
caro, carnis, f., flesh
castitas, -tatis, f., chastity; sexual purity
castra, -orum, n., fort
casurum, see **cado**
catena, -ae, f., chain
causa, -ae, f., legal case; crime
celeriter, swiftly
cenaculum, -i, n., dining hall
centum, one hundred
centurio, -onis, m., centurion; captain
certus, -a, -um, sure; fixed; **certus fio,** to be informed; learn
certissime, with great assurance
certius, neuter accusative singular comparative from certus
cervix, -cis, f., neck
cesso (1), to cease
ceterus, -a, -um, other
chorus, -i, m., the northwest
Christianus, -i, m., Christian
Christus, -i, m., anointed one; Messiah
cibus, -i, m., food; meal
circa + accusative, around; for
circiter, around; approximately
circuitus, -us, m., circle; circuit
circumcido (3), -cidĭdi, -cīsum, to circumcise
circumcisio, -onis, f., circumcision
circumdo, -ăre, -dedi, -datus, put on; tie up
circumeo (4), -ii or -ivi, -itum, to go around
circumfulgeo (2), -fulsi, -fulsum, to flash around
circumlego (3), -legi, -lectum, to pick one's way around; sail carefully
circumsto (1), -steti, -statum, to stand around
circumvenio (4), -vēni, -ventum, to exploit
cito (1), to arouse
civis, -is, m/f., citizen
civitas, -atis, f., city; legal status (of citizenship)
clamo (1), to cry out; shout

clamor, -oris, m., a shout
clarifico (1), to glorify
claritas, -tatis, f., brilliance
claudus, -a, -um, lame; crippled
clausus, -a, -um, closed
clementia, -ae, f., mercy; indulgence
coago (3), -egi, -actum, to force; order
coepi, -isse, -tum, to begin
cogitatio, -onis, f., thought
cogito (1), to think
cognatio, -onis, f., kindred
cognatus, -a, -um, related; kindred
cognitio, -onis, f., in a legal sense, a trial
cognomino (1), to give as a second name; give as a nickname
cognosco (3), -novi, -notum, to come to know
cohors, -hortis, f., a batallion (of about 600 soldiers)
colligo (3), -legi, -lectum, to assemble; to gather together + **reflexive pronoun**
collum, -i, n., neck
colo (3), -ui, cultum, to worship; tend; devote oneself to
colonia, -ae, f., colony
comitor, -ari, comitatus sum, to accompany
comes, -itis, m., companion
commemoro (1), to call to mind
commendo (1), to commit; hand over for protection; commend; entrust
comminor, -ari, comminatus sum + dative, to curse; threaten
committo (3), -misi, -missum, to entrust
commoratio, -onis, f., a dwelling; a lasting place
commoror, -ari, commoratus sum, to delay; dwell
commoveo (2), -movi, -motum, to be in motion; aroused; stirred up
communicatio, -onis, f., a sharing; making common
communis, -e, common; unwashed
conor, -ari, conatus sum, to try; **in sailing,** to hold course

conburo (3), -busi, -bustum, to burn up
concilium, -ii, n., council; assembly
concito (1), to stir up
concludo (3), -clusi, -clusum, to encompass; close up on
concordo (1), to agree with
concupo (3), -ii, or **-ivi, -cupitum,** to long for
concurro (3), -curri, -cursum, to run together; assemble
concursio, -onis, f., a gathering
concursus, -us, m., assembly; gathering
conductum, -i, n., an apartment; lodgings
confero, -ferre, -tuli, -latum, to make plans; confer; bring together
confestim, immediately
confirmo (1), to strengthen
confiteor, -eri, confessus sum, to confess; admit
conforto (1), to strengthen
confugio (3), -fūgi, -fugiturum, to take refuge
confundo (3), -fudi, -fusum, to bewilder; put into an uproar
confusio, -onis, f., confusion; perplexity
congrego (1), to gather; assemble together with
coniungo (3), -iunxi, -iunctum, to join together
coniuratio, -onis, f., conspiracy
conlactaneus, -i, m., childhood friend
conlaudo (1), to praise enthusiastically
connumero (1), to count in; include
conpello -ere, -puli, -pulsum, to force
conperio (4), -peri, -pertum, to find
comperto quod, at the realization that
conpleo (3), -plevi, -pletum, to fulfill; complete
conplector, -i, conplexus sum, to embrace
conprehendo (3), -di, -prehensum, to arrest
conprimo (3), -pressi, -pressum, to close
conpungo (3), -pugi, -punctum, to grieve; disturb
conputo (1), to add up; calculate

conquiro (3), -ii or -ivi, -quisitum, to ask questions; wonder
conquisitio, -onis, f., dispute; quarrel
conscius, -a, -um, aware; knowing
conscientia, -ae, f., conscience
conscindo (3), -scidi, -scisum, to tear apart; wrend
consequor, -i, consecutus sum, to follow
consentio (4), -sensi, -sensum, to agree with
considero (1), to examine thoroughly
consilium, -i, n., plan; advice
consolo (1), to cheer; give advice; **can also be deponent, consolor**
consolatio, -onis, f., consolation
consolido (1), to strengthen
conspectus, -us, m., sight; view
constans, -ntis, firm; resolved
constanter, firmly; steadily
constantia, -ae, f., fixed resolve
constituo (3), -stitui, -stutum, to decide upon; to establish; order
consuetudo, -inis, f., habit; custom
consul, -is, m., consul
consummo (1), to bring about; accomplish; complete
contaminatio, -onis, f., defilement
contemptor, -oris, m., one who looks down; despiser
contestor, -ari, contestatus sum, to call to witness
contigerat, see contingo
contineo (2), -tinui, -tentum, to contain; close up
contingo (3), -tigi, -tactum, to come about; **used impersonally,** to happen to
continuo, directly, immediately
contionor, -ari, contionatus sum, to convene with
contra, to the other side
contradico (3), -dixi, -dictum, to speak against
contrarius, -a, -um, contrary; opposing
contumelia, -ae, f., insult; abuse
conturbo (1), to confuse; disturb
convalesco (3), -valui, to get better
conveniens, -ntis, consistent; in agreement
convenio (4), -vēni, -ventum, to come together; **convēnit,** it came in mind to do something + **dative** + **infinitive**
conversio, -onis, f., conversion
conversor, -ari, consersatus sum, to stay; remain
converto (3), -verti, -versum, to turn toward
convescor, -i, to eat; eat with
convoco (1), to call together; summon
copiosus, -a, -um, well supplied
cor, cordis, n., heart
coram + ablative, before; in front of
coriarius, -ii, m., leather worker
corona, -ae, f., crown; garland
corpus, -oris, n., body
corrigo (3), -rexi, -rectum, to set right
corripio (3), -ripui, -reptum, to take; seize
corruptio, -onis, f., decay
cotidianus, -a, -um, daily
cotidie, daily
cras, tomorrow
crastinus, -a, -um, of the next day; **used as a noun,** the next day
credo (3), -credidi, creditum, to believe; believe in
crepo (3), -ui, crepitum, to make a loud noise; explode
cresco (3), crevi, cretum, to grow; increase
crimen, -inis, n., crime
crucifigo (3), -fixi, -fixum, to crucify
cubiculum, -i, n., dining room; **in a political sense,** cabinet
cui, see qui
cuicumque, see quicumque
cuique, see quisque
cuius, see qui
cuiusdam, see quidam
cultrix, -icis, f., worshipper
cum + ablative, with; **can be attached to the end of a personal pronoun,**

mecum, tecum, secum, etc.
cum, when; since; although
cunctus, -a, -um, all
cur, why
cura, -ae, f., concern; anxiety
curiosus, -a, -um, odd; curious; mystical
curo (1), to heal
curro (3), cucurri, cursum, to run
currus, -us, m., chariot
cursus, -us, m., journey
custodia, -ae, f., guard house; watch; a guard; prisoner
custodio (4), -ii or -ivi, -itum, to guard; watch over
custos, -odis, m., guard

D

daemonium, -i, n., demon
damnatio, -onis, f., condemnation; guilty verdict
damno (1), to convict
damnum, -i, n., harm; loss
de + ablative, from; about
dealbatus, white-washed
dea, -ae, f., goddess
debeo (2), -ui, -itum, to owe; ought
decem, ten
decerno (3), decrevi, decretum, to decide upon; decree
decido (3), -cĭdi, -casum, to fall down
decreverunt, see **decerno**
decurro (3), -cursi, -cursum, to pass to the leeward side of
dedo, -are, dedi, deditum, to give over; devote
deduco (3), -duxi, -ductum, to lead out
defendo (3), -di, -fensum, to defend; protect
definio (4), -ii or -ivi, -itum, to determine
definitus, -a, -um, exact
defungor, -i, defunctus sum, to die; be dead
deinceps, one after another
deleo (2), delevi, deletum, to erase

demento (1), to drive mad
demoror, -ari, -moratus sum, to stay; live in
denarius, -ii, m., a Roman denarius
denuntio (1), to order; command
dens, -ntis, m., tooth
deorsum, down from; downward
depono (3), -posui, -positum, to set down; take down
deprecor, -ari, -precatus sum, to beg
derelictus, see **derelinquo**
derelinquo (3), -liqui, -lictum, to abandon; forsake; leave behind
descendo (3), -di, -scensum, to descend
desertum, -i, n., wilderness
deservio (4), -servi or -servivi, -seritum, to serve earnestly
desiderium, -ii, n., longing; desire
desidero (1), to wish; desire
desino (3), -sivi, -situm, to leave off from; cease
desolatio, -onis, f., desolation
despicio (3), -spexi, -spectum, to overlook; disregard
destruo (3), struxi, -structum, to pull down; destroy
detraho (3), -traxi, -tractum, to drag away
defero, -ferre, -tuli, -latum, to bring; indict
deus, -i, m., God; god
devasto (1), to lay waste
devenio (4), -vēni, -ventum, to arrive at
devotio, -onis, f., devotedness; a consecration; oath
devovo (3), -vovi, -votum, to swear (a religious oath); promise solemnly
dexter, -tra, -trum, or, -tera, -terum, right; the right (hand)
dico (3), dixi, dictum, to say; speak
dictum, -i, n., a saying; something said
dies, -ei, m./f., day
diffundo (3), -fusi, -fusum, to spill out
dignus, -a, -um, worthy; worthy of; worthy to + **genitive, ablative, or infinitive**
diiudico (1), to judge

dilatio, -onis, f., delay
diligenter, carefully
diligentia, -ae, f., care; diligence
diligentius, very carefully
diluculum, -i, n., dawn
dimitto (3), -misi, -missum, to dismiss; forgive; set free
diruo (3), -rui, -rutum, to demolish
discedo (3), -cessi, -cessum, to leave; get away
discepto (1), to make an investigation
discerpo (3), -cerpsi, -cerptum, to tear apart; revile; rip into
discessio, -onis, f., separation; departure
discipulus/a, -i/ae, m/f, student
discerno (3), -crevi, -cretum, to distinguish; perceive as different
disperdo (3), -perdidi, -perditum, to perish
dispertio (4), -ii or -ivi, -itum, to apportion out; divide
disperitus, -a, -um, disperate
dispicio (3), -spexi, -spectum, to pick out; neglect
dispono (3), -posui, -positum, to set in order
dispositio, -onis, f., arrangement
disposuit, see **dispono**
disputo (1), to explain; dispute
disseco (1), to cut to the heart
dissemino (1), to spread around
dissensio, -onis, f., disagreement; quarrel
dissero (3), -serui, -sertum, to discuss
dissipo (1), to disperse; scatter
dissolvo (3), -vi, -utum, to break down; destroy; take apart
distribuo (3), -tribui, -tributum, to distribute
differo, -ferre, distuli, dilatum, to scatter apart; break up; dismiss
diu, for a long time
diutius, see **diu**
divido, -videre, -visi, -visum, to divvy up
divino (1), to make predictions
divinus, -a, -um, divine

divulgo (1), to spread around; divulge; publish
do, dăre, dedi, datum, to give
doceo (2), -ui, -tum, to teach; preach
doctor, -oris, m., teacher
doctrina, -ae, f., teaching
dogma, -atis, n., teaching; dogma
doleo (2), dolui, dolitum, to feel pain; grieve; be distressed
dolor, -oris, m., pain; grief
dolus, -i, m., deceit; trick
domesticus, -a, -um, belong to a household
dominor, -ari, dominatus sum, + ablative or genitive, to gain mastery of; overpower
dominus, -i, m., lord; Lord God
domus, -us or -i, m., home
dono (1), to give as a gift
donec, while; **+ subjunctive,** until
donum, -i, n., gift
dormio (4), -ii or -ivi, -itum, to sleep
dubitatio, -onis, f., hesitation
ducenti, -ae, -a, two hundred
duco, ducere, duxi, ductum, to lead; think
dum, while; **+ subjunctive,** until
dummodo, while; until
duo, duae, duo, two
duodecim, twelve
durus, -a, -um, hard
dux, ducis, m., leader
dysenteria, -ae, f., dysentery

e(x) + ablative, out of
ebrius, -a, -um, drunk
ecce, behold
ecclesia, -ae, f., meeting; gathering
educo (3), -duxi, -ductum, to draw out
effero, -ferre, extuli, elatum, to carry out
effugio (3), -fūgi, -fugiturum, to escape
effundo (3), -fudi, -fusum, to pour out
egeo (3), -ui, to need **+ ablative**
egit, see **ago**
ego, mei, mihi, me, me, first person sin-

gular pronoun
egredior, -i, egressus sum, to go out; depart
eicio (3), -ieci, -iectum, to throw out; send out; dismiss
eiusmodi, of this sort
electio, -onis, f., choice
elemosyna, -ae, f., act of mercy; alms
elevo (1), to lift up
eligo (3), -legi, -lectum, to pick out; select; choose
eloquens, -ntis, good at speaking; eloquent
eloquor, -i, elocutus sum, to speak out
emo (3), emi, emptum, to buy
enarro (1), to recount; narrate
enato (1), to swim away
enavigo (1), to sail out
enim, for; truly
enutrio (4), -ii or -ivi, -nutritum, to rear; raise
eo, ire, ii or ivi, -itum, to go
eo, to where; **in eo quod,** because of what
ephesius, -a, -um, of Ephesus; Ephesian
epicureus, -i, m., an Epicurean philosopher
episcopus, -i, m., an overseer; bishop
epistula, -ae, f., letter
equites, -ium, m., cavalrymen; the cavalry
ergo, therefore
erigo (3), -rexi, -rectum, to set up right; set back up
eripio (3), -ripui, -reptum, to rescue
erudio (4), -ii or -ivi, -itum, to instruct
eruditus, -a, -um, educated
esto, estote, imperatives of **sum**
esurio (4), —, -tum, to be hungry
et, and; even; **et . . . et,** both . . . and
etiam, even still; be that as it may
eunuchus, -i, m., eunuch; court official
euroaquilus, -i, m., northwest wind
evado (3), -vasi, -vasum, to escape
evagino (1), to unsheathe (a sword)
evangelista, -ae, m., evangelist
evangelium, -ii, n., good news; good report
evangelizo (1), to preach; spread the word about
evenio (4), -vēni, -ventum, to occur; happen to
everto (3), -verti, -versum, to overturn; upset
exalto (1), to raise up; exult
exaudio (4), -ii or -ivi, -ditum, to hear clearly
excelsus, -a, -um, high; heavenly
excessus, -us, m., a departure
excĭdo (3), -cĭdi, -casum, to fall down; sink
excito (1), to rouse; awaken
exclamo (1), to shout out
excutio (3), -cussi, -cussum, to shake off
exeo (4), -ii or -ivi, -itum, to go out; leave
exercitus, -us, m., army
exhibeo (3), -ui, -itum, to hold forth; deliver; offer
exhortatio, -onis, f., encouragement
exhortor, -ari, exhortatus sum, to exhort; urge
exiguus, -a, -um, small
exilio (4), -ui, to spring up; jump up
exinde, next; thereupon
existimo (1), to wonder
exorcista, -ae, m., exorcist
expectatio, -onis, f., expectation
expecto (1), to await; expect
expello (3), -puli, -pulsum, to expel; throw out
expergefacio (3), -feci, -factum, to arouse
expleo (3), -plevi, -pletum, to fulfill; complete
expletio, -onis, f., fulfillment
explicitus, -a, -um, completed
expono (3), -posui, -positum, to set out; bring forth; deliver
expugno (1), to fight again
exspiro (1), to expire; die
exsurgo (3), -surrexi, -surrectum, to rise up
extasus, -a, -um, stunned
extendo (3), -di, -tus or -sum, to extend; reach out

exter, -a, -um, outlying
extermino (1), to drive out
exto, -are, -titi, -tatum, to rise up; appear
extra + accusative, besides; out of; not including; **with foras,** outside
extremum, -i, n., last; **in extremis,** in the final moments of life; extreme suffering
extulerunt, see effero
exultatio, -onis, f. exultation

F

facies, -ei, f., face; presence
facinus. -eris, n., crime; evil deed
facio (3), feci, factum, to do; make
fallacia, -ae, f., deceit
falsus, -a, -um, untrue; false
fames, -is, f., famine
familia, -ae, f., family
fas, indeclinable adjective, permitted; right
febris, -is, f., fever
fellis, -is, f., bile; gall
fenestra, -ae, f., window
fere, almost; nearly
fero, ferre, tuli, ablatum, to bear; carry
ferreus, -a, -um, iron
ferveo (3), fervi, to burn; be impetuous; driven
festino (1), to hurry
fidelis, -e, faithful; loyal
fides, -ei, f., faith
fiducia, -ae, f., trustworthiness
fiducialiter, confidently; forcefully; earnestly
figura, -ae, f., image; figure
filia, -ae, f., daughter
filius, -i, m., son
fines, -ium, f. pl., borders; land
finis, -is, m., end
fio, fieri, factus est, to be made; to happen
figo (3), fixi, fixum, to stick; fasten
flagello (1), to whip
flagellum, -ii, n., a whip
flamma, -ae, f., flame; fire
flo (1), to blow

flatus, -us, m., blast of air
fleo (2), -evi, -etum, to cry
fletus, -us, m., weeping
flumen, -inis, n., river
foras, outside (with **extra + accusative**)
forensis, -e, public; outside; legal
fornicatio, -onis, f., adultery
forte, by chance; perhaps
fortiter, powerfully
fortitudo, -inis, f., strength; courage
forum, -i, n., marketplace
fractio, -onis, f., breaking
frango (3), fregi, fractum, to break
frater, -tris, m., brother
fraudo (1), to deceive
fremo (3), -ui, -itum, to growl
frequenter, frequently; often
fretum, -i, n., strait; body of water
frigus, -oris, n., cold
fructiferus, -a, -um, fruit bearing
fructus, -us, m., fruit
frumentum, -i, n., fruit; produce; crop
fugio, fugere, fugi, fugiturum, to flee
fumus, -i, m., smoke
fundamentum, -i, n., foundation
fundo (3), -fudi, -fusum, to pour out
funis, -is, m., rope; line
futurus, -a, -um, future; about to be; coming

G

gallica, -ae, f., boot
gaudeo (2), gavisus sum, to rejoice; be pleased
gaudium, -ii, n., joy
gaza, -ae, f., treasury; richess
gemitus, -us, m., sigh; groan
generatio, -onis, f., generation; nation
genero (1), see gigno
gens, -ntis, f., nation; non-Jewish people
Gentilis, -e, Gentile; non-Jewish
genu, -us, n., knee
gigno (3), genui, genitus, to give birth to
genus, -eris, n., race

gero (3), gessi, gestum, to do; **in the passive,** to happen
gladius, -ii, m., sword
gloria, -ae, f., glory
glorifico (1), to glorify
grabattum, -i, n., stretcher
gradus, -us, m., step; stairway
graece, in the Greek language
gratia, -ae, f., thanks; grace
gratis, freely
gratus, -a, -um, dear to + **dative**
gravis, -e, heavy; serious
graviter, seriously
grex, gregis, m., flock; herd
gubernaculum, -i, n., rudder
gubernator, -oris, m., helmsman
gusto (1), to taste; eat

H

habeo (2), -ui, -itum, to have; consider
habitaculum, -i, n., small room; cell
habito (1), to inhabit
haec, see **hic**
haesito (1), to hesitate; doubt
hebraeus, -a, -um, Hebrew, Aramaic
hebraicus, -a, -um, see **hebraeus**
heresis, -is, f., sect
heri, yesterday
hereditas, -tatis, f., inheritance
hic, haec, hoc, this/these
hiemo (1), to spend the winter
hiems, -is, f., winter
Hierosolymitas, -ae, m., resident of the city of Jerusalem
hodie, today
hodiernus, -a, -um, of this day; today's
homicida, -ae, m., a murderer
homo, -inis, m., human being; man
honestus, -a, -um, of good standing; well placed; high society
honestas, -tatis, f., respectability
honorabilis, -e, respectable
honor, -oris, m., honor
honorifico (1), to honor; glorify
honoro (1), to honor
hora, -ae, f., time; hour
hortor, -ari, hortatus sum, to encourage; exhort
hospitor, -ari, hospitatus sum, to be a guest
hospes, -itis, m/**f.,** visitor; guest
hospitium, -ii, n., hospitality
hostia, -ae, f., sacrificial animal
huc, to this place; hither
huiusmodi, of this kind
humane, kindly; humanely
humanitas, -tatis, f., human decency
humilio (1), to humble
humilitas, -tatis, f., humbleness

I

iaceo (2), -cui, -itum, to be lying down
iacto (1), to buffet; shake; brandish
iactura, -ae, f., a discarding; loss
iactus, -us, m., a throwing out
iam, already; straightaway; by now
ianua, -ae, f., door; gate
ibat, see **eo**
ibi, there, in that place
id, see **is**
īdem, eadem, idem, the same
ideo, on this account; therefore
idiota, -ae, m., layperson; common man
idolatria, -ae, f., idol worship
idolum, -i, n., image; idol
ieiunatio, -onis, f., fasting; time without eating
ieiunium, -ii, n., hunger
ieiuno (1), to fast
ieiunus, -a, -um, fasting; hungry
igitur, therefore
ignis, -is, m., fire
ignorantia, -ae, f., ignorance
ignoro (1), not to know; be ignorant of
ignotus, -a, -um, unknown
ille, illa, illud, that/those
illic, there; in that place
illuc, see **illic**

imber, ibris, m., rain
immolo (1), to slay as a sacrifice
impetus, -us, m., a sudden rush; movement against; an attack
impleo (2), -evi, -etum, to fill up; fulfill
in + ablative, in; on; + accusative, into
inanis, -e, empty; void
incido (3), -cĭdi, -cāsum, to fall into; reach
incipio (3), -cepi, -ceptum, to begin
incircumcisus, -a, -um, uncircumscised
incito (1), to stir up; arouse
includo (3), -clusi, -clusum, to lock up
incola, -ae, m., inhabitant; resident
incrasso (1), to thicken
incredibilis, -e, unbelievable
incredulus, -a, -um, not believing; incredulous
incubuo (3), -cubui, -cubitum, to lay on; lie on
inde, thereupon
indemnatus, -a, -um, unconvicted
indico (3), -dixi, -dictum, to call for
indico (1), to explain; reveal
indigeo (3), -ui, to be in need of + **ablative**
indignus, -a, -um, unworthy + **genitive**
induco (3), -duxi, -ductum, to lead in
induro (1), to harden
infans, -ntis, m., child; infant
infernum, -i, n., the underworld
infero, -ferre, -tuli, -latum, to bring into
infirmatus, -a, -um, weakened; ill
infirmitas, -tatis, f., illness
ingredior, -i, ingressus sum, to enter into; walk in
inhabito (1), to live in
inicio (3), -ieci, -iectum, to lay upon; throw onto
inimicus, -i, m., enemy
iniquitas, -tatis, f., injustice
iniquus, -a, -um, unjust
initium, -i, n., beginning; edge; corner
iniuria, -ae, f., injury
inmineo (2), to hang over; threaten; be near
inmobilis, -e, unmovable
inmundus, -a, -um, impure; unclean

inpingo (3), inpigi, inpactum, to force upon; run aground
inpendo (3), -di, -pensum, to pay
inpono (3), -posui, -positum, to place on
inpositio, -onis, f., laying on
inpossibilis, -e, impossible
inquieto (1), to inopportune; disturb
inquiro (3), -quisivi, -quisitum, to ask about; request
inquisitio, -onis, f., examination
inquit, inquunt, he/she/it says; they say
inrideo (3), -risi, -risum, to laugh at
insania, -ae, f., madness
insanio (4), -ivi or **-ii, -itum,** to be crazy; rage
insidiae, -arum, f., plot
insidior, -ari, insidiatus sum, to plot against + **dative**
insigne, -is, n., insignia
insilio (4), -ui, to jump toward or in; attack
insinuo (1), to make known
inspiro (1), to inspire; to excite
inspiratio, -onis, f., inspiration
instans, -ntis, be devoted to
insto, -stare, -stiti, -statum, to press on urgently; be devoted to
insula, -ae, f., insland
insuper, moreover
insurgo (3), -surrexi, -surrectum, to rise up
integer, -gra, -grum, pure; whole
intellego (3), -lexi, -lectum, to understand
intendo (3), -di, -tentum, to pay close attention to; stare at
inter + accusative, among; between
interemo (3), -emi, -emptum, to take out; kill
interficio (3), -feci, -fectum, to kill
interior, -ius, inside
intermissio, -onis, f., break; rest
interpello (1), to interrupt; confront
interpono (3), -posui, -positum, to bring up; make manifest; put forth
interpretor, -ari, interpretatus sum, to explain; translate

interrogatio, -onis, f., a questioning; interrogation
intra + accusative, within
intro (1), to enter into
intro, inside
introduco (3), -duxi, -ductum, to lead into
introeo (4), -ii or -ivi, -itum, to enter
introgredior, -i, introgressus sum, to enter
intueor, -ēri, intuitus sum, to look upon carefully
intus, within
invado (3), vasi, vasum, to enter upon; fall upon
invalesco (3), -valui, to grow strong; prevail
invenio (4), -vēni, -ventum, to find
invicem, in turn; see also **ad invicem**
invoco (1), to invoke
ipse, ipsa, ipsum, the very; self
ira, -ae, f., anger
iracundia, -ae, f., anger
iratus, -a, -um, angered
ire, see **eo**
is, ea, id, he/she/it; this
iste, ista, istud, that/this; these/those
ita, thus; so
itaque, and so; also
iter, itineris, n., road; journey
iterum, again
iubeo (2), iussi, iussum, to command; order
iucunditas, -tatis, f., joy; delight
iudex, -icis, m., judge
iudicium, -ii, n., judgment
iudico (1), to judge; pass judgement
iugum, -i, n., yoke
iumentum, -i, n., draught animal
iungo (3), iunxi, iunctum, to join together
iunctura, -ae, f., binding; rope
iuro (1), to swear an oath
iusiurandum, iurisiurandi, n., oath
iustitia, -ae, f., divine will; justice
iustus, -a, -um, just
iuvenis, -is, m/f. a young person
iuventus, -tutis, f., childhood
iuxta + **accusative,** close to; in accordance with

L

laboro (1), to struggle
lacrima, -ae, f., tear
laetor, -ari, laetatus sum, to be joyful; take delight
laetitia, -ae, f., joy; happiness
lampas, -adis, f., lamp
lancearius, -ii, m., lancer
languidus, -a, -um, sick
languor, -oris, m., disease; ailment
lapido (1), to stone
lapis, -idis, m., stone
lateo (2), -ui, to be concealed; hidden
latus, lateris, n., side
laudo (1), to praise
laus, laudis, f., praise
lavo, (1), lavatus or lotum, to wash
laxo (1), to untie
lectio, -onis, f., a reading
lectulum, -i, n., cot
legitimus, -a, -um, lawful
lego (3), legi, lectum, to pick; read; **in sailing**, to sail near the coast of
levo (1), to lift up
lex, legis, f., law; **when capitalized**, the Pentateuch
libellus, -i, m., little book; writ
libenter, freely; willingly; with pleasure
liber, -bri, m., book
libero (1), to set free
libertinus, -i, m., a freeman; manumitted former slave
licet, -ere, licuit, it is permitted + **dative and infinitive**
lictor, -oris, m., lictor
lignum, -i, n., wood; wooden club
ligo (1), to tie; bind
lingua, -ae, f., tongue; language

linteum, -i, n., linen cloth; table cloth
litigo (1), to quarrel
littera, -ae, f., a letter of the alphabet; **in the plural,** writing; literature, a letter
litus, -oris, n., shore
locus, -i, m., place; **in the plural, loca, -orum, n.,** places
longe, far from
loquor, -i, locutus sum, to speak
lorum, -i, n., rope; strap
lucrum, -i, n., gain; profit; goods
lumbus, -i, m., loin
lumen, -inis, n., light
luna, -ae, f., moon
lupus, -i, m., wolf
lux, lucis, m., light; dawn
lycaonice, in the Lycaonian language

M

magicus, -a, -um, magic
magis, more; even more; greater
magistratus, -us, m., official, magistrate
magnalia, -ium, n., great things
magnifico (1), to fuss over; make a big deal of
magnus, -a, -um, great; large
magus, -i, m., sorcerer
maiestas, -tatis, f., majesty; grandeur
maior, maius, greater; **maiores natu,** elders
malus, -a, -um, bad; evil
male, badly
maledico (3), -dixi, -dictum, to curse + **dative**
mandatum, -i, n., command
manduco (1), to eat
mane, f., indeclinable, morning; **as an adverb,** at dawn
maneo (2), -si, -sum, to remain; await
manifeste, openly; clearly
manifesto (1), to make clear; reveal; expose
manifestus, -a, -um, clear; obvious
manufactus, -a, -um, made by hand

manus, -us, f., hand
mare, -is, n., sea
mater, -tris, f., mother
maturius, soon enough; shortly
maxime, greatly; especially
maximus, -a, -um, greatest; largest
me, see **ego**
mecum, see **cum**
meditor, -ari, meditatus sum, to ponder; think about
medius, -a, -um, midst; middle
melior, -ius, better
mimini, meminisse, to remember + **genitive**
memoria, -ae, f., memory
mens, -ntis, f., mind
mensa, -ae, f., table
mensis, -is, m., month
mentior, -iri, mentitus sum, to lie; deceive; misrepresent
merces, -cedis, f., price; reward; payment
mergo (3), mersi, mersum, to cause to sink; **in the passive,** to sink
meridianus, -a, -um, midday; southern; **contra meridianum,** southward
metuo (3), -ui, -utum, to fear; respect
metus, -us, m., fear
meus, -a, -um, my; mine
migro (1), to depart; move
miles, -itis, m., soldier
milia, -ium, n. pl., + **genitive,** thousands
militia, -ae, f., service; military service
mina, -ae, f., threat
mino (1), to threaten
minime, hardly
minimus, -a, -um, least; smallest
minister, -tri, m., servant; assistant
ministerium, -ii, n., service; aid
ministro (1) + **dative,** to take care of; tend to
minus, see **quo** + **minus**
miror, -ari, miratus sum, to be astonished at
mitto (3), misi, missum, to send; send a message to

modicus, -a, -um, a little; **in modico,** shortly
modo, just now; recently
momentum, -i, n., moment; exact time
moneo (2), -ui, -itum, to warn; advise
mons, montis, m., mountain
monstro (1), to point out; show
monumentum, -i, n., grave; tomb
mora, -ae, f., delay
moror, -ari, moratus sum, to remain; stay
mos, moris, m., custom; in plural, character
morior, -i, mortuus sum, to die
mors, mortis, f., death
mortalis, -e, mortal
mortuus, -a, -um, dead
moveo (2), movi, motum, to move
mulier, -is, f., woman; wife
multiplico (1), to increase
multitudo, -inis, f., crowd of people
multus, -a, -um, much; many
multum, greatly; much
mundo (1), to heal; make clean
mundus, -a, -um, clean; innocent
mundus, -i, m. the world
municeps, -is, m., resident of a city
murmur, -is, n., murmur; grumbling
murus, -i, m., city wall
mustum, -i, n., new wine
muto (1), to change

N

nam, for
narro (1), to tell; narrate
nascor, -i, natus sum, to be born
nato (1), to swim
natio, -onis, f., nation
natus, -us, m., birth; **maiores natu,** greater in birth = ancestors
nauclerius, -i, m., ship's owner
nauta, -ae, m., sailor
navigatio, -onis, f., sailing
navigo (1), to sail; navigate
navis, -is, f., boat
ne, lest; not
nec, nor; **ne . . . ne,** neither . . . nor
necessarius, -a, -um, necessary; **as a noun,** relative
nex, necis, f., death; murder
nego (1), to deny; say . . . not
nemo, -inis, m./f., no one
nequam, indeclinable adjective, useless; worthless
nequaquam, hardly; not at all
neque, and not; **neque . . . neque,** neither . . . nor
nequitia, -ae, f., evildoing
nescio (4), -ii or -ivi, -itus, not to know
nihil, nothing
nihilum, see nihil
nisi, unless; if not
nobilior, -ius, more decent
nobilis, -e, well born; noble; worthy
nobiscum, see cum
noceo (2), -ui, nocitum, to harm
nolo, nolle, nolui, not to want; **imperatives noli or nolite with infinitive as the negative imperative; eg., nolite turbari,** don't be troubled
nomen, -inis, **n.,** name
non, not
nondum, not yet
nonne, no?, right? is it not so that?
nonus, -a, -um, ninth
nos, nostri/nostrum, nobis, nos, nobis, we, of us, etc.
nosco (3), novi, notum, to come to know; recognize; know how to + **infinitive**
nosse, = novisse < nosco
noster, -tra, -trum, our; ours
nosti, = novisti < nosco
notus, -a, -um, known; familiar
novissimus, -a, -um, most recent; last
novus, -a, -um, new
nox, noctis, f., night
nubis, -is, f., cloud
nudius, adverb from nudus, just barely
nudo (1), to strip bare; uncover

nudus, -a, -um, naked
nullus, -a, -um, no; none; not any
numerus, -i, m., number
numquam, never
numquid, interrogative to begin a question, what
nunc, now
nuntio (1), to announce; proclaim
nuper, recently
nutrio (4), -ii or -ivi, -itum, to raise; bring up

O

O, interjection, Oh
ob + accusative, on account of
obdormio (4), -ivi or -ii, -itum, to fall asleep
obeo (4), -ii or -ivi, -itum, to go meet; perish
obfero, -ferre, obtuli, oblatum, to bring before; offer; exhibit
oblatio, -onis, f., an offering
obligatio, -onis, f., obligation
obnoxius, -a, -um, punishable by + **genitive**
oboedio (4), -ivi, -itum, to be obedient to + **dative**
obsecro (1), to implore; beg
obstupesco (3), -pui, to be astonished
obtentus, -us, m., pretense
obtineo (2), -tinui, -tentum, to hold fast
obumbro (1), to cast a shadow on
obvio (1), to impede; confront; meet
obvius, -a, -um, at hand to meet
occido (3), -cidi, -casum, to fall, sink; sit down
occīdo (3), -cīdi, -cīsum, to kill
occisio, -onis, f., slaughter
occulte, secretly
occurro (3), -curri or -cucurri, -cursum, to meet; encounter + **dative**
octavus, -a, -um, eighth
octo, eight
oculus, -i, m., eye

offendiculum, -i, n., a trifling offense
omnino, entirely
omnis, -e, all; each; every
onus, -eris, n., burden; freight
operor, -ari, operatus sum, to perform
opifex, -cis, m., worker; craftsmen
oportet (2), -uit, to be necessary; appropriate
opportunus, -a, -um, opportune; suitable
opprimo (3), -pressi, -pressum, to afflict; overwhelm
opto (1), to wish; pray for
optimus, -a, -um, best
opus, -eris, n., work; task; duty; a need for + **dative**
oratio, -onis, f., prayer
orator, -oris, m., speaker; lawyer
orbis, -is, m., orb; **orbis terrarum,** the world
ordo, -inis, m., line; order
oro (1), to pray
os, oris, n., mouth; face; presence
osculor, -ari, osculatus sum, to kiss
ostendo (3), -i, -tus or -sum, to show
ostium, -i, n., door; entrance
ovis, -is, f., sheep

P

paene, almost
paenitentia, -ae, f., repentance
paeniteor, -eri, to repent
panis, -is, m., bread; loaf
paralyticus, -i, m., paralytic
parceo (3), -ui, to spare + **dative**
pareo (3), -ui, -itum, to appear; be at hand; be obedient to; arrive at
paries, parietis, m., wall
pariter, equally; alongside
paro (1), to make ready; prepare
pars, partis, f., part; area
parvus, -a, -um, small
Pascha, -atis, f., Passover
pasco (3), pavi, pastum, to feed; pasture;

in the passive voice, to graze
passibilis, -e, capable of suffering; suffering
passio, -onis, f., suffering
passus, -us, m., a step; pace; five feet
pater, -tris, m., father
paternus, -a, -um, paternal
patienter, with endurance; submissively
patior, -i, passus sum, to suffer; endure
patria, -ae, f., fatherland
patriarcha, -ae, m., patriarch
patrius, -a, -um, fatherly
pauci, -ae, -a, few
pax, pacis, f., peace
peccator, -oris, m., a sinner
peccatum, -i, n., a sin
pecco (1), to sin
pecunia, -ae, f., money
pelagus, -i, n., sea
pendeo (2), pependi, to depend; hang down from
Pentecoste, accusative, -n, + dies, the Day of Pentecost
pentecostes, fifty
per + accusative, through; by means of; **per ter,** a third time
perago (3), -egi, -actum, to complete
peragro (1), to walk through; traverse
perambulo (1), to journey
percipio (3), -cepi, -ceptum, to receive; perceive
percutio (3), -cussi, -cussum, to strike; beat
perditio, -onis, f., waste; perdition
perduco (3), -duxi, -ductum, to lead through
perduro (1), to abide; remain
pergo (3), -rexi, -rectum, to travel through; come; go
perhibeo (3), -ui, -hibitum, to hold forth; offer; tell
pereo (4), -ii or -ivi, -itum, to perish
periclito (1), to be in danger
perfero, -ferre, -tuli, -latum, to bring to
permaneo (2), -mansi, -mansum, to remain to the end; endure

permissus, -us, m., permission
permitto (3), -misi, -missum, to allow + **dative**
persequor, -i, persecutus sum, to follow after; look for; persecute; hound
persevero (1), to persist; persevere
persona, -ae, f., person
perspicio (4), -spexi, -spectum, to see through; understand
persuadeo (2), -si, -sum, to persuade + **dative**
pertranseo (4), -ii or -ivi, -itum, to pass through
pervenio (4), -veni, -ventum, to arrive
perversus, -a, -um, evil; wrong
pes, pedis, m., foot
pessimus, -a, -um, worse
pestiferus, -a, -um, obnoxious; destructive
peto (3), -ii or -ivi, -itum, to seek; ask for
Pharisaeus, -i, m., a Pharisee
philosophus, -i, m., philosopher
pietas, -tatis, f., piety
pigritor, -ari, pigritatus sum, to be slow; delay
placeo (3), -ui, -itum, to be pleasing to + **dative**
plaga, -ae, f., wound; blow; ailment
planctus, -us, m., wailing; grieving
planta, -ae, f., sole of the foot
platea, -ae, f., broad street; major road
plebs, -is, f., the people; crowd
plene, fully
plenus, -a, -um, filled by; full of + **ablative or genitive**
plurimus, -a, -um, very many; very much; **in the plural,** the majority
plus, pluris, more
pluvia, -ae, f., rain
poeta, -ae, m., poet
pono (3), posui, positum, to put; place
ponticus, -a, -um, of Pontus
populus, -i, m., people; the common people
porta, -ae, f., gate
porticus, -us, f., portico; walkway
porto (1), to bring; carry

portus, -us, m., harbor; port
possessio, -onis, f., possession; land
possessor, -oris, m., owner
possibilis, -e, doable; possible
possideo (3), -sedi, -sessum, to own
possum, posse, potui, to be able
post + accusative, after; behind; **as an adv.,** after
posteaquam, after
posterus, -a, -um, following; after; next
postquam, after
postulo (1), to ask for; seek
potens, -ntis, powerful
potestas, -tatis, f., power; authority
potius, rather
prae + ablative, before; in front of; **as an adv.,** before; previously
praebeo (2), -bui, -bitum, to present; show
praecedo (3), -cessi, -cessum, to go on before; lead the way
praeceptum, -i, n., commandment; order; precept; teaching
praecingo (3), -cinxi, -cinctum, to bind up
praecipio (3), -cepi, -ceptum, to instruct; order + **dative**
praedium, -ii, n., estate
praedico (1), to preach
praedico (3), -dixi, -dictum, to predict
praenuntio (1), to foretell; announce beforehand + **de + ablative**
praeordino (1), to chose beforehand; preordain
praeparo (1), to make ready; equip
praepositus, -i, m., superintendent; chief
praeputium, -ii, n., foreskin
praescio (4), -ivi, -scitum, to know before; already know
praescientia, -ae, f., foreknowledge
praesens, -ntis, ready at hand; present
praeses, -idis, m., governor; ruler of a district
praesto (1), -stiti, -statum, to stand; maintain; present to
praesto, indeclinable adjective, available; at hand

praeter + accusative, besides; except for
praetereo (4), -ii or -ivi, -itum, to pass by; make one's way
praeteritus, -a, -um, previous
praeterquam, besides; other than
praetorium, -ii, n., governor's headquarters; governor's body guard; governor's custody
praevaricor, -ari, praevaricatus sum, to deceive; dissemble; lie
pravus, -a, -um, depraved
precor, -ari, precatus sum, to pray
presbyterus, -i, m., an elder
pretium, -ii, n. price
pretiosiorem, see pretiosus
pretiosus, -a, -um, valuable
primus, -a, -um, first
princeps, -cipis, m., leader
principalis, -e, leading; most important
priusquam, before
pro + ablative, before; on behalf of; **as an adverb,** before
probo (1), to approve; prove
procedo (3), -cessi, -cessum, to go forth
procido (3), -cidi, to fall before; fall forward
proconsul, -is, m., governor
procumbo (3), -cubui, -cubitum, to lean down; fall forward
prodigium, -ii, n., prodigy; wonderous sign
proditor, -oris, m., traitor
produco (3), -duxi, -ductum, to lead forth; put on display
professio, -onis, f., acknowledgement; declaration
proficiscor, -i, profectus sum, to set out
prohibeo (3), -hibui, -hibitum, to prevent; hold back
proicio (3), -ieci, -iectum, to cast out in front of
proles, -is, f., child
promissio, -onis, f., promise
promissus, -us, m., a promise; an order
prope, nearby

propello (3), -puli, -pulsum, to drive on
propheta, -ae, m., prophet
propheto (1), to prophesy
propono (3), -posui, -positum, to place before; prefer
propositum, -i, n., resolution; objective
propter + accusative, on account of
propterea, for that reason; **propterea quod,** because
prora, -ae, f., the front of a ship
protestor, -ari, protestatus sum, to declare publicly
protinus, immediately
protraho (3), -traxi, -tractum, to draw out; extend
prout, insofar as
provideo (2), -vidi, -visum, to foresee
providentia, -ae, f., foresight
provincia, -ae, f., province
proximus, -a, -um, nearby
proximus, -i, m., a neighbor
prudens, -ntis, having foreknowledge; wise
psalmus, -i, m., a psalm; **Psalmi, -orum, m. pl.,** (the book of) Psalms
pseudopropheta, -ae, m., false prophet
publicus, -a, -um, public
publice, openly; publicly
puella, -ae, f., girl
puer, -i, m., boy
pugno (1), to fight
pulso (1), to beat; pound
pulvis, -eris, m., dust
punio (4), -ivi, -itum, to punish
puppis, -is, f., stern
purifico (1), to clean
purificatio, -onis, f., the act of cleaning; purification
purpurarius, -a, -um, having to do with purple dye; a purple dye merchant
pusillum, a little
puto (1), to think; reckon
pyra, -ae, f., a (controlled) fire; camp fire
python, -onis, prophetic

Q

quadraginta, forty
quadringenti, -ae, -a, forty
quadrupedius, -a, -um, four-footed
quaero (3), quaesivi, quaestum, to ask for; seek
quaestio, -onis, f., inquiry; question
quaestus, -us, m., gain; livelihood; occupation
qualis, -e, what sort; such a sort
qualiter, just as; in what manner
quam, how; than
quamvis, however much
quantus, -a, -um, how many; as many
quapropter, for which reason
quartadecimus, -a, -um, fourteenth
quare, why
quartanus, -a, -um, fourth
quasi, as if; like; about
quaternio, -onis, f., body of four soldiers
quattuor, four
quemadmodum, just as; how
qui, quae, quod, who, which
quia, because; since; that
quicumque, quaecumque, quodcumque, whosoever; whatsoever
quid, why? what?
quidam, quaedam, quod[d]am, a certain; some; a/n
quidem, indeed; in fact
quidnam, what?; whatsover?
quiesco (3), quievi, quietum, to rest; keep still
quindecim, fifteen
quinquaginta, fifty
quinque, five
quis, quid, who, what?
quislibet, quidlibet, who/what have you; ordinary
quisnam, quidnam, whoever, whatever
quisquam, quaequam, quicquam or

quidquam, anyone; anything
quisquis, quidquid, whosoever, whatsoever
quo, whereby; to what place; whither
quoadusque, up until; until which point
quod, because; that; **quod si**, but if; **or a form of qui**
quominus, that not; from
quomodo, how
quoniam, since; that
quoque, and also
quot, how many
quotquot, as many as

R

rado (3), rasi, rasum, to shave
rapio (3), -ui, -tum, to carry off by force; steal; rescue
ratio, -onis, f., account; explanation; **sine ratione**, inappropriate
reaedifico (1), to rebuild
recedo (3), -cessi, -cessum, to withdraw
recipio (3), -cepi, -ceptum, to take back; recover
reconcilio (1), to restore; bring back
recordor, -ari, recordatus sum, to remember
recte, correctly; properly
rectus, -a, -um, straight
recumbo (3), -cubui, to lay down; recline at a table
recuso (1), to refuse; deny
redigo (3), -egi, -actum, to reduce to; bring back
redargutio, -onis, f., refutation
reddo (3), -didi, -ditum, to give back; render; offer up
redemptor, -oris, m., redeemer
redeo (4), -ii or -ivi, -itum, to go back; return
refero, -ferre, rettuli, relatum, to bear back; report
reficio (3), -feci, -fectum, to restore

refrigerium, -i, n., cooling; renewal
refulgeo (3), -si, to shine
rego (3), regi, rectum, to rule over
regia, -ae, f., palace
regius, -a, -um, royal
rex, regis, m., king
regina, -ae, f., queen
regio, -onis, f., area; region
regnum, -i, n., kingdom
religio, -onis, f., religion; religious practice
religiosus, -a, -um, devout; observant
relinquo (3), -liqui, -lectum, to leave behind
reliquus, -a, -um, the remaining; the other
remaneo (3), -mansi, -mansum, to stay behind
remissio, -onis, f., forgiveness; remission
remitto (3), -misi, -missum, to send back
reppello (3), -puli, -pulsum, to push back; reject
repente, suddenly
repleo (2), -evi, -etum, to fill up
reppulit, see repello
reprobo (1), to disapprove of; condemn; reject
repromitto (3), -misi, -missum, to make a promise again
repromissio, -onis, f., a promise
reptile, -is, n., snake
repugno (1), to fight against; resist
reputo (1), to think of; reckon
requies, -ei, f., silence; calm; rest
requiesco (3), -evi, -etum, to rest
requietio, -onis, f., rest; repose
requiro (3), -quisii or -quisivi, -quisitum, to look for; ask for
res, rei, f., matter
rescindo (3), -scidi, -scissum, to rescind; repeal
rescio (4), -scivi, -scitum, to come to know; know for sure
resideo (3), -sedi, resessum, to sit; to sit up
resisto (3), -sisti, -sistum, to resist + dative
respicio (3), -spexi, -spectum, to have

thought for; consider; look at; face
respondeo (3), -di, -sum, to answer
responsum, -i, **n.,** answer
restituo (3), -stitui, -stitutum, to restore; make whole
restitutio, -onis, f., restoration
resurgo (3), -rexi, -rectum, to rise up again
resurrectio, -onis, f., resurrection
resuscito (1), to revive; renew
retineo (3), -tinui, -tentum, to hold back; keep
rettulerunt see refero
revertor, -i, reversus sum, to turn back; return; go away
revinco (3), -vici, -victum, to defeat thoroughly
rex, regis, m., king
rogo (1), to ask
Romanus, -a, -um, Roman
ruber, -bra, -brum, red
rubus, -i, **m.,** bush
rursum, rursus, again

Sabbatum, -i, **n.,** the Sabbath; also **Sabbata**
sacerdos, -otis, m., priest; temple official
sacerdotalis, -e, pristly
sacrifico (1), to offer a sacrifice
sacrilegus, -a, -um, impious
Sadduces, -ei, m., a Sadducee
saeculum, -i, **n.,** generation; age; the people of an age
saltim, at least; at any event
salus, -utis, f. safety; salvation
salutare, -is, n., salvation
saluto (1), to greet; bless; pay ones repects to
salvator, -oris, m., savior
salvo, (1), to save
salvus, -a, -um, safe; saved
sanctifico (1), to make holy; sanctify; purify
sanctus, -a, -um, holy
sanguis, -inis, m., blood
sanitas, -tatis, -i, health
sano (1), to heal; make whole
sanus, -a, -um, healthy; whole
sapientia, -ae, f., wisdom
sapio (3), -ivi or -ii, to know; be wise about
sarmentorum, -i, **n.,** twig; small branch
satio (1), to fulfill; satiate
satis, enough
satisfacio (3), -feci, -factum, to fulfill; satisfy
scabillum, -i, **n.,** footstool
scapha, -ae, f., small boat; skiff
scenofactoria, -ae, f., tent making
scevas, -ae, m., exorcist
scindo (3), scidi, scissum, to cut; tear
scio (4), -ii or -ivi, -itum, to know
scola, -ae, f., school
scriba, -ae, m., a scribe
scribo (3), scripsi, scriptum, to write
scriptura, -ae, f., writing; Scripture
scruto (1), to search
secedo (3), -cessi, -cessum, to go away; depart; go apart
secta, -ae, f., sect
sector, -ari, sectatus sum, to follow eagerly; run after
secum, see cum
secundum + accusative, according to; along
secundus, -a, -um, following; second; favorable; **secundo,** a second time
secus + accusative, along; near
sed, but
sedeo (3), sedi, sessum, to sit
sedis, -is, f., seat; chair; throne
seditio, -onis, f., insurrection; disagreement
sedo (1), to calm; settle; calm
seduco (3), -duxi, -ductum, to lead astray
segrego, (1), to separate out
semen, -inis, n., seed

semet, compound intensive pronoun from **se** + **met,** his/her/their very self/selves. Note also forms such as **temet, vosmet,** etc. (often with the corresponding form of **ipse, -a, -um** attached at the end)
semicintium, -ii, n., work apron
seminiverbius, -i, m., a word-seeder; one who spreads new words around
semper, always
senior, -is, m., an elder; **seniores,** elders
sententia, -ae, f., thought; opinion
sentio (4), sensi, sensum, to feel; perceive
seorsum, apart; separately; privately
separo (1), to separate; go away
sepelio (4), -ii or -ivi, sepultum, to bury; give the funeral rites
septem, seven
septimus, -a, -um, seventh
septuaginta, seventy
sepulcrum, -i, n., tomb
sepultus, see **sepelio**
sequor, -i, secutus sum, to follow; come next
sermo, -onis, m., talk; speech
serpens, -ntis, m./f., serpent; snake
servio (4), -ivi, -itum, to serve + **dative**
servitus, -tutis, f., service; slavery
servo (1), to save; keep
servus, -i, m., slave; servant
sex, six
sextus, -a, -um, six
si, if
sibimet, see **semet**
sic, thus; so
sicarius, -ii, m., knife man; assassin
sicco (1), to dry out
sicut, thus; just as
Sidonius, -a, -um, of the city of Sidon; inhabitant of Sidon
sidus, -eris, n., star
significo (1), to indicate; signify
signum, -i, n., sign; evidence
silentium, -ii, n., silence
similis, -e, like; similar to
simplicitas, -tatis, f., simplicity

simul, at the same time
simulacrum, -i, n., image; idol
sine + ablative, without
singulis, one at a time, individually
singulus, -a, -um, single; individual; **per singula,** in detail; point by point
sinister, -tra, -trum, left; on the left
sino (3), sivi, situm, to allow, permit
sinum, -i, n., bay
sobrietas, -tatis, f., sobriety; prudence
sol, -is, m., sun
solitudo, -inis, f., solitude; wilderness
solummodo, alone; individually
solus, -a, -um, alone; sole; only
solvo (3), -ui or -ii, -utum, to set free; break up; untie; break apart
somnio (1), to dream
somnium, -ii, n., dream
somnus, -i, m., sleep
sonus, -i, m., sound
soror, -oris, f., sister
sors, sortis, f., lot; roll of the dice
sortior, -iri, sortitus sum, to obtain by lot
spatium, -ii, n., space; time
speciosus, -a, -um, beautiful
spero (1), to hope; expect
spes, -ei, f., expectation; hope
spiritus, -us, m., spirit
splendor, -oris, m., brightness
sporta, -ae, f., basket
squama, -ae, f., scale
statim, immediately
statuo (3), statui, statutum, to set up; fix; determine
sterno (3), stravi, stratum, to spread; roll up; make [a bed]
stimulus, -i, m., goad; proad
stŏ (1), steti, statum, to stand
stoicus, -i, m., a stoic philosopher
strideo (3), -i, to hiss; shriek
stringo (3), strinxi, strictum, to tie up
studeo (3), -ui, to be eager for; study + **dative**
stupefacio (3), -feci, -factum, to strike dumb; stun

stupeo (3), -ui, to be astonished
stupor, -oris, m., astonishment
suadeo (3), -si, -sum, to persuade
sub + ablative, under
subduco (3), -duxi, -ductum, to bring up; dock
subicio (3), -ieci, -iectum, to throw underneath; submit; subject
subito, immediately
submitto (3), -misi, -missum, to put underneath; bring as evidence; **in sailing,** lower a sounding line
subnavigo (1), to sail on the leeward side
subsequor, -i, -secutum, to follow from behind
substantia, -ae, f., resource; wealth
subterfugio (3), -fūgi, to escape; evade
subtraho (3), -traxi, -tractum, to withhold
subverto (3), -verti, -versum, to subvert; cause to rebel
successor, -oris, m., successor
sudarium, -ii, n., hankerchief
suffero, -ferre, sustuli, sublatum, to endure; suffer
suffoco (1), to strangle; suffocate
sui, sibi, se, se, 3rd person reflexive pronoun
sum, esse, fui, futurum, to be
summa, -ae, f., sum total; sum (of money)
sumo (3), sumpsi, sumptum, to take up
super + **accusative or ablative,** upon; on; concerning
superior, -ius, higher
superstitio, -onis, f., belief; superstition
superstitiosus, -a, -um, superstitious; credulous
supervenio (4), -vēni, -ventum, to come to; come upon; intervene
supra, adverb or adjective, above; beyond
suprascriptio, -onis, f., inscription
surgo (3), -rexi, -rectum, to get up; rise up
sursum, upward
suscipio (3), -cepi, -ceptum, to undertake; take on; receive
suscito (1), to awaken
suspendo (3), -di, -sum, to hang on; fix on
suspicio (3), -spexi, -spectum, to look up to; honor
suspicor, -ari, suspicatus sum, to mistrust; suspect
sustineo (2), -tinui, to hold up and wait for; stop
sustul- , **see tollo**
suus, -a, -um, his/her/its own
synagoga, -ae, f., synagogue; gathering place
Syrtis, -is, f., the Syrtis sandbar

tabernaculum, -i, n., tent
taberna, -ae, f., hut
tabula, -ae, f., board; plank
taceo (3), -ui, -itum, to be silent
talis, -e, such; so great a(n)
tamquam, as; like; as if
tantum, only
tantus, -a, -um, such; so great
tarde, slowly; late
tardus, -a, -um, slow
taurus, -i, m., bull
tecum, see cum
temere, rashly
temetipsum, see semetipsum
tempestas, -atis, f., storm; weather
templum, -i, n., temple; **when capitalized,** the temple in Jerusalem
temptatio, -onis, f., temptation; test, trial
tempto, (1), to tempt; put to the test
tempus, -oris, n., time
tendo (3), tetendi, tensus or **tentum,** to stretch out; strive to
tenebra, -ae, f., darkness; gloom
teneo (2), -ui, -ntum, to hold
ter, per ter, a third time
terminus, -i, m., boundary line
terra, -ae, f., land; earth
terraemotus, -i, m., earthquake
tertius, -a, -um, third

testificor, -ari, testificatus sum, to bear witness; attest
testimonium, -i, n., witness; evidence
testis, -is, m./f., witness
testor, -ari, testatus sum, to testify; bear witness
tetrarcha, -ae, m., tetrarch
theatrum, -i, n., theater
timefactus, -a, -um, frightened
timor, -oris, m., fear
timoratus, -a, -um, reverent; devout
timeo (3), -ui, to be reverent toward; fear
tollo (3), sustuli, sublatum, to raise up; rescue; **in sailing**, set sail
tollo (3), sustuli, sublatum, to lift up; destroy
torqueo (3), -si, -tum, to torture
tondeo (3), totondi, tonsum, to cut one's hair off; tonsure
totus, -a, -um, whole; entire
tracto (1), to treat; consider
traditio, -onis, f., a handing over; surrender
trado (3), -didi, -ditum, to hand over; betray
traho (3), traxi, tractum, to draw; drag
trans + accusative, across; through
transigo (3), -egi, -actum, to conclude; bring to an end; go through
transeo (4), -ii or -ivi, -itum, to pass through
transfero, -ferre, -tuli, -latum, to carry across; transport
transfreto (1), to transport; cross over
transnavigo (1), to sail through; sail by
transpono (3), -posui, -positum, to conduct to; put on
tremefactus, -a, -um, terrified
tres, tria, three
tribulatio, -onis, f., tribulation
tribunal, -is, n., tribunal
tribunus, -i, m., tribune; politician
tribus, -us, m., tribe
triduum, -i, n., three days
triennium, three years

triticum, -i, n., grain; wheat
tu, tui, tibi, te, te, you (sg.), of you, etc.
tumor, -oris, m., a swelling
tumultus, -us, m., uproar
tunc, then; thereupon
tunica, -ae, f., tunic; shirt
turba, -ae, f., crowd
turbatio, -onis, f., disturbance
turbo (1), to stir up; disturb
tutus, -a, um, safe
tuus, -a, -um, your (sg.); yours
typhonicus, -a, -um, gale force

u

ubi, where; when
ubique, everywhere
ullus, -a, -um, any; anyone, anything
ultimus, -a, -um, farthest; most remote.
ultio, -onis, f., revenge
ultra + accusative, beyond
ultra, any longer, anymore
ultro, on its own
umbra, -ae, f., shade
unā + cum, together with
unde, whence
undecim, eleven
ungo (3), unxi, unctum, to annoint; give power to
unianimis, -e, of one mind
unianimiter, in one mind; unanimously
universus, -a, -um, all; entire
unus, -a, -um, one
unusquisque, unaquisque, unumquidque, each one
urbs, -is, f., town
usque, up until + **ad** or **in**; **usque ad tempus**, for a while
ut, + indicative, when; since; + **subjunctive**, that, so that
utor, -i, usus sum, to use
uterus, -i, m., womb
uterque, utraque, utrumque, each one; both

uti, see ut
utilis, -e, useful; valuable
utique, most assuredly
uxor, -oris, f., wife

vaco (1), to make time for
vado (3), to go; walk
valde, really; very much; powerfully
valedico (3), to say good-bye
valefaciens, bidding farewell
valeo (3), -ui, valiturum, to be healthy; prevail
valide, see valde
validus, -a, -um, powerful
vanus, -a, -um, vain
vapor, -oris, m., exhalation; billow
vas, vasis, n., baggage
vehementer, violently
vehemens, -ntis, furious; powerful
vel, or; either; perhaps
velint, see volo
velociter, swiftly
velut, like
vendo (3), vendidi, venditum, to sell
venio (4), vēni, ventum, to come
ventus, -i, m., wind; a windstorm
venundatum, -i, n., money from a sale; profit
verbum, -i, n., word; speech
vere, truly
vereor, -ēri, veritus sum, to fear
veritas, -tatis, f., truth
vermis, -is, m., worm
vero, truly; but
verus, -a, -um, true; real
vespera, -ae, f., evening
vester, -tra, -trum, you (pl.); yours
vestimentum, -i, n., clothes
vestio (4), -ii or -ivi, -itum, to dress
vestis, -is, f., clothing; attire
vestitus, -a, -um, dressed
veto (1), to prevent; deny

vexo (1), to disturb; make ill; torment
via, -ae, f., way; road
vicinus, -a, -um, neighboring
victima, -ae, f., sacrificial victim; offering
vicus, -i, m., village; district
video (2), vidi, visum, to see; videtur, it seems right
vidua, -ae, f., widow
vigilo (1), to be awake; be on guard; keep watch
viginti, twenty
vincio (4), vinxi, -ctum, to bind
vinctus, -i, m., a prisoner
vinculum, -i, n., chain
vindico (1), to defend; avenge + dative
vinum, -i, n., wine
violo (1), to injure; dishonor
vipera, -ae, f., snake
vir, -i, m., man
virga, -ae, f., walking stick; rod
virgo, -inis, f., young girl; daughter
virtus, -tutis, f., power
vis, vis, —, accusative vim, ablative vi, power; violence
viscera, -orum, n., innards; internal organs; guts
visio, -onis, f., vision
visito (1), to pay a visit to
visus, -us, m., vision; dream
vita, -ae, f., life
vitulus, -i, m., male calf
vivifico (1), to revive; live
vivo (3), vixi, victum, to live
vix, scarcely
vobiscum, see cum
vocifero (1), to raise a shout
voco (1), to call
volatilis, -e, flying
volo, velle, volui, voliturum, to wish; want
voluntas, -tatis, f., will
vos, vestri/vestrum/vobis, vos, vobis, you (pl.), of you, etc.
votum, -i, n., prayer; offering
vox, -cis, f., voice

vulgus, -i, m., mob; crowd
vulnero (1), to wound
vultis, 2nd person plural present indicative of volo

Z

zelo (1), to be eager; enthusiastic
zelotes, -ae, m., an eager one
zelus, -i, m., zeal; passion
zona, -ae, f., belt

APPENDIX A: THREE ACCOUNTS OF PAUL'S CONVERSION

	A	B	C
1	9:3-20 Luke tells the story	22:6-16 Paul's own words before the Jerusalem Brethren	26:12-18 Paul's own words before the Roman governor
	³ Et cum iter [Saulus] faceret, contigit ut adpropinquaret Damasco. Et subito circumfulsit eum lux de caelo.	⁶ Factum est autem eunte me et adpropinquante Damasco mediā die subito de caelo circumfulsit me lux copiosa,	¹² In quibus dum irem Damascum cum potestate et permissu principum sacerdotum, ¹³die mediā in viā vidi, rex, de caelo supra splendorem solis circumfulsisse me lumen et eos qui mecum simul erant.
2	⁴ Et cadens in terram audivit vocem, dicentem sibi, "Saule, Saule! Quid me persequĕris?"	⁷ et decidens in terram audivi vocem dicentem mihi, "Saule, Saule! Quid me persequĕris?"	¹⁴ Omnesque nos cum decidissemus in terram, audivi vocem loquentem mihi hebraicā linguā: "Saule, Saule, quid me persequeris?
3			¹⁵ Durum est tibi contra stimulum calcitrare."
4	⁵ Qui dixit, "Quis es, Domine?" Et ille [dixit], "Ego sum Iesus, quem tu persequĕris."	⁸ Ego autem respondi, "Quis es, Domine?" Dixitque ad me, "Ego sum Iesus Nazarenus quem tu persequĕris."	Ego autem dixi, "Quis es, Domine?" Dominus autem dixit, "Ego sum Iesus, quem tu persequĕris.¹⁶
5		⁹ Et qui mecum erant lumen quidem viderunt, vocem autem non audierunt eius qui loquebatur mecum.	
6	⁶ Et tremens ac stupdens dixit, "Domine, quid me vis facere?"	¹⁰ Et dixi, "Quid faciam, Domine?"	
7	⁷ "Sed surge et ingredere civitatem, et dicetur tibi quid te oporteat facere."	Dominus autem dixit ad me, "Surgens, vade Damascum, et ibi tibi dicetur de omnibus quae te oporteat facere."	Sed exsurge, et sta super pedes tuos.
8			Ad hoc enim apparui tibi, ut constituam te ministrum et testem eorum quae vidisti et eorum quibus apparebo tibi, ¹⁷ eripiens te de populo et Gentibus, in quas nunc ego mitto te ¹⁸ aperire oculos eorum ut convertantur a tenebris ad lucem et de potestate Satanae ad Deum, ut accipiant remissionem peccatorum et sortem inter sanctos per fidem quae est in me."
9	Viri autem illi qui comitabantur cum eo stabant stupefacti, audientes quidem vocem, neminem autem videntes.		

10	⁸Surrexit autem Saulus de terrā apertisque oculis nihil videbat. Ad manūs autem illum trahentes introduxerunt Damascum.	¹¹Et cum non viderem prae claritate luminis illius, ad manum deductus a comitibus veni Damascum.	
11	⁹Et erat tribus diebus non videns, et non manducavit neque bibit.		
12	¹⁰Erat autem quidam discipulus Damasci, nomine Ananias,	¹²Ananias autem quidam, vir secundum Legem testimonium habens ab omnibus habitantibus Iudaeis,	
13	et dixit ad illum in visu Dominus, "Anania?" At ille ait, "Ecce: ego, Domine." ¹¹Et Dominus ad illum, "Surgens, vade in vicum qui vocatur Rectus, et quaere in domo Iudae Saulum nomine, Tarsensem. Ecce enim: orat."		
14	¹²Et vidit virum, Ananiam nomine, introeuntem et inponentem sibi manūs ut visum recipiat. ¹³Respondit autem Ananias, "Domine, audivi a multis de viro hōc quanta mala sanctis tuis fecerit in Hierusalem, ¹⁴et hic habet potestatem a principibus sacerdotum alligandi omnes qui invocant nomen tuum." ¹⁵Dixit autem ad eum Dominus, "Vade, quoniam vas electionis est mihi iste, ut portet nomen meum coram gentibus et regibus et filiis Israhel. ¹⁶Ego enim ostendam illi quanta oporteat eum pro nomine meo pati."		
15	¹⁷Et abiit Ananias, et introivit in domum, et inponens ei manūs dixit, "Saule, frater, Dominus misit me Iesus qui apparuit tibi in viā quā veniebas, ut videas et implearis Spiritu Sancto. ¹⁸Et confestim ceciderunt ab oculis eius tamquam squamae, et visum recepit.	¹³veniens ad me et adstans dixit mihi, "Saule, frater, respice." Et ego eādem horā respexi in eum.	
16		¹⁴At ille dixit, "Deus patrum nostrorum praeordinavit te ut cognosceres voluntatem eius, et videres iustum et audires vocem ex ore eius¹⁵ quia eris testis illius ad omnes homines eorum quae vidisti et audisti.	
17	Et surgens baptizatus est. ¹⁹Et cum accepisset cibum, confortatus est. Fuit autem cum discipulis qui erant Damasci per dies aliquot. ²⁰Et continuo in synagogis praedicabat Iesum, quoniam hic est Filius Dei.	¹⁶Et nunc quid moraris? Exsurge, baptizare et ablue peccata tua, invocato nomine ipsius."	

APPENDIX A

Most of the discrepancies in the three accounts are insignificant or the result of the different contexts in which they were narrated. One, however, has been thought to be more important.

Line 8C in this table, *ad hoc enim apparui tibi* begins a major departure from the first two accounts where Jesus explains Paul's mission first to Ananias, which Ananias then passes on to Paul.

In this last version, Ananias is completely omitted from the story and Jesus explains his mission to Paul directly. But we should not forget the setting of this account. Paul is making his defense before the newly installed Roman governor, Festus. He wouldn't have benefited in the least from knowing that there was an intermediary between Jesus and Paul. Inasmuch as Ananias got his information from Jesus in the other versions, it's very much the same to say Paul heard it from Jesus. He would have seen no reason to clutter up his speech with a small point that would have not advanced his defense before a Roman.

APPENDIX B: SOURCES FOR PAUL'S DEATH

Acts appears to modern readers to end abruptly. Paul has arrived in Rome, but Luke tells us nothing about his trial, what other travels he might have had, or his ultimate fate. There are hints in his letters (particularly Timothy) that suggest Paul was released by Nero at the trial in Rome and went on a fourth missionary journey to Spain, Crete, Ephesus, Miletus, Troas, various cities in Macedonia, and Corinth. He was then rearrested somewhere and brought back to Rome, this time to be executed. The following are some of the major but non-canonical sources for his death.

Clement of Rome

Clement is traditionally held to be the first bishop of Rome, an office he held from AD 88 until his death in AD 99. Sometime during his tenure, he wrote a letter to Christians in Corinth concerning a matter that had come up over church organization. The letter, called 1 Clement (written in Greek), is the earliest non-canonical Christian text we have. In his letter, he mentions Peter and Paul in a context that suggests they were among the first Christian martyrs. We don't know whether he had firsthand knowledge of their martyrdom, or was simply repeating what he had heard from others.

> 5:5 By reason of jealousy and strife Paul by his example pointed out the prize of patient endurance. After that he had been seven times in bonds, had been driven into exile, had been stoned, had preached in the East and in the West, he won the noble renown which was the reward of his faith, 5:6 having taught righteousness unto the whole world and having reached the farthest bounds of the West;* and when he had borne his testimony** before the rulers, so he departed from the world and went unto the holy place, having been found a notable pattern of patient endurance. 6:1 Unto these men of holy lives was gathered a vast multitude of the elect, who through many indignities and tortures, being the victims of jealousy, set a brave example among ourselves.

---

*Perhaps this is evidence that he preached in Spain, which would have been considered "the farthest bounds of the West."
** Clement uses the expression "to bear testimony" to mean "to be martyred" here and elsewhere.

Ignatius of Antioch

Ignatius served as the bishop of Antioch in the late first century. On his way to Rome, where he would be martyred in AD 107, he wrote a series of letters (in Greek) to Christian churches in Asia Minor. In chapter 12 of his letter to the Ephesians, he refers to Paul as having been martyred.

> You are initiated into the mysteries of the gospel with Paul, the holy, the martyred, the deservedly most happy, at whose feet may I be found, when I shall attain to God; who in all his epistles makes mention of you in Christ Jesus.

Dionysius of Corinth

Dionysius was bishop of Corinth from AD 166 to 174. He is reported by other early Christian sources to have written seven letters, extracts from only one of which survive. They all deal with his coming, or hoped for, martyrdom. In it he makes references to Peter and Paul's martyrdom, presumably in Rome.

> You also by this instruction have mingled together the Romans and Corinthians who are the planting of Peter and Paul. For they both came to our Corinth and planted us, and taught alike; and alike going to Italy and teaching there, were martyred at the same time.

The Acts of Paul

The most detailed account of Paul's fate comes from the fragments of the Acts of Paul, written around AD 160. It tells the story of extensive conversations between Paul and the emperor Nero. In the end, Nero had Paul decapitated.

V. And while they [Nero and some others] were still talking, Nero sent one Parthenius and Pheres to see if Paul had already been beheaded. They found him still alive. [Paul] called out to them and said, "Believe in the living God, which raises me and everyone who believes in him from the dead." And they said, "We're going to Nero. When you die and rise again, then we'll believe in your God." And as Longus and Cestus [the soldiers who were guarding Paul and overseeing his execution] asked him to tell them more about salvation, he said to them: Come to my grave in the morning and you will find two men praying, Titus and Luke. They will give you the seal in the Lord."*

Then Paul stood with his face to the east and raised up his hands to heaven and prayed a long time. In his prayer he spoke Hebrew with the fathers, and then stretched forth his neck without speaking. When the executioner struck off his head, milk spurted upon the cloak of the soldier. The soldier and all that were there present were amazed and glorified God who had given such glory unto Paul. They went and told Caesar what had happened.

VI. When he heard it, Nero marveled for a long and was perplexed. Paul came about the ninth hour, when many philosophers and the centurion were standing with Caesar. He stood before them all and said, "Caesar, behold, I, Paul, the soldier of God, am not dead, but live in my God. But many evils and great punishment will befall you in a few days, you wretched man, because you spilled the blood of the righteous." Having said that, Paul departed from him.**

---

* I.e., they will instruct and baptize you.
** As instructed, the two soldiers find Titus and Luke at Paul's grave and are baptized.

Later Sources

AD 200 : Tertullian (*Prescription Against Heretics*) says Paul was martyred in Rome (chapter 36).

AD 318 : Lactantius (*Of the Manner in Which the Persecutors Died*) wrote that Nero "crucified Peter, and slew Paul" (chapter 2).

AD 392 : Jerome (*De Viris Illustribus*) states that Paul was beheaded at Rome (chapter 5).

APPENDIX C: SUGGESTIONS FOR FURTHER READING

Introduction
Johnson, Luke Timothy. *The Writings of the New Testament: An Interpretation*. 3rd ed. Minneapolis: Fortress, 2010.

> *For students new to texts of the New Testament, Johnson offers an exemplary and fair-minded introduction. His discussion of Luke-Acts is can be found on pp. 187–225, which includes a short bibliography for more reading.*

Shillington, V. George. *An Introduction to the Study of Luke-Acts*. T&T Clark Approaches to Biblical Studies. London: T&T Clark, 2007.

> *I personally benefitted immensely from this book when first beginning to study this fascinating but often frustrating text. It also succintly reviews major trends in scholarship in clear language.*

Witherington, III. Ben. *Invitation to the New Testament: First Things*. 2nd ed. Oxford: University Press, 2017.

> *Witherington's widely used introduction has been rightly praised for striking a balance between a faith-based approach to Scripture and an accurate representation of problems uncovered by academic scholarship. Chapter 7 treats Luke-Acts.*

Commentary on Acts
Ricciotti, Giuseppe. *The Acts of the Apostles: Text and Commentary*. Milwaukee : Bruce Publishing, 1958.

> *There are numerous line-by-line commentaries available on Acts. I will cite only the one I found myself returning to most often while preparing this text. It spent more time open before me on my desk than it did on my shelf. While by no means a modern commentary, it nevertheless deftly combines useful scholarship with the storyteller's art. I highly recommend his introduction. The book is sadly out of print, but my university's library fortunately had a copy. Eventually I used it so often that I purchased a used copy on ebay.*